KU-164-031

Contents

IS GOD STILL AN ENGLISHMAN?

How Britain Lost Its Faith (But Found New Soul)

COLE MORETON

ABACUS

First published in Great Britain in 2010 by Little, Brown
This paperback edition published in 2011 by Abacus

A CIP catalogue record for this book
is available from the British Library.

ISBN 978-0-349-12224-3

Typeset in Bembo by M Rules
Printed and bound in Great Britain by
Clays Ltd, St Ives plc

Abacus
An imprint of
Little, Brown Book Group
100 Victoria Embankment
London EC4Y 0DY

An Hachette UK Company
www.hachette.co.uk

www.littlebrown.co.uk

S he was lying on my bed when she asked the question. Ali, my beautiful friend, stretching out under the open window, lit by the sunshine of a summer afternoon.

'Where am I going?'

'Up the motorway,' I said, not really thinking. That was the best way back to London. Her daughter and mine were sharing a bath in the next room and I was standing in the doorway, watching them, sometimes turning back to her. Downstairs, the table was being cleared after a riotous Sunday roast.

'No.'

Her hand was up to shield her eyes from the sunlight, but I knew she was looking at me. Lovely Ali, elegant even in t-shirt and jeans, even when she was salt-stained and tired after a day at the beach. Her soulmate was down in the kitchen: Chris, the chalk to her cheese, the yang to her yin, who would have been a hermit if he hadn't met this talker, this listener, this woman who made glittery magpie art and who loved to party.

'Where am I going?'

Oh God. Now I got it.

'Sorry,' she said, after the silence. 'It's all I think about.'

Of course. I pulled the bathroom door almost shut. Our kids could cope on their own for a moment, splashing away. Their laughter had filled the weekend. In the adult moments, stolen over coffee, over ice-cream, over late-night wine and port, Ali had talked about them and about her art, about the sea, about anything but this one thing. Out with it, then. She was dying.

The cancer in her body was winning. The battle was almost lost. My memory of this moment says you wouldn't have believed it, to have seen her lying on the bed, curvy and sexy, fringe falling over one eye. That was Ali. I don't want to think about how she might really have looked that day, still less about what came later, when her head was stubbled and her skin was paper thin, so you could see the veins and the bones beneath. Once, towards the end, she said: 'Some women would die to be this thin.' It wasn't funny. Not at forty. The wasting away of a precious friend, as if the sun had risen one morning as pale as the moon.

'Where am I going?'

How do you answer a question like that? She was the one with all the faith, the godmother of my child. Long ago, as teenagers, we had both been zealous believers, on fire for the Lord. It was one of the things we had in common: embarrassment at having once been so keen to save the world, and so sure we were the people to do it. That was before faith was dashed against the rocks of real life. Ali had managed to gather up the pieces and make something out of hers: she worked with refugees and broken families in one of the poorest, most chaotic parts of London, because she still believed that God helped the suffering through the hands of the faithful. And now she had cancer. Was that her reward? The bastard.

'Don't say, "Heaven,"' she said. 'I know all that, but what does it mean? What is it going to be like? I'm afraid.'

I lay down on the bed beside her. We were close, side by side, but not touching. The kids were making a lot of happy noise, oblivious.

'I'm not afraid of heaven, don't get me wrong. Or of dying.'

She went quiet, then. For a moment, I thought she was

2

regretting the question. Would she sit up and make some stupid joke and say we should go and get drunk? I really hoped so. No.

'It's this,' she said, propping herself up on an elbow. 'Somebody said something the other day that I think was meant to comfort me, but it just made me panic. They said I'd always be there, able to watch the kids grow up.'

'Some people find that a helpful thought,' I said weakly, way out of my depth.

'It's awful. Imagine having to watch your son get hurt, or make the mistakes he is bound to, because we all do, and not be able to go to him and hold him and tell him, "It's okay, everything will work out. Be strong, Mummy's here." You'd just have to watch, like standing at a shop window with your hands and face pressed up against the glass, unable to be heard or to touch. Is that what it's like?'

Surely not. That would be hell. Her eyes were wet. She was trembling. I didn't know what to say. Her adult faith had always seemed so honest and admirable and out of my reach. Her question was not hypothetical, as it had been on those nights when we had sat up late, musing on the soul. Here and now, it was practical. This was not a matter of religion or tradition, it was about skin and bone, flesh and blood, tissue and phlegm and the essence of Ali inside that warm, living body, and what happened when the body went cold. What would she see, for real, when the light faded? Where would she go? Would the stories we told on the streets as teenage evangelists turn out to be true, or would they all be revealed as delusions? Was there nothing waiting for her but nothing? Moments like these confront us with the assumptions we make every day, and the values upon which our life is based. Who are we, and what do we believe? We must find our own answers, and live and die by them. So what could I say to Ali that would help? What, as I lay beside her, did I know?

Nothing. Absolutely nothing.

Once, I would have answered with a clear eye and certain tone. 'Believe and pray,' I would have said. 'Ask the Lord to heal you, but be assured that heaven is waiting. It's just like going home.' I was a teenage know-it-all, a cocky young Christian fuelled by a high-octane blend of adolescent insecurity, desperation to belong and the absolute conviction that what I knew was not just right, it was the only right. I was a teenage fundamentalist who spoke with the tongues of angels, received visions from the Lord and gave prophecies. I cast out demons, I prayed for healing, I sought miracles. And now? If, by some magic, my teenage self had come into that room to share his certainties, his warnings of damnation and his promises of salvation, I know exactly what I would have done. The only thing possible.

I would have punched his lights out.

Ali died early one morning, in her own bed, with the people she loved sitting at her feet singing songs of hope, through their tears. She had become convinced she was going to a good place with no more pain. She was carried out of the house in a wicker coffin. Those of us she had left behind told stories of the good times. We wept again. We talked about our confusion, how everything felt wrong. Numb from it all, I did something I had not done in years. Something I knew I would regret. I just couldn't stop myself.

I went to church.

It was rash, I know. The impulse took me by surprise. The rain was lashing down on that particular day, it looked cold out there and it was warm and cosy in my room, with *The Archers* on the radio and the Sunday papers spread out on the bed. Coffee in the mug, bacon in the sarnie. The only really quiet moment of the weekend, with the kids watching television. Why go to church when there were so many better things to do, like stretching out under the covers, wiggling my toes and wondering why Ruth Archer stuck with David? Because I felt a sense of shame at not having been able to give Ali a more comforting answer. A sense of nostalgia, too, for the certainties we had both enjoyed when we were young. Was I missing something now, by not going to church? I had to find out. So I did. I found out the answer to that question.

The answer was no.

They say that more people go shopping at IKEA on a Sunday than go to a church. Who can blame them? I would rather queue in flat-pack hell and eat reindeer balls than go back to St Gabriel and All Angels. I went there that day because it was nearest and because I do like an angel: it was (apparently) seeing one of them that got me into faith, years ago. I was late, of course. Only five minutes, but it was enough. They had started, so I thought, Fine, I'll just stay in the porch with the notices and the flowers, then sneak in under cover of the music when they start a hymn. Only they didn't. The introduction went on for ages, until I either had to walk away or go in . . . right in the middle of prayers. Some churches are welcoming. Some have comfortable chairs, subtle lighting and carpets in nice, warm tones. Not this one. My shoes slapped on stone and each step echoed as I made my way through the gloom towards the congregation, such as it was. One old man and two old ladies, sitting among pews that had once held a hundred, muttering 'Amen' with their eyes open. Up in the pulpit, looking down on all this emptiness and me, was Father Insipid. He smiled a watery smile. I smiled back and sat down. The pew creaked and the three fish-eyed septuagenarians turned slowly and stared.

We sang a hymn I had never heard before, to an electric organ played by the vicar. One lady trilled like a songbird lying injured by the roadside, or it may have been her chest whistling. There was a sermon about . . . well, homosexuality was mentioned, and not in a nice way. After the service, when hot water was being added to coffee powder in little plastic cups and the worshippers were ignoring me, presumably out of fear, the priest came over and gripped my arm tightly and spoke so close to my face that specks of saliva prickled my cheek. He whispered something, urgently. I could only just make it out. 'Help!' he seemed to be saying. 'I can't stand it any more. Please, get me out of here!'

As I fled, leaving the priest to the mercy of his elderly captors, I realised I was not the only one eager to be elsewhere. The roads were busy with people-carriers heading for the shops, the park, the cycle trail, anywhere that wasn't a place of worship. The latest research suggests that between three and four million people go to church on any given Sunday, across the whole of Britain. That includes everyone, from the crowds at mass in Westminster Cathedral to the half-dozen faithful in our local gospel hall. It's not many. Three million people belong to the National Trust. Four million buy a copy of the *News of the World*. So, is that it? Have we all stopped believing? The answer, again, is no.

Every time anyone asks, for a poll or some such, about two-thirds of us say we believe in God or a higher power of some kind. The figures vary, depending on how the question is put, but the usual result is about two in every three people. Richard Dawkins might not like it, he might think it's all a delusion (and he might be right, who really knows? Nobody, not even the Ayatollah of Atheism), but many of those people pray. They ask for help. They might go and buy a flat-pack on a Sunday morning but it is their god they call out to when they lose the only Allen key. It could be Christ or Jehovah or Allah or Krishna or Freya or any other, because we have more choice than ever, but if you take them all as representations of the divine, at least in the minds of their followers, and include everyone who has their own personal faith in a higher power, however loose, then there are about forty million believers in Britain. Now, consider this: that is twice as many people as there were in the whole country when Victoria was Queen, when the mania for church building was at its most intense.

You can't turn a corner without coming across a church of some kind, because they are everywhere: old ones, modernist ones, flat-tops or spiky ones, Norman towers or Gothic spires. Their presence is an indication that we were once entranced by evensong, seduced by the psalms, pacified by the Book of Common Prayer. And yet, on the whole, they now stand empty. How did we come to believe, with such conviction, that snoozing or washing the car or playing football or screaming at the kids playing football or queueing to buy Rawlplugs or climbing mountains or walking or washing up or having sex or watching telly or doing nothing much at all, just staring into space, was so much better than going to church?

Why did it take us so long to find out? That's another way of putting it, I suppose. It is tempting to think that it doesn't matter, this sudden absence of something that was once so much part of our lives, but it really does. It changes everything. However you feel about it, personally speaking, our common way of life in this country has long been based on Christianity. Our myths and legends, our collective assumptions, our values, our government and our law were all formed and influenced by our own, unique and local understanding of the faith, bound up as it is in tradition, class and power. Take it away, as something we do and share and know about and obey, however unthinkingly, and this is suddenly a different place. All the old certainties are gone.

The change didn't happen in Victorian times, as people think. It didn't happen during the First or even the Second World War, although they certainly put a bomb under the state religion. Churchgoing dropped off dramatically during the sixties, but this book is about something much more dramatic and recent than that. It's not about the churches and the Christians, it's about all of us. There has been a shift in the national DNA. A mutation, as the flu-chasing scientists would put it. We were something, then we became something radically different, without anybody noticing. It happened in my lifetime, and probably yours.

I was educated in a state school during the seventies and early eighties, in a society still dominated by Christianity. It was assumed that most people believed in Jesus in some way, that going to church was a normal thing to do, that Bible stories were our common heritage and that the country was organised and run in accordance with principles set out in the Word of God. When I became a teenage convert, I joined a Church that many of its members believed was on the verge of a great revival. Millions would take its message to heart, we were told. Society would be transformed. Even the Archbishop of Canterbury believed it, and told his people to work towards this goal. What happened? Look around you.

We now live in a post-Christian society. Jesus is just one of many prophets, going to church is seen as an odd thing to do, Bible stories have been forgotten (removing the resonance from so much of our language and literature) and the way the country is organised and run looks archaic, inadequate and even disturbing. The next coronation service surely won't declare that the monarch has been chosen by God to lead the nation and defend the one true Protestant faith. Not very long ago, it was assumed that everyone in Britain was a Christian unless they said they were not. Now the opposite is true. Faith is a marketplace and the churches occupy just a corner of it. The stallholders seem more interested in fighting each other than selling anything.

Meanwhile, the rest of us are trying to work out a way to live together with our different gods, different cultures and different ways of seeing the world.

I'm not complaining about this. Far from it. I love it, for the possibilities it offers and for the fun of seeing it evolve.

Yesterday I was on the Western Lawns in Eastbourne, long known as God's waiting room and one of the most conservative and traditionally Christian towns in the country. There were thirty-foot statues of the pagan god and goddess Herne and Andred swaying down the promenade, past the war memorial. There were witches and warlocks and children waving willow wands for no other reason than that Harry Potter does, and there were several hundred other people – some committed, some curious, some just there for the spectacle – walking to the sound of the Pentacle drummers, who hammered on the skins of their marching drums and made the rain bounce upwards. They were all on their way to mark the harvest festival of Lammas, one of the eight great moments in the pagan calendar, with a ritual dance enacting the cutting down of a figure called John Barleycorn who represents the sun deity, the masculine side of God. There were men and women from a Morris side called Hunter's Moon, dressed in black rags with blacked-up faces so they looked like a bunch of ragged crows after mating with Hell's Angels, and they hopped and skipped and jangled and smashed willow sticks together with a roar, in a way that left nobody in doubt that theirs was a fertility dance and the sticks were each representing an excitable part of the body. They were funny and loud and nothing like the white-clad, hankie-waving Morris men everyone thinks they know.

This raggle-taggle procession crossed the road in front of a coach full of women in Islamic dress, who laughed and smiled and shook their heads. Parked up along the seafront I saw minibuses carrying the names of an African Pentecostal church from East London, a Sikh welfare society and a Muslim youth charity, all of which had apparently come on day trips looking for old-fashioned sun, sea and ice-cream. The weather had let them down, but what else had they expected in the middle of summer? When most of the pagan marchers had made it to the beer tent, a band of young, well-spoken white boys in pork-pie hats started playing acoustic guitar and bass and fiddle and singing a raucous gypsy song, in Polish.

This was England. What a strange and wonderful place it has become. The last part of this book will explore and celebrate the way the country is growing into its new soul. I do, though, want to know how, when and why the great change happened. That's what I have to find out.

This book covers the last thirty years, roughly, during which time half of the people who were going to church have stopped. We begin back in an age of relative certainty, looking at where English belief (and the self-belief so closely linked to it) came from and discovering just how flimsy it was. The second section investigates how everything fell apart, uncovering a remarkable secret history of blunders and battles over sex, money and power. The third part asks what we are becoming now.

My need for answers is personal. I want some solid ground on which to place my feet. I have moved during the course of my life from extreme certainty of faith into doubt and on into wondering whether it is still possible to believe in anything at all. That is what I want to know, but when I write about my personal experiences it will be to illustrate and inform the much bigger, far more important story, and to show how the cultural shifts described here have an impact on individual lives. I meet so many men and women who say they have been through similar things.

They used to be so sure of what they believed – whether that was because their parents taught them or they had come to their own conclusions – but they lost it all somewhere along the line. They don't really know why. They don't know how. Maybe that's you. I don't think it's a bad thing. I think we often feel nostalgia for old certainties, because they made life simpler, but we forget to celebrate mystery, and miss the thrill of seeing that there are more things in heaven and earth than are dreamed of in our philosophies. As I say, this story is not just about or for believers, although I hope they will find it challenging, entertaining and maybe even useful. I set out to write this for all of us, including the atheists, because whether we like it or not, so much of what we do – our language, literature, art, films, television, clothes, even the way we play sport – has been shaped over centuries by shared values that are now, suddenly, gone. I want to know when that happened, and why, and what is taking their place. The way the world is changing around us brings up questions that demand to be answered. They drive this book, as they have driven my thoughts since that sunlit, ominous afternoon with Ali.

Who are we? What do we really believe in? And where are we going?

CREATION

The ordinary Britisher imagines that God is an Englishman.

George Bernard Shaw

1

How God became an Englishman

I am English. Sorry. Blame the parents. Don't expect tea and cucumber sandwiches, though. I'm not that sort of Englishman. Nor am I a foul-mouthed thug, an Old Etonian or a cold-eyed criminal mastermind about to be thwarted by a Hollywood hero in a dirty vest. I'm not any of those things that other people apparently think of when they think of the English, and neither are my English friends.

What are we then? It's hard to say. People born within the borders of England, certainly, but that isn't much to shout about these days. It often seems less a country and more of an administrative region jammed in between Scotland, Ireland, Wales and France. I have good friends from all those places, many of whom have a strong sense of national identity. I hope they enjoy this book, because much of what I am writing about affects us all. As for the English, though, our identity has been kidnapped several times over. If we're not being typecast then we're being shamed by fascists who refuse to recognise that the boys in the England shirts are playing for an Italian manager, under the flag of a saint from Palestine. Actually, that's one of the things that is pretty glorious about the modern English: we're all mixed up. We're Morris men with maypoles, but we're dubstep and dancehall too.

We're roast beef and Yorkshire pudding, but we're chicken balti, born in Brum. There is honey still for tea, but supper is rice and peas. Which is lovely, and it's new. A new England is being born, and that is very exciting. This book is going to explore it, but first we have to find out what happened to the old one. How come there has been such a huge shift in the shape of our national soul?

If you are from England, that word may be a little distressing. Apologies. 'Soul' is a word no English person can use without feeling uncomfortable, or at the very least a powerful urge to self-deprecate. Soul is something Americans have, particularly the black ones. Aretha has soul. Barack Obama has soul. David Cameron has the ability to appear natural on a bicycle. That's not the same thing at all.

This book is about the soul of England, but can a nation have such a thing? I think so, yes. It exists in our collective imagination, our history, our traditions, our low desires and high ideals, our responses, our ways of living and our systems of power and control, so many of which have come, in the past, from our belief in God. Not just any old deity either, but one of our own making. The English God. The one who bends His will to meet our needs, as people first began to say during the reign of Elizabeth I.

The idea that Catholicism was heresy and the English had God on their side as they sought to protect the true faith was a powerful way of motivating people to fight the Spanish. The dramatist John Lyly suggested England was the modern equivalent of the Tribe of Israel in the Bible, a nation set apart by God. 'So tender a care hath he always had of that England,' wrote Lyly in 1580, that the English were 'His chosen and peculiar people'. I can think of plenty of Scots, and others, who would agree with that 'peculiar', but in this case it means special. This was even before God sent storms to destroy the apparently invincible

Armada. A year after that remarkable victory, in 1589, a hardline Bishop of London put the new wisdom directly: 'God is English.'

And that was that. The specific comparison with Israel was taken more or less seriously over the centuries, but the sense of England as special and chosen did not disappear. It was taken as an explanation for the spread of the language across the world, and the widespread recognition of the poetry and authority of the King James Bible. One group of people did more than any other to keep the idea alive, claiming to be the keepers of the mystic soul of England. They were, and still are, a strange, ancient, mysterious bunch with peculiar rituals, arcane histories and a power way beyond what could be seen, reaching into the darkest and highest corners. Their organisation had members everywhere, from deep dungeons to palace bedrooms, whispering their creed and holding sway over the nation in a way that even Dan Brown could not have invented without inviting ridicule. The name of this all-influencing sect?

No, not the Women's Institute. Close, though.

Who presumed to speak for the God who appointed kings? Who ran a national network of preachers, propagandists and petty spies that was – before television, the wireless or even the printed word – the best way for a monarch to get a message across to the people? Whose word was named, by royal command for five centuries, as the one true version of God's holy writ? Who helped lay down the law, and enforce it? Who were given unique rights to hold their own courts and automatically take up seats in Parliament? Whose defining articles also defined the belief system of our militant, ambitious, imperial island race?

It certainly wasn't the Quakers.

The Church of England dominated as the English God evolved. (Which is ironic, when you consider what a hard time he was to get from Charles Darwin.) The destroyer of Catholics became a burner of witches, a royalist then a republican then a royalist again, a tamer of dark savages, a conqueror of foreign lands, a righteous warrior, a slaver and an abolitionist, the God of Wilberforce and Shaftesbury but also Kitchener and Haig. His followers proved themselves capable of great violence, oppression, cruelty and bigotry during the days of empire, when faith appeared to be at its most fervent, Britannia ruled the waves and the map of the world was pink; but the Lord did not complain. On the contrary, the English God was said to endorse, sponsor and empower His chosen people as they strove to conquer, command and subjugate the planet, seizing and suckling on everyone else's natural resources in the name of righteousness. His people were suitably, dutifully, grateful: a census taken in 1851 suggested that 60 per cent of the British population was at church on Sunday. This was very sensible if your parson happened to be your landlord, or his son, as was often the case. The numbers fell as the Industrial Revolution continued to drive more people to the cities and away from parishes where their families had always lived: by 1900, attendance was down to 27 per cent. That did not, however, alter the convictions of those in charge of the empire. They were Christians and Christianity was theirs. They served the Lord, however brutally, and He favoured them.

'The message is carved in granite,' said Lord Curzon, the Viceroy of India, in 1905. 'It is hewn out of the rock of doom – that our work is righteous and that it shall endure.' George Curzon was the second son of the Baron Scarsdale, a great landowner who also happened to be the rector of Kedleston in Derbyshire (where the tenants were surely careful never to fall asleep during the sermon). Educated at Eton and Oxford, Curzon became – in the words of the historian David Gilmour – 'the last and in many ways the greatest of Victorian viceroys' in 1899. The Raj was never mightier, nor more full of pomp. Six

18

years later, at his farewell speech in Bombay, he told those who were staying behind to rule India: 'Remember, the Almighty has placed your hand on the greatest of His ploughs.' Their aim should be 'to drive the blade a little forward in your time, and to feel that somewhere among these millions you have left a little justice or happiness or prosperity, a sense of manliness or moral dignity, a spring of patriotism, a dawn of intellectual enlightenment, or a stirring of duty, where it did not before exist'. That was 'the Englishman's justification in India'.

Such swagger. Such self-righteousness, nailed by that brilliant Irishman George Bernard Shaw when he told the *New York Times* in 1911: 'The English think God is an Englishman.'

Whatever His allegiances, the Lord was powerless to stop the slaughter at the Somme. The best He could do was to send a priest with the nickname Woodbine Willie to give out cigarettes to those who were about to go over the top, but the English God did not die in the mud and blood along with a million men, as might have been expected. He survived thanks to His training in the public schools, the source of so many gentleman priests over the years, such as Baron Scarsdale. Games, beatings and cold showers drove a muscular Christianity into the boys. Upper lips were always stiff. Snivelling was for girls. If violence was necessary, it had to be swift and unemotional, and overwhelming but fair. These were the values taken into the pulpit and into battle by men who believed in stoicism, patriotism and fair play above all else, as seen to vivid effect in Sir Henry John Newbolt's poem 'Vitaï Lampada'. It is set in the desert, where the sand is red with the blood of fallen comrades, including the commanding officer. One soldier remains. His machine gun is jammed, but in the fury of it all he remembers a school cricket match, when he was the last boy in and his duty was to survive at the crease for an hour to win the match for his team. He recalls the hand of his cricket captain on his shoulder, and the words he spoke. The doomed soldier calls them out again, across the battlefield: 'Play up! Play up! And play the game!'

The poem was written before the Great War in which so many of the pupils who learned it by heart were killed. The Imperial War Museum in London displays a letter written by a soldier to the parents of a friend in June 1917: 'Let me tell you that he died as I knew he would: like a real Englishman. He was struck in the chest and simply said: "I'm done, boys."' He died like a real Englishman. Playing the game to the last.

Some of those who were not scythed down became priests. In time they would become bishops and archbishops, alongside old schoolfriends who became doctors, judges, cabinet ministers and lords. Their attitudes were tempered by what they had seen, naturally, but the core values remained, and helped the post-war Church of England become known – in the exasperated phrase of the suffragette and preacher Maude Royden – as 'the Conservative Party at prayer'.

Having made it through the carnage, though, the English God emerged with a less ferocious character: part Father Christmas, part W.G. Grace, a thoroughly decent, sporting sort of chap to have woven into your language, culture, society and governance at every level. He now avoided confrontation wherever possible, preferring compromise and influence to the terrible alternative He knew so well. The middle ground had always been His: right from the beginning, Anglicans defined themselves as being neither the ritualistic Catholics nor the austere Lutherans but something in between, unique. This attitude waxed and waned (and was sometimes very vicious indeed towards the Catholics) but in time it widened into an instinct for moderation, which meant that on the whole England tolerated more dissent than is usual under a state religion. The instinct became stronger than ever after the shock of world war. The English God was still a moralist, still ready to oppose the heathen and the foreign, and if a selfless sacrifice was needed then He was ready to make it, like a batsman who applauds the bowler and walks before he is given out; but in peace time, the wizened warrior put down His gun and became instead the Lord of Good Manners. His emblem was a jolly good Victoria sponge on a paper doily at the village fayre.

The men who preached His word helped promote the self-image of the English as stoic, well-mannered folk who would always muddle through, never complaining but trusting that things would turn out all right in the end, as long as everyone knew their place and did their bit. Under their influence, the English shied away from extremes such as fascism and communism, preferring a nice quiet cup of tea to any fuss (although they were also very fond of simmering resentment, backbiting and plotting against the neighbours). When Chamberlain returned from Germany in 1938 with a piece of paper and a signed agreement that all would be well, he was behaving very much like an English vicar trying to sort out a dispute over the hedgerows. And he was just as effective.

The Second World War should have knocked the English God's middle stump out for good, but it didn't. Not quite. While some people sought to rebuild the nation as a socialist land fit for heroes, others looked backwards to a mythical time of pre-war peace and prosperity. The presence of a priest in every parish was a fortifying reminder of England's past strength at the heart of the great kingdom, as Jeremy Paxman has written: 'The Church of England, bells tolling from the ivy-clad tower to summon the labourers to Harvest Festival, is part of the folk memory of the summer of British greatness, a pastoral counterpoint to stories of wars, conquests and colonies.'

The fifties have been called an Anglican decade, because the Church flourished in the immediate aftermath of war. It slowly became obvious, though, that attempts to rebuild the old order were doomed. Priests and bishops were among the last to realise it (and some still haven't), even though churchgoing was down to 19 per cent by 1960. In response to this, young members of the clergy said it was time to be 'radical' and 'relevant' and took to riding motorbikes and running boys' clubs in an attempt to prove they were. Others were too fond of their status in conventional circles to give it up quite so quickly. Sipping sherry with the Lady Mayoress or saying grace at the garden party, a vicar was still usually among the best-educated and poshest people in his community. You dusted off the best china, chopped off the crusts and sliced the cucumber thinly when he came calling. Locally or nationally, a dog collar meant you were part of the Establishment.

The *Oxford English Dictionary* says this phrase was first used in writing, in the modern sense, in 1955, although the meaning was understood before then. It appeared in an article in the *Spectator* by Henry Fairlie, who wrote: 'By "the Establishment" I do not mean only the centres of official power – though they are certainly part of it – but rather the whole matrix of official and social relations within which power is exercised.' This use of the word 'Establishment' comes from Christianity having been 'established by law' as the faith of the land. We'll investigate that more later, but by the time Peter Cook opened the Establishment Comedy Club in Soho, the name stood for a more modern concept. His target was the network of assumptions, privileges and titles through which power was maintained. Cook and his fellow satirists went after the landed, the aristocratic, the peers, the ministers, the civil servants, the newly wealthy, the old money, the royal family but also the bishops and archbishops who were forever telling society how to behave: all those who perpetuated the notion of England as a civilised Christian nation in which tradition mattered and old ways were not to be challenged.

We were all expected to play our part and be satisfied, as satirised in that famous comedy sketch first seen on *Frost Over England*. You know the one. Three men are standing in a row. The tallest, on the left, is John Cleese, imperious in a pinstriped suit and a bowler hat. He towers over Ronnie Barker, who is less expensively dressed and has a trilby. 'I look up to him,' says Barker, doing just that, 'because he is upper class.' He turns his face towards Ronnie Corbett, tiny and ragged in a flat cap and costermonger's scarf. 'But I look down on him, because he is working class. I am middle class.' Corbett says, forlornly: 'I know my place.'

Upper-Class Man has breeding, but admits he has no money. Middle-Class Man has money, but knows he is vulgar. Not as vulgar, though, as Working-Class Man, who sighs and says again that he knows his place. What do they get out of this arrangement? Upper-Class Man gets a feeling of superiority. Middle-Class Man gets a feeling of inferiority on one side, but superiority on the other. Working-Class Man strains to look up at them both, as they look down on him, then says: 'I get a pain in the back of my neck.'

There has always been a strong tradition of dissident faith in England, proposing a God whose bounty is for all the people, not just the people in power. That is very important to our story, but it has usually been pushed to the fringes of society and not allowed near 'the English God' – by which I mean the idea of God most prevalent in England at any given time, in public and official life but also in language, law and everyday customs. For

23

most of the last five hundred years, this has been the God defined and promoted by the Establishment, evident in the English way of life from the highest ritual to the lowest curse. That was even true in the sixties and seventies. Any doubt that Christianity served the status quo could have been removed by picking a school at random, walking through the doors in time for assembly and hearing the children sing, as so many did, 'All Things Bright and Beautiful'. The words suggested that the class divisions satirised by Cleese, Barker and Corbett were just as God intended: 'The rich man at his castle, the poor man at his gate, God made them high or lowly and ordered their estate.'

We know that the children of the wartime generation rebelled against what their parents stood for, striking a blow for individual freedoms in matters of sexuality, politics, class and religion. That is the story that is always told. It was perhaps easier to believe at the time if you were sitting with the Beatles and the Maharishi in a haze of hash smoke, looking forward to some free love; but a bit more difficult to accept if you were, say, a fishmonger's apprentice in Grimsby whose only experience of swinging was when he pulled down another smoked haddock. They say that if you can remember the sixties, you weren't there. The truth is that the social revolution has been hyped up by people who can remember it very well, thank you, but would rather pretend they can't. It was all too groovy, man, on the King's Road, but not so transcendental in King's Lynn.

The English God was not about to run from a whiff of patchouli oil. He still had allies. There were, for example, old soldiers everywhere in the seventies. Men and women with experience of war were in the government, in the town hall, in the bank manager's office, running the Scout troop, writing for the papers, presenting the news, delivering the milk, fixing the boiler, collecting their pensions. There was still a collective memory of a time when England (and Scotland, Wales and Ireland) had been severely tested. These people knew how to follow orders, march in time and keep mum (for better or worse, given that there was so much they could have questioned). The language and imagery they used to grapple with life and death, war and suffering, loss and remembrance, in private and at the grandest public occasions, were those of Christianity and the Bible, even if they had no personal belief left in God. Their values had been learned from stories like the parable of the Good Samaritan that cause blank faces among children now. The national anthem was still played at the end of films in the cinema. I remember being hauled to my feet at the end of a rerun of *The Battle of Britain* at the Walthamstow Granada in the mid-seventies, seeing mice scurry along under the screen as we sang 'God Save the Queen'. It was a polite reminder that He really ought to look after Her Majesty, as He had put her on the throne in the first place. We sang it at our school, an ordinary state primary, and said the Lord's Prayer every day in assembly. By 1980, only 13 per cent of the population went to church but, culturally speaking, the English God was still a powerful force.

The legacy of His long-held dominance was a set of common values identified by the social anthropologist Kate Fox as the 'fundamental guiding principles' of Englishness. First among them is fair play. Fox calls it a 'national quasi-religious obsession' that governs the way we drive, queue, flirt, buy a round, do business and always support the underdog. Breaches of fair play provoke 'more righteous indignation than any other sin', she says (and notice the religious language). It's not socialism, we don't want everyone to have equal rights (perish the thought), but we do want everyone to have a fair crack of the whip. 'We accept that there will be winners and losers,' says Fox, 'but feel that everyone should be given a fair chance, providing they observe the rules and don't cheat or shirk their responsibilities.' That takes us back to the playing fields and the battleground, playing up and playing the game. What looks like tolerance towards other religions and cultures is actually the instinct for fair play combined with moderation, which Fox describes as 'our avoidance of extremes, excess and intensity of any kind. Our fear of change. Our fear of fuss.' Caution, conservatism and apathy are parts of this, even now. Our MPs don't get caught embezzling fortunes out of the public purse to pay for bacchanalian orgies and parties in paradise, as they do in other countries. They are found guilty of claiming the cost of building a little house on a lake for some ducks.

Modesty is another of Fox's core values. It's not that the English are more modest than other nationalities, just that we place a much higher value on appearing to be. Everyone knows that self-deprecation often means the opposite of what is being said. 'Well, I suppose I know a bit about that' often means 'I'm the acknowledged world expert.'

Then there is courtesy, so deeply ingrained it is almost a knee-jerk response. It comes from being deeply uneasy in social situations, which Fox describes as a disease at the heart of what it means to be English. We try to cope by following a complicated set of rules: 'Excuse me, I'm terribly sorry, but you seem to be standing on my foot.' The idea is that if you go outside, run down the street with your head down and your arms flailing and charge straight into a stranger, they will almost certainly step back and say, 'Sorry.'

Try that in my street and you'd better wear a stab vest. And what about the yob who spits between your feet on the bus? Some of the patterns of behaviour acknowledged by Fox in *Watching the English* in 2004 are dying off, but that's not a surprise. They are echoes of the past, things we learned to do when the English God was in His pomp and have not quite forgotten. Yet. The values and habits we learned from Him still hang around like ghosts in our lives, affecting our culture, our laws, our language and even the way we play our sport, whether we're believers or not. They are fading fast. Soon they will be gone. Some church leaders say, with ungodly bitterness, that we have become a secular society; but the current head of the Church of England, Rowan Williams, says that's not the case. Instead, he says we are 'haunted by the memory of religion'. That suggests – rather bleakly, you might think, for an Archbishop of Canterbury – that the English God is dead. Is it true? Or has He pulled off His old trick of evolving again, into something more in keeping with the way most of us live our lives, shaped by the things that frighten or inspire us?

To find out, we need to go back to the last time anyone saw Him alive: the last great festival of English certainty, when England seemed to know what it was and what it stood for. Looking back, it all seems like a fairytale . . .

2

Once upon a time

It *was* a fairytale. Everybody said so. The palace said so. The papers said so. The printers of tea towels and manufacturers of commemorative plates said so . . . and the people agreed, rushing to buy them. My mother said so, as we sat on the sofa with the curtains drawn against the sunshine, so that we could see the picture on the new Rediffusion more clearly. Even my father's socialist mates down at the club said so, pretending to be ironic. The Prince was in need of a wife and he had found the loveliest young bride in the country to be his own. 'This is a wonderful, fairytale sight,' said the BBC commentator Tom Fleming, speaking to the largest television audience of all time: 750 million of us, from Buckingham Palace to Bangalore, on 29 July 1981. Usually the provider of solemn reflection at the Cenotaph on Remembrance Day, Fleming was caught up in the emotion of the day and could not resist the f-word. Nor could the Archbishop of Canterbury, rehearsing his sermon: 'This is the stuff of fairytales . . .'

Diana scrubbed floors, just like Cinderella, for a pound an hour at her sister's house. She was a good-hearted girl who lived off Harvest Crunch cereal and chocolate bars in a shared flat. She had no qualifications at all, academically, but that didn't matter:

she had been chosen, like Cinders. The story, as it was told and believed by most people that year, had an ancient power. If someone like that could become a princess, then couldn't anyone?

Five days after final kisses and cuddles at the kindergarten where she worked part time, Diana was sitting in the Glass Coach, knee to knee with her father, waist deep in ivory silk. The dress was worth £9000, more than the average wage of a working man and certainly more than she had ever earned for herself. Ten thousand mother-of-pearl sequins had been sewn on by hand. She was driven out of the gates of Clarence House behind a coachman in scarlet and gold, and two magnificent horses, into the sunlight and an immense noise. Cheers, yells, screams of 'Lady Di!' More than half a million people were along the route, hoping to see her in person. So many Union Flags, each one bearing a portrait of herself and the Prince. She was, suddenly, a superstar. She couldn't back out now, her sisters had said so: 'Your face is on the tea towels.'

'She is gift-wrapped!' said Tom Fleming, gushing as the carriage door opened at the cathedral and Lady Diana Spencer stepped out. 'She looks absolutely lovely!' The dress was styled after the golden age of royal weddings, two centuries earlier; but it also had the puffed sleeves and frilled collars of the summer of 1981, when romance and extravagance were coming back into fashion as a reaction to the dreary, worrying real world. She was like a princess bride drawn by Walt Disney, with a dash of Disco Di. Women were already wearing Lady Di haircuts with heavy fringes, and Lady Di blue blouses with Lady Di bow collars. The dress would be copied, but perhaps not the train: it went on and on as the bridesmaids unfurled it like a sail. Taking fistfuls of silk to keep from tripping on her skirt, Diana climbed the steps of the cathedral.

Prince Charming was waiting. He was not, let's be honest,

handsome; but many young women had allowed themselves to become convinced of his desirability. This may have been because he was as fit as a polo player should be. It may have been because he was the Earl of Chester, Duke of Cornwall, Duke of Rothesay, Earl of Carrick, Baron Renfrew, Lord of the Isles, Prince and Great Steward of Scotland and Prince of Wales. Oh, and heir to the throne. His chosen bride was to be Queen.

The fanfare blared. Way back in the cathedral, under the portico, the bride stood still while the designer of the dress fussed over her collars. The aisle was long, it would take more than three minutes to get to the altar, under the gaze of 2600 guests. Most of the crown heads of Europe were present, having been led in procession by Princess Grace of Monaco, the world's most glamorous royal . . . until today. As the trumpets played the 'Prince of Denmark's March', Diana stepped forward, focusing on helping her father, who was beside her. His presence was a triumph of will, as he had not fully recovered from a cerebral haemorrhage. As she moved towards the altar, surrounded by pomp and ceremony, she told herself she was happy. She was happy. Nothing could spoil it. Nothing.

The first hymn they sang was her choice. It spoke of how duty to God and to the nation were woven together in the soul of England. 'I vow to thee my country . . . the service of my love.' It was a hymn from the playing fields, from the public schools, from the battle lines:

> The love that asks no questions,
> The love that stands the test,
> That lays upon the altar the dearest and the best.
> The love that never falters,
> The love that pays the price.
> The love that makes, undaunted, the final sacrifice.

Once upon a time

The Archbishop of Canterbury, Dr Robert Runcie, came gliding over the carpet in a new silver stole and mitre decorated with glittering stars. 'I require and charge you both,' he said in a drift-away voice that served him badly, 'as ye will answer at the dreadful Day of Judgement, when all hearts shall be disclosed, that if either of ye know of any impediment why ye may not be joined together in matrimony, ye do now confess it.' Dr Runcie sounded as if a dewdrop was about to fall from his nose into his Campari, but never mind. The language of the liturgy, the prayers, the anthems and the hymns was monumental and commanding. 'Christ Is Made the Sure Foundation', they sang. 'Let the People Praise Thee', sang the choir. 'Look,' the Church of England was saying, 'these important people – the royal family – do what our God tells them to do. We're in charge here.'

The Church still had a grip on the culture of England in the summer of 1981. On a normal Saturday, without a royal wedding to watch, we would all have been making a mad dash for the high street, cramming all our shopping, browsing and meeting people into a few hours (or rushing to football matches, which always kicked off at three o'clock) in the knowledge that the following morning, when all right-thinking men and women were meant to be at worship, the country would be closed down completely. No shops. No DIY stores. No sport. No pubs until noon, and then only for two hours. The Church did all that. Its influence was the reason for the survival of the Defence of the Realm Act of 1914, passed when there was a war to win and it was necessary to ban such dangerous practices as flying a kite, buying binoculars or feeding bread to the ducks. Now it was used to preserve a little of our pre-war piety. There were anomalies, wonderful ones: you could buy vodka but not baby food; you could buy a plant but not a pot to put it in; you could buy a copy of *Playboy* magazine on a Sunday, at one of the newsagents allowed to open briefly in the morning, but you could not buy a copy of the Bible. Church leaders told their opponents that if they wanted one so badly there were plenty available in the pews. The churches didn't want the law to change. The shop workers didn't want it either, nor did the unions, and the Confederation of British Industry wasn't keen on the cost of all that overtime. Even the *Guardian* was glad we could all enjoy one day 'free from the seductions and hustle of material goods and the pressure of work'. That didn't really apply to all those mums who had to peel the spuds, but no doubt it was the principle of the thing.

The licensing laws were supposed to give families a chance to spend time together, but what if you didn't want that? What if you wound each other up just by being in the same room? Tough. There was not much distraction to be found on the television, with only three channels. The Sunday schedules were taken up with religion, farming, weather and more religion. The prime-time show was *Songs of Praise*, in which Thora Hird sat listening as a bank manager from Pinner told her why he loved 'Oh God Our Help in Ages Past'. Afterwards there was a suitably uplifting film, such as *The Greatest Story Ever Told*. Later, at close down, a homily from the Reverend Ernest Barely-Awake. Time for bed, citizens. It was nearly eleven. When the revolving globe appeared, and just before it vanished to a little white dot, there was the national anthem again. 'Long to reign over us, God save the Queen.'

Back at the wedding, Her Majesty was in bed with the Archbishop. Not literally, although it's a lovely thought –

'Your Majesty, may I remove the royal undergarments?'

'My Lord Archbishop, I trust your hands have been warmed in prayer?'

– but metaphorically, as the service made visible a very old partnership at the heart of England. The deal was that the Queen would protect the Church, placing it at the heart of national life by allowing it to conduct the great events of state; and in return the Church would declare once more that Her Majesty had been chosen by the Lord to rule over us all. This was a five-hundred-year-old pact to protect a vision of one nation under God, worshipping in the one Church, led by the monarch. It was designed to preserve, as one writer put it at the time: 'The identity of the English nation as one unique and even mystical social, tribal, political and spiritual community.' These two needed each other like lovers in a storm. Neither liked to mention that their special relationship, which had defined the nation of England for so long, had been conceived long ago in a bedroom, borne out of love and lust.

Without the naked flesh and heavy breathing of Henry VIII and Anne Boleyn, there would have been no independent Church of England. Henry, captivated by the lady in waiting (in every sense), asked the Pope to annul his marriage to Catherine of Aragon, who had not been able to give him a male heir. Catherine was, in the words of one male historian, 'too bleak to content the bounding energy of the king'. Poor woman. The Pope said no, of course. He was more or less being held captive by Catherine's emperor nephew at the time. So, as every schoolboy used to know, Henry declared himself to be the new Supreme Head of the Church of England, which from now on would appoint its own bishops and pay no heed to Rome. Men of God who refused to swear an oath of allegiance would lose their heads. So would Anne, in the end, because she could give him only a daughter, Elizabeth. Henry was like that. Then again, so were his girls.

Elizabethan England was as extreme in its faith as a modern

Islamic state: within a year of the Queen coming to the throne, a law was passed ordering everyone to go to church every Sunday or pay a fine equivalent to half the average weekly wage. Elizabeth softened her title to that of Supreme Governor, but she still used the Church as an instrument of state control. Every priest had to follow what was written in the Book of Common Prayer, so that all services used the same phrases and declared the same, state-ordained truths. The network of pulpits was used to pass messages from the throne to the people. Few of those present could read, but they could all listen. They had to. Even if you were rich or powerful enough to shrug off the fine, the local bishop could get you excommunicated. You could go to prison, where you became unable in law to challenge anyone who took your land. These new dictats were not always enforced (a servant could go to church on behalf of a household), but the intention was that everyone should be made to worship in the same way. Atheism was not an option. The existence of God was not to be denied, at least in public. Nobody would dare.

The comparison with Israel as a chosen nation was used to supercharge the belief that England's fight with Catholic enemies was right. 'God is English,' said the Bishop of London, John Aylmer, 'for you fight not only in the quarrel of your country but also, and chiefly, in defence of His true religion and of His dear son Christ.' The exact nature of the faith worth dying for was set down in writing in an Elizabethan mission statement called the Thirty-Nine Articles, a list that included specific attacks on 'repugnant' papal error such as priestly celibacy and the Latin mass. The Thirty-Nine Articles survived the English Civil War and acted as the basis for the exclusion and persecution of people who didn't agree with them, whether they were Catholics or nonconformists. Over time England developed a reputation for religious tolerance, but it is still true that until the Victorian era you could not go to Oxford or Cambridge universities or take up any kind of political or civil position of influence without swearing by the Articles. All clergymen and -women still have to, which rules them out of being republicans (unless they cross their fingers).

The Articles are detailed at the back of the Book of Common Prayer, still the main service book used by many congregations, which declares: 'The King's Majesty hath the chief power in this Realm of England.' They have been a prime instrument of the Crown, the Church and the State working together, each being as helpful and essential to the others and to the English God as a cricketer's bat, pads and box. You can make up your own joke about protecting the Crown Jewels.

When the young Elizabeth Windsor was crowned in 1953 she vowed to uphold the historic creeds of England as faithfully as her namesake. The props they gave her were glorious: the Rod with the Dove; the Supertunica; the Bracelets of Sincerity and Wisdom. This was a costume worthy of Wonder Woman. The language of the liturgy and the readings was equally dressy, but the meaning was clear: 'As Solomon was anointed King, so be thou anointed, blessed and consecrated Queen, over the Peoples whom the Lord thy God hath given thee to rule and govern.' The Archbishop of Canterbury at the time, Dr Geoffrey Fisher, had placed the crown upon her head 'for a sign of royal majesty'. Everything inherited by Elizabeth – the palaces, the footmen, the money, the land – had been given by God. And by the God of Christianity, you must understand. The God of the Bible. Specifically, the God of the Church of England. The English God, although her subjects elsewhere were generously allowed to share in Him. No Catholic was involved; and certainly no Muslim, Hindu, Sikh or Jew.

Elizabeth's faith has always appeared to be personal and sincere.

'The teachings of Christ,' she once said, 'and my own personal accountability before God, provide a framework in which I try to lead my life.' We can only guess at how the wealthiest woman in Britain interprets the bit about it being easier for a camel to make it through the eye of a needle than for a rich person to enter the kingdom of heaven, but it is undeniable that Elizabeth was raised as more of a Christian than most. We don't all get to be baptised by the Archbishop of Canterbury. Cosmo Lang, the man who wetted her forehead, believed his Church was 'witness to some ultimate sanction to which the nation looks, some ultimate ideal to which it professes'. It was the keeper of the soul of England, in other words. Elizabeth was brought up to believe that. She swore at the coronation to 'preserve inviolably the settlement of the Church of England' which had given it so many special privileges. Its version of Christianity was the official version and it had a presence in every community, through the parish priest. The Church had the right to make its own laws and hold its own courts. It also had a unique influence over secular politics and law-making, through the automatic presence of bishops in the House of Lords. Elizabeth promised to 'uphold the rights and privileges of the bishops and clergy'. She vowed to 'maintain the Laws of God and the true profession of the Gospel'. And so the deal was made once more, for the Atomic Age. She swore to be Defender of the Faith, and that didn't mean some vague notion of a nice old bearded chap on a cloud: it meant the faith defined in the Thirty-Nine Articles, down to every last anti-papal cough and spit. She has never since given any indication of changing her mind. It seems inconceivable that her son will take the same vows.

On the day of his wedding, the Queen had never been more popular. She had adapted to modern times by allowing just a little light in on the magic of the monarchy, beginning with a television documentary series during the sixties. The Windsors were walking a fine line between seeming ordinary ('They're just like us, bless 'em') and seeming, well, ordinary ('They're no better than us, damn it'). The strategy required them to appear a model family, embodying the best of us all, and on that day in July 1981 at least, people seemed to believe it. This was, after all, a fairytale. Almost everybody said so. Those who were less certain had their doubts drowned out by the cheers.

3

The land of make believe

Fairytales change in the telling. Details emerge and meanings shift, so let's look at this one again. Cinderella was not all she seemed: Diana Spencer was really very posh indeed. This was not the story we were sold, of a transcendent love between a prince and a commoner whose elevation to the palace could enable every girl to dream. Diana belonged to one of only a hundred or so families in the kingdom whose daughters were considered by the royal family to be suitable for marriage to the Prince, on the grounds that they had acquired their titles before the Industrial Revolution (when it had become possible for vulgar industrialists to buy their way into the ruling classes). This was 1981, but within the House of Windsor the rules of previous centuries still applied. Stability, security, succession were what was desired. She could not be a Roman Catholic, by law. Ideally, she would be a confirmed member of the Church of England. Americans were definitely out, they had caused enough trouble. The bride had to be a sweet, malleable virgin, but committed to the idea of having children. The line had to go on.

How would you find such a girl in the eighties? By looking for a junior aristocrat who had put a poster of the Prince on her bedroom wall and kept herself to herself, sexually speaking, despite the attentions of countless Right Honourables, for reasons that only she knew. Diana was not the brightest girl around (they called her Two Amp at school), but that did not really matter. She belonged to a group in English society that still considered itself born to rule.

So, what of her prince? Charles Philip Arthur George, known as Charlie to his people but never to his face, had been told by his uncle and mentor, Lord Louis Mountbatten, that someone in his position should 'sow his wild oats and have as many affairs as he can before settling down'. His emotional life was unusual, to say the least, having been brought up with little physical contact from his parents, sent to a brutal boarding school he later compared to a concentration camp, then issued with servants who would satisfy his every whim, including squeezing his toothpaste tube in the morning. He was not ideally equipped to be a generous, understanding husband, but he was going to be King.

'He is depressed,' said a chaplain who was close to him, shortly before the wedding. 'You can tell by the tone of his voice.' The main reason for this gloom was taken to be the terrible fate of his Uncle Dickie, the beloved Mountbatten, who had been blown up by the IRA in 1979. A bomb had been planted on his yacht while it was moored, against the advice of his security men, in Sligo. The assassination was a heavy blow to the heart of the Prince, who reacted by doing what he knew Uncle Dickie had wanted all along: he asked Mountbatten's granddaughter, Amanda, to become his wife. She was also in shock and swamped by grief, and said no. So it was that Charles found himself single and lonely a year after the murder, in the autumn of 1980, as he sat on a bale of hay at a barbecue organised by a friend and listened to that young Spencer girl he knew vaguely.

'You looked so sad,' she said of the funeral, which she had seen on television. 'My heart bled for you when I watched. I thought,

It's wrong. You're lonely. You should be with somebody to look after you.'

Diana offered sympathy, understanding and doe-eyed obeisance. 'For a wife,' Uncle Dickie had written, 'choose a suitable, attractive and sweet-charactered girl before she has met anyone else she might fall for.' Enquiries were made. Diana was still intact, it seemed. She was very young but not unsuitable. This was hardly surprising, as, without Charles knowing it, their encounter at the party had been engineered by a group of concerned women, including his grandmother. Diana was good enough, they had decided. She would do.

She was terrified. Quite rightly. From this distance, it seems astonishing that she was given so little protection. The royal love affair, 'whatever "love" meant', was made public by the announcement of their engagement in February 1981. After that, photographers began chasing Diana down the street and camping outside her flat in Earl's Court, so she rang the press office at Buckingham Palace to plead for help. Sorry, she was told, there was nothing they could do. She was not yet a royal. That was the way things worked: boundaries had to be respected, whatever the cost. Here was that old English unemotional, expedient approach again. The personal feelings of a frightened nineteen-year-old girl were not relevant. She must play up, and play the game. There was much more at stake than her own predicament, she had to understand that. She was joining a family that had done more than any other to promote and protect the Establishment and its characteristic response to all things: show as little sign of weakness as possible, but rather do one's duty, however difficult, to preserve the privilege and power gifted by God.

Diana was already slim, but she lost another six inches from her waist between the engagement and the wedding day. She did eat, sometimes voraciously, but she also stuck her fingers down her throat and threw the food up again. Nobody seems to have noticed, or cared enough to try to stop her. Perhaps they just didn't think about it, which would also be the most generous way of excusing what they did to Diana on the eve of her wedding.

She was staying with the Prince's grandmother at Clarence House. It has many bedrooms, but for some reason (malicious or stupid, it is hard to know) the bride-to-be was given a room overlooking the Mall. Normally it would have been quiet, but everybody had seen the crowds that had already gathered out there, in advance of the big day. They were waiting for her. Talking, laughing, singing. All night, just outside her window. They didn't know they were keeping her up. They would have been horrified.

Diana was barely able to sleep. She had eaten everything she could lay her hands on the night before and thrown it up. At five in the morning she woke for good, stomach clenched but deadly calm. There was no way of getting out of this, even though she knew her future husband to be in love with someone else. Diana suspected they had every intention of going on seeing each other. Orange juice was all she could manage for breakfast. She did laugh and talk when the dress was being put on, nerves making her loud. She watched the television, not quite believing the scale of what she was seeing. Then the time came and she was in the coach, escorted by mounted policemen. They were the sort who rode into riots.

Diana was dwarfed by symbolism at St Paul's. The dome of the cathedral, which had famously survived German bombs during the Second World War, towered over her, speaking of endurance, the strength of the old ways, the powerful union of faith, government and monarchy at the head of the country. This was a temple of certainty. She climbed the steps of the cathedral, an innocent delivered up to those appointed by God. To do with as

they chose. As she went from the bright sunlight into the darkness, the dazzling white train, the virginal trail, spread across a
carpet as red as blood. She would remember the moment always.
'I felt I was a lamb to the slaughter.'

Prince Charming was in the dress uniform of a naval commander, although a fellow sailor had said he couldn't park a ship
without crashing it. Thick gold braid was looped over his right
shoulder and gold stitching stiffened his high collar. On his hip
was a sword, although he had never been to war. On his left
breast were two medals. They looked like combat honours, but
the first marked his mother's coronation and the second her silver
jubilee. These medals had been given for attending his mother's
parties.

The large, embroidered silver star on his chest identified him
as a Knight of the Most Noble Order of the Garter. The white
enamel Maltese cross at his throat showed him to be Grand
Master and Principal Knight Grand Cross of the Most
Honourable Order of the Bath, named after the tradition of ritual
bathing before the acceptance of an honour from the monarch.
The star and the cross were high honours indeed, awarded to
those who had served their country very well, or earned the
favour of the Queen in some other way. Such as being her eldest
son. He was dressed like a warrior, but his costume was straight
out of the dressing-up box.

His job was to wait. And wait. His purpose in life was to
become King, but all he could do for now was to wait with as
much dignity as possible, open things and visit things, and – most
importantly of all – marry the right girl. Love had nothing to do
with it.

She loved him, or thought she did. She made it down the aisle,
still holding the arm of her father, still telling herself she was
happy. Nothing would spoil it. Then she saw a woman in grey,

in a pillar-box hat. A boy was standing on a chair beside her. Camilla Parker Bowles and her son. Diana knew, suddenly, that her suspicions were right. As she reached the altar, she was furious.

The first hymn they sang was her choice, but the second verse was left out for being too bloody. The words had been written before the slaughter of the First World War, but seemed to see it coming and rush over the top with enthusiasm for the mother country. 'Round her feet are lying the dying and the dead.'

The Archbishop of Canterbury, who came gliding over the carpet in silver, had sipped tea with the bride and groom, individually and together, listened to them and tried to prepare them for marriage, and he had come to the conclusion that their partnership was a disaster. He had not felt, however, that he could say so. For the Church to confront the Crown would only weaken both. He watched as the Dean of Westminster reminded the couple, in front of the world, that Holy Matrimony was 'an honourable estate instituted of God Himself, signifying unto us the mystical union that is betwixt Christ and His Church'. It was to be undertaken 'reverently, discreetly, soberly and in the fear of God'.

As this was said, the cameras saw the Prince scratch first one side of his nose, then the other. He rubbed under one eye, then the other. Any trainee psychologist might have recognised evasive tells, the things a person does — usually subconsciously — when nervous about a secret or being economical with the truth. The Prince messed up his words, too. Instead of vowing to share all his worldly goods with his wife, he said: 'All thy goods with thee I share.' That was really not the deal at all. She didn't have much. He could probably amuse himself in her company with her old red Mini Metro and a pair of marigold rubber gloves — what man couldn't? — but not for long.

The sound of the crowd cheering outside drifted into the cathedral and down the long aisle, where it made Charles smile. It was impossible to see Diana's reaction, as her face was still covered by the veil. They did not kiss, even after the Archbishop declared: 'Those whom God has joined together, let no man put asunder.' He asked God the Father, God the Son and God the Holy Spirit to preserve and keep them, and so on, and so on. When George Thomas, Speaker of the House of Commons, read a passage from the Bible about love being not easily provoked, the Queen Mother – architect of this union – leaned over in the most obvious way to catch the eye of the bride. Behave yourself, girl, her eyes seemed to say. Know your place. Not that the family expected anything else of the shy Sloane Ranger whose only real passion – as far as they knew – was for looking after children.

'Here,' said the Archbishop at the beginning of his sermon, 'is the stuff of which fairytales are made.' Those who knew Robert Runcie expected to hear him qualify this in some way, but he never did. He was still in his own honeymoon period with the press, and on this day he seemed to have been seduced by the illusion. 'The Prince and Princess on their wedding day.' He was supporting the myth. The deal was being played out again. The closest he got to realism was to say that marriage was not 'the happy ever after' but the beginning of an adventure. Then he told the Prince and new Princess of Wales they were surrounded 'by the sincere affection, and the active prayer, of millions of friends'.

There was still no kiss. Not in church, not on the steps outside, not in the open-topped carriage, not even on the balcony of Buckingham Palace, as they looked down on the crowds filling the Mall and the parks for as far as they could see and heard the people singing 'You'll Never Walk Alone'. It was right for the moment, that sentimental song. Right for a fairytale. 'God Save the Queen' was sung next, inevitably. The wedding party disappeared back inside, but re-emerged to thunderous cheers a few moments later. Inside again, and out again. And again. No kiss, still.

'We want the Queen!' the people chanted. They got her, on her own on the balcony, waving and smiling.

'We want Di!'

She was miserable in the shadows, dizzy, sick, unable to get through to her husband, who wouldn't even touch her. But when she stepped back on to the balcony, it was different. The look on her face changed. The cameras caught it: the first real-isation that half a million people were in love with her, and their energy was something she could suck up and feed upon. Suddenly, Diana had the look of someone who realised her own strength.

'They want us to kiss,' she said now to the Prince, as the lip readers revealed. This girl, who had called him 'Sir' all through their courtship, was telling him what to do. He stood where he was, straight as his sword, and made her lean across him, stretch-ing her neck upwards. It was over in a moment and they moved apart, while the crowd was still going mad. Fairytales indeed. Everything was simple and certain. Love ruled. The sun was shin-ing. God was in His heaven. The people began to sing again 'Happy and glorious . . .' It was a powerful sound, much louder than the mutterings and shouts of all those who had missed the moment and were saying: 'What? Did they kiss? Crikey, that was quick. Is that it, then? Is that it?'

One of the bright and fizzy pop bands that Diana liked most in the summer of 1981 was Bucks Fizz, who had won the Eurovision Song Contest by whipping off their skirts. They were making a follow-up album including a song that would describe, quite accidentally, the state of the nation: 'The Land of Make Believe'. The royal bride believed she was Cinderella. She believed she would be loved and looked after. The groom believed she would do her duty with no fuss. The family believed it was treating Diana in a reasonable way. The Queen believed she was on her throne by divine appointment. The people believed their deep affection for her and her children was mutual. The Archbishop believed England was still a Christian nation and would go on being so. Everyone was fooling themselves. The whole thing was like a wedding cake with a hollow bottom tier: sooner or later it was going to collapse. Nothing would ever be this certain again. Not for Charles, not for Diana, not for Elizabeth, not for anyone. Change was coming. Doubt was lurking, growing. Soon, things that were taken for granted would be revealed as illusions. New certainties were about to challenge the old ones, and those who held them would be as passionate, persuasive and powerful as anyone the Establishment could offer.

The Bucks Fizz song was about a child caught up in a dream world that seemed perfect, when actually there was something nasty lurking in the garden. In real life, the nastiness wasn't waiting patiently, as the song said. Not at all. It was coming straight down the middle of the road, through the crowds, prepared to mow down anyone who got in its way.

4

People gettin' angry

The Land-Rover did not stop. The police officer at the wheel had been told to keep going, into the crowd and through it. 'They know what will happen if they get in the way,' his boss had said, ordering the use of the heavy vehicle to disperse rioters when bricks and flaming bottles were flying. The tactic had worked in Ulster, but this was Liverpool on the eve of the royal wedding. While the rest of the country was engaged in a story of love, patriotism and joy, here there was trouble. There had been all month, on and off, following earlier riots in Manchester, Bristol and Brixton. So the driver kept going. Somebody was bound to get hurt. Somebody did.

The rumour spread fast the following day, because of all the street parties. Somebody told somebody else down in London, who told my father as he was opening the Party Seven: 'Heard what happened in Liverpool last night? Somebody died.' A young black man in a wheelchair, he couldn't get out of the way in time. Those bastards. The first person, the only person, to be killed as a direct result of the riots had died in hospital while the bunting was being put up in his street. There would be no ale and sandwiches for him. His family would not be singing 'God Save the Queen'. He was not named in the brief reports on the news bulletins, because his death was not as important as the wedding. Of course not. That was a regal occasion, something good and true and bright in a gloomy time. The sun was shining and the red, white and blue was bold. Unemployment was higher than 2.5 million and rising. Inflation was strong. The government was falling down on the job, failing with its fiscal shock tactics. We needed distraction.

We needed make believe, and so both sides told fairytales: the police in their evasion of blame and the protesters in their fury. The young man who died was not in a wheelchair at all; in truth, he just had a slight limp. He wasn't black, either. He was white. A local lad, or so I have been told by a policeman who was there that day and knew him. That isn't the story people tell, even now. The Chief Constable of Merseyside was sure he knew who was to blame for the trouble in his city, and said so: 'Black hooligans.'

Here is another certainty that was dominant in the burning summer of 1981: England was white. Yes, there were immigrants and angry young people of colour but the overwhelming majority, the good people, the hard-working and law-abiding ones, were white. Or so it was believed, in a country that had only just given up laughing at the words 'honky' and 'nig-nog' in the TV show *Love Thy Neighbour*. The widely held assumption surfaced accidentally during royal wedding day, in a moment that went unnoticed at the time but is a jaw-dropper now. A BBC presenter was standing on a balcony in Whitehall, with a million pink faces behind and below him. The mood was happy despite the heat and crowding, in contrast with the so-called black riots that were obviously on his mind. 'At a time when crowds taking to the street makes the whole nation nervous,' he said to the camera, 'this is a crowd of a different complexion.'

Oh dear. People get sacked for less these days. Let's be fair, he probably only meant to contrast the behaviour of the two groups, but it was not a smart thing to say. That phrase 'the whole nation' co-opts the viewer. It says: 'You and me, we're peaceful people. Loyal, law-abiding people like the ones behind me. White people. We're England. Not those other people, those trouble-makers, those rioters. They are outsiders. They are not us. They are not England.' His message was accidental and subconscious, but in the institutions of the Establishment, it was explicit. The first black bishop would not take office for four more years. The first black MP was six years from being elected. The first black High Court judge was only just being called to the Bar and would not achieve that great office for another twenty-three years.

Black people had lived in Liverpool for two centuries and played an important part in the making of a great Victorian port, yet they were still expected to live in ghettos and be grateful for the worst of jobs. There were riots in the city because work was hard to find, money was scarce and homes were overcrowded or falling down; and the police were heavy handed, using sus laws for fun. 'For years I have been saying that the conditions are not tolerable,' said Margaret Simey, chair of the Merseyside Police Committee. 'It is not fair play. There is social unrest in the area and I would regard the people as apathetic if they didn't riot.' The Chief Constable and the Prime Minister regarded her as a trai-tor for that, but notice the use of the phrase 'fair play'. Even amid the street battles, the values of the English God were present. According to local legend, both sides called an abrupt halt in the middle of one riot when they noticed that an old people's home was burning down. They helped the ambulance service get the elderly residents out, then went back to knocking seven bells out of each other.

Fair play had nothing to do with the way immigrants were treated. West Indians had come here by invitation to help boost the workforce after the war, and many had brought with them an emotional allegiance to what they called the mother country. As post-colonial Christians, most believed in the English God, but they were not treated as equals. Nor were their children. The same was true of those who came from Asia. The English wouldn't really let them in, emotionally or at an official level. Margaret Thatcher had been elected by sailing close to the ugly wind that filled the sails of the National Front. 'People are really rather afraid,' she said, 'that this country might be rather swamped by people with a different culture.'

Some might call that prophetic, if they subscribe to the politics of fear, but at the time it generated alarm that was not justified by the numbers. The biggest immigrant group was the Indians, but they still made up only 1.5 per cent of the population. Pakistanis accounted for less than 1 per cent, as did black Caribbeans. Africans and Chinese were down around a third of a per cent. Overall, England was 95 per cent white. In the places that were mixed, things were happening that the Prime Minister could neither see nor understand. If she was threatened by a multicultural future, some of us were already living it. There was nothing political about my friendship with Delon and Sunil at a battered comprehensive in the East End of London. It was just natural, like Tucker being friends with Benny on *Grange Hill*. The three of us – whose parents had been born in Kingston, Karachi and Hackney – sat in the same classroom as boys who scratched 'NF' on the desks. Some of them were very confused, and things could get bizarre. Marksy, who had scabs on his shaven head where he had tried to tattoo 'NF' with a compass needle, once came charging down the school playground with a tennis ball at his feet, sent it fizzing between the posts that had been painted on the wall, then stood there with his hands in the air like he'd won the cup for Spurs again, shouting, 'Yes! Crooks!'

Garth Crooks was black.

'Yeah,' said Marksy. 'But he's brilliant. Black bastard.'

The rioters were the footsoldiers of another England, whose values had never been taught at Eton or preached from the Anglican pulpit, and certainly never acknowledged by the House of Windsor. Most people know that George Orwell found the soul of England in 'long shadows on county grounds, warm beer, invincible green suburbs, dog lovers and old maids bicycling to Holy Communion through the morning mist'. Which is lovely, except he didn't. Those words do not come from Orwell at all but from a misquote by John Major. The writer himself actually prefaced the bit about the old girl on her bike with 'the clatter of clogs in the Lancashire mill towns, the to-and-fro of the lorries on the Great North Road, the queues outside the Labour Exchanges, the rattle of pin tables in the Soho pubs'. Not quite so idyllic, is it?

The pin tables are fruit machines now. The Great North Road has ceded its importance to the Great Car Park otherwise known as the M1. The clogs don't clatter and the mills are closed, but otherwise, Orwell still has a point: the soul of England was never just to be found in the beauty of a village green on a summer's evening. It was never just about elegance and tradition and respectability, castles and cream teas. Those are the propaganda tools of the England we have mostly been exploring until now, the one created by the Church, the State and the Crown and sustained by the Tourist Board, the advertising agency and the heritage industry. This Establishment England put on a party in the summer of 1981 whose noise drowned out almost all the dissent. Just like the Queen's silver jubilee, the wedding offered the chance to enlist the temporary but fervent support of its rival, which we could call – with a little ironic nod to what was to come – the People's England.

I don't just mean the working classes, although for a long time this version of Englishness did survive best hidden among them, while the other held the golf clubs and suburbs. The People's England was – and always had been – feisty, argumentative, icon-oclastic, collective, populist and improvised, particularly in the way it related to God. The Diggers, the Ranters, the Seekers and the Muggletonians were not characters from Harry Potter books but members of sects in the seventeenth century with different ideas about who God was and how we should live. Collectively known as the Dissenters, they had their day during the reign of Oliver Cromwell. After that, when the monarchy and the State Church were restored and Charles II again made it the law in 1662 that all priests should be licensed and preach only the the-ology laid down in the Thirty-Nine Articles, nearly two thousand clergymen left. They became part of the nonconformist movement, which included Baptists, Quakers and eventually Methodists.

John Wesley and his band of unlicensed, unregulated spiritual revolutionaries were seen as a threat by both the Church and the State in the 1700s, because they preached that people had to make their own individual decisions about faith and become active converts rather than passive members of a religious insti-tution corrupted by its closeness to power. As the historian Callum Brown says, this form of Christianity was democratic:

It was a leveller, tearing the formal expression of religiosity from the serried ranks of churchgoers in the landlord's parish church and ceding it to the personal experience of high and low, wherever they might feel it. It deregulated religion . . . 'privatising' it, opening up the saving of souls to any passing evangelist or preacher and denying the authority and control of ecclesiastical regulation.

People gettin' angry

These agitators had a great deal in common with others who opposed the established order of things in English society, even when it was not for explicitly religious reasons: the leader of the Tolpuddle Martyrs, for example, was a Methodist lay preacher called George Loveless. This group of farm labourers swore an oath to each other under a tree in Dorset and formed a prototype union to protest against a drop in farm wages. Seven of them were sentenced to transportation to Australia. The trade union movement still holds a festival to remember what they did, which was a point of contact between dissident faith and the fine tradition of atheist resistance. Without both of those, there would have been no Labour Party.

The People's England was not always pious. It was also bawdy, boozy and lewd, with a love of saucy jokes and naughty fun. Where could it be seen in the summer of 1981? Dancing to 'Knees up Mother Brown' at the street parties – 'If I catch you bending, I'll saw your knees right off' – but also on the streets of Toxteth, throwing bottles. Waving a flag and hoping for a glimpse of Di, but also in a curtained, smoke-filled room, plotting to bring down Thatcher. On the beach, wrestling with a windbreak and eating sand-and-fishpaste sandwiches, but also kissing quickly in the gay clubs, defying prejudice and the law. It was at the dogs or fighting on the terraces, or putting on the slap for a big night out. The People's England had a faith of its own, an old and secret faith that would grow strong again in the future, but for now it paid lip service to the English God sustained by the Establishment, put down 'C of E' on the forms and got on with life. It was about Diana Dors flashing her massive cleavage next to Adam Ant in the video for 'Prince Charming', all brash and wonderful; or Boy George dressing like a what-is-that-a-man-or-a-woman?

But it wasn't all hedonism. There was anger. There were black

53

boys and white boys driving around in a Vauxhall Cresta, in the video for 'Ghost Town'. The number-one single in the week of the royal wedding, in the week the riots claimed their only life, was a powerfully political song which claimed that the hostility was coming from the government, not the people. It opened with the howling of the wind across a wasteland, as the Specials drove through a deserted city at night. 'This town . . . is coming like a ghost town,' said a voice, with a hoarse honesty seldom heard in the charts. Then a shout: 'Why must the youth fight against themselves? Government leaving the youth on the shelf.' The singers were from Coventry, a town in which the car industry was being destroyed. 'This place is coming like a ghost town. No job to be found in this country. Can't go on no more . . .' Then that ominous voice again: 'People gettin' angry.'

Who really cared, though? Two Tone terrified nobody. Ska couldn't skewer the government. Sticks and stones were proving useless against the people in power; even bricks and petrol bombs had made no impression on their solid certainties. It would take something much more startling than riots to bring those down.

5

Gotcha!

Every fairytale needs a wicked witch, and Margaret Thatcher made Sleeping Beauty's stepmother look cuddly – but there is one thing about her that many people forget when they are discussing the poison that some say ran in her veins, the second head that was hidden under the bow collar of her blouse and the apparent fact that if you added up the number of letters in her name, divided the total by three and multiplied it by twenty-seven you got the number of the Beast. It is how explicitly she presented herself as a Christian.

It was there right from the start, on the steps of Downing Street after she came to power in 1979, when she paraphrased St Francis of Assisi: 'Where there is discord, may we bring harmony. Where there is error, may we bring truth. Where there is doubt, may we bring faith. And where there is despair, may we bring hope.' Well no, it didn't really turn out that way, but she was sincere. 'The Christian religion – which, of course, embodies many of the great spiritual and moral truths of Judaism – is a fundamental part of our national heritage,' she once said. 'For centuries it has been our very lifeblood. Indeed we are a nation whose ideals are founded on the Bible. Also, it is quite impossible to understand our history or literature without grasping this fact.'

You might think that a Conservative Prime Minister who spoke in those terms would be a champion for the English God, a protector and preserver of the historic faith with all its powers and privileges. Wrong. She was going to do more than anyone else to kill it, through example, through policy and through changes in the law. Mrs Thatcher had her own, compelling certainties at odds with the old ones. She had a new morality, centred on wealth creation; she had a new understanding of society, as a collection of individuals motivated to look out for themselves and their families rather than the common good; and she had a faith that was, at heart, anti-Establishment.

Margaret Thatcher was an outsider, a grocer's daughter, raised in a flat above the shop. However posh she made herself sound, however many elocution lessons she took, however much she sought allies who were One of Us, she was never One of Them. Alfred and Beatrice Roberts, her father and mother, were Methodists, and therefore members of a faith that considered a dustman the same as a duke under God. Their Margaret would smash the system so that class would no longer be the defining factor in British life. Unfortunately, her replacement as the measure of worth was wealth, which was probably not what the preacher at the chapel the Roberts family attended would have wanted. Self-help was at the heart of everything she tried to do, as she once told David Frost:

The essence of human rights is that each person can choose between right and wrong. That is the essence of morality, that is the essence of religion. If you were to take away so much in tax that people did not have the choice, if you take away from them responsibility for their families and their children, I would say that that is wrong. How can you develop your character, develop your responsibilities, if you are not allowed the

right to choose? As I understand it the right to choose is the essence of Christianity.

Not fair play, modesty and courtesy, then. The core values of the English God did not suit her. Fair play applied in the sense of giving everyone a chance in the free market, but after that it was every man and woman – or at least every family unit – for themselves. Modesty was not necessary; indeed, what was wrong with telling the world you were a success? The nation must become great again, and for that she needed Great Britons. And courtesy? Not unless it had a purpose. Not if she thought you were a fool. And not in the City, where calling your rival rude names was becoming okay as long as you then crushed him beneath your heel.

Taxing the rich to help the poor was too constricting for her. People must be given the freedom to become as wealthy as possible, so that they could choose to help the less fortunate. If they wanted to. 'How could we respond to the many calls for help, or invest for the future, or support the wonderful artists or craftsmen whose work also glorifies God, unless we had first worked hard and used our talents to create the necessary wealth?' She outraged some people, who called that the Creed of Greed.

Margaret Thatcher had yet to articulate her philosophy fully in the summer of 1981, but at fifty-five years of age, the Prime Minister was limbering up for a long and bloody battle with the doubters, the cynics, the wets, the unions and anyone else who got in her way. Who would dare?

The answer was absurd. The Labour Party was a mess, the Liberals unimportant. The main opposition voice against Margaret Thatcher and her policies at the start of the eighties was the man in the silver cope, the man whose voice was wetter than the bottom of an open-air swimming pool on a very rainy day.

The Archbishop of Canterbury, Robert Runcie, who had wimped out at the wedding and simpered along with the illusion of a love story. The teller of fairytales. Like Margaret, he was an outsider, born in Crosby on Merseyside, where his dad was an electrical engineer at the Tate and Lyle sugar factory. Dad went blind when Robert was seventeen, and had to take early retirement, which put them on their uppers. This was not the usual sort of background for an archbishop. He was the first of modern times to have killed someone, as a tank commander during the war: 'A German standing up bravely with a bazooka and you training your gun on him and just blowing him to smithereens as you went through.' When anti-hunt campaigners asked the Archbishop if he had ever killed an animal, he said no. Only humans. 'When I'd been very successful in knocking out a German tank, I went up to it and saw four young men dead. I felt a bit sick. Well, I was sick, actually.' His head also contained memories of the concentration camps, as he was one of the first British soldiers to enter Belsen. He spoke of 'the terrible, terrible grey skeleton figures' but did not say much else about it. He was a child of his times, trained to keep it all in.

Runcie was almost as reticent about his Military Cross, won for two acts of bravery in Normandy. The first was to climb into a burning tank, while shells were falling all around, and turn the turret so that the driver could be pulled out. The next morning he risked making his own tank an easy target by taking it out on to open ground, so that he could destroy a major gun emplacement. 'I didn't expect to get decorated,' he said. 'I was totally surprised.' The wartime Runcie was a risk-taker: he even had a girlfriend who had been in the Nazi Youth, whose previous boyfriend had died fighting for the SS. His relationship with her was against all the rules. When one of his fellow officers heard he was going into the Church he said, 'What a waste.'

His wife Lindy was also unusual, a pianist who refused to be the tame clergy companion and once said: 'Too much religion makes me go pop.' They were both alarmed when he was offered the top job in 1980, he said. 'I didn't think I was good enough for it. I wasn't spiritual enough.' As he was trying to make up his mind what to do, a fellow clergyman watched him during a service in St Albans Cathedral. 'We were kneeling there in the candlelight . . . and I know we were all thinking, That poor bugger!'

The trouble with being Archbishop of Canterbury is that everybody thinks you have real power, like the Pope, and you just don't. You can't tell your people what to do at all, only offer suggestions, at most. And they won't thank you for it. They'll blame you when it all goes wrong. The writer Andrew Brown describes the situation well: 'An Archbishop of Canterbury has little more power than the King of Poland . . . to lead such a body is like taking a large collection of dogs for a walk in the country without enough leads.' Actually, he says, in this case, 'the pack of good-natured, energetic, English dogs is augmented by an elephant or two, some very touchy rodents and perhaps a hippogriff'.

The press loved Runcie for the first couple of years. One of his most remarkable early acts was to kneel and pray in Canterbury Cathedral in 1982 with Pope John Paul II, during the first papal visit to England since the Reformation. 'The wilder rantings of Ian Paisley would have made perfect sense to almost everybody in this country 100 years ago,' wrote Brown. 'Runcie's gracious, generous and intelligent handling of these matters was hugely important in showing that attitudes had changed, as well as in changing them.' The Roman Catholic Church was still excluded from the Establishment by ancient prejudice, but that was now to its benefit. Catholics were younger and more likely to be working class than Anglicans. They were enjoying revolutionary changes brought about by the Second Vatican Council, including the mass being said in English. Men and women who were not priests were allowed to lead services, and to worship with other Christians, sometimes. The English could now hardly tell the difference between an Anglican priest and a Catholic one – except that if the latter had a woman on his arm, he was heading for trouble.

The Pope was a superstar, and people of both faiths and none lined the streets for him, even if he did arrive bang in the middle of Britain's surprising fight with a Catholic nation, Argentina, over the sovereignty of the Falkland Islands. The conflict allowed Margaret Thatcher to present herself as Britannia with a bouffant, while Robert Runcie was to become a figure of tabloid loathing. 'Gotcha!' screamed the front-page headline of the *Sun* when the *General Belgrano* was sunk, killing 368 men. Roy Greenslade, who was working there at the time, remembers the news editor wearing a naval officer's cap. The *Sun's* coverage of the war was 'xenophobic, bloody-minded, ruthless, often reckless, black-humoured and ultimately triumphalist', he says, but it 'captured the zeitgeist. Here was a new Britain, and new kind of newspaper heralding the emergence of a transformed culture.'

When victory had been won and a service was held at St Paul's, the Prime Minister sat with the heads of the armed services and representatives of all the units that had fought, top brass gleaming, expecting to be led in thanking God for a glorious triumph. Robert Runcie knew more about the horrific realities of all-out combat than many people there, and certainly more than Margaret Thatcher. He reminded the congregation that people were 'mourning on both sides in this conflict'. A year earlier, in the same place, he had spoken of fairytales. Now he sounded more like himself: 'Those who dare to interpret God's will must never claim Him as an asset for one nation or group rather than another.' Listening to this, Margaret Thatcher was livid. 'The boss is spitting blood,' said her husband that evening. She had fought the Argentinian junta, she was not afraid of an infernal clergyman. If the Church did not agree with her view of what was right and wrong, then she would do to liberal English Christianity what she had done to the *General Belgrano*: sink it.

6

The final countdown

Some of us had bigger things to worry about than strange little wars in the South Atlantic. The end of the world was nigh. The Bomb was big. The Campaign for Nuclear Disarmament had never been more fashionable: membership was climbing towards an all-time high and the badge was a symbol of cool as well as solidarity. Some of the teachers at my school spent far longer in class than they should have done showing us what the blast and fallout had done to Japanese children at Hiroshima and Nagasaki. They told us the Americans were using an airbase called Greenham Common as a base for warheads that could each do far more damage than had been done in 1945. The teachers pulled down the blinds and screened the film *The War Game*, banned by the BBC for being too horrifying. Too right. We watched as the screen shifted shadows to show two boys our age screaming and holding their faces after the blast. 'At this distance,' the sinister voice of the narrator said, 'the temperature is sufficient to cause melting of the upturned eyeball.' Ginger, the maths tyrant, smiled in the half light, knowing there would be a few more young members at the next CND meeting, where he would be sitting up front with Bubble, the science teacher. Not that he ever got to park his missiles on her base: she gave up her job to join the women's peace camp at Greenham.

Fear has always propelled people into faith. Fear of sickness, fear of death, fear of natural forces beyond understanding. Fear of the Bomb was our generational nightmare, the apocalypse that plagued our thoughts as global warming does for children today. The difference is that the propaganda tells you it is possible to do something to prevent eco-oblivion, by changing the way you use energy, the car you drive, even a light bulb. No such response was possible to the prospect of nuclear meltdown. You could campaign, which would make you feel better, but nobody was listening. The Bomb was a potent symbol of the gulf between the people with power and the rest of us. They had their certainties and we would suffer for them. They'd be in their underground bunkers with the doors locked, and we would fry.

The only other thing we could do was pray. For this reason, surprising numbers of young people were drawn to churches of all kinds during this second coming of CND, whether to the pacifist Quakers or the Catholics who had given us the inspirational anti-nuclear campaigner Monsignor Bruce Kent. The same was also true in left-wing politics. There were not enough new recruits to slow the downward slide, but they did provide the energy to keep things going for a while. The important thing for our story is that the version of faith that was given a shot in the arm by all of this believed the Establishment's English God to be an offensive, dangerous distortion of the truth.

The fear of the Lord is the beginning of wisdom, the Book of Proverbs says, drawing on a knowledge more ancient than the Bible. The fear of the Lord is the fear of the sky, fear of the dark, fear of the wind, the waves, the water. Fear is there at the heart of the most influential theory of religious conversion in modern times, published in 1965 by John Lofland and Rodney Stark, after a study of people joining the Moonies. The theory has been revised and challenged many times, but still underpins research into faith. It says that the process often starts with tensions in the life of the person who is going to convert. They've got problems they can't solve on their own, worries that won't go away. Fears they cannot beat. They start searching for answers, for a way of looking at the world that will give some comfort and protection, and the idea of a religion – a creed based on a higher power of some kind – appeals to them. They reach a point where they feel the need to make big changes in their life. Then they meet the followers of a specific faith and find them very attractive. The appeal is in the certainty, perhaps, or the sense of purpose. The community. They respond, start going along to meetings and gradually start seeing their other friends less often. The feeling of being part of a select group of people with the truth leads to a full conversion. Some people are easily led, others will go into it completely voluntarily.

The process is not entirely universal, of course, but it does seem to describe what happens when you are converted or drawn more deeply into a powerful faith or belief system, such as Islam or Christianity, as happened to me. I was drawn by degrees into the deepest heart of the faith that still ruled the country, and eventually into a version of it that said God could be my friend, my confidant, my healer, even my lover. It started because I was afraid. The end of the world was nigh.

The end of the world came at twenty past two on a Tuesday afternoon. My friend Stu and I were bunking off school. We'd finished our chips and run out of coins for Space Invaders, so we were just wandering about, arguing.

'No way. Just look at him. He's going to be rubbish.'

'Shut up. Give him a chance.'

'You don't know nothing.'

This heated discussion was about whether the new Dr Who

would be as good as the old one. The scarf had gone, the hat had gone, the wicked grin had gone, and in their place was a wet-looking bloke in a cricket outfit. I knew Stu was right, but that foppish, linen-clad Oxford look was big in 1982, with *Chariots of Fire* long out and *Brideshead* being revisited on TV. Black was our thing, though. Skinny jeans, t-shirts with the sleeves cut off, black leather and studs on our wrists. We were a bit punk, a bit metal and a bit into this new stuff called Goth. Somehow – the warm sun, a full stomach and a distracting billboard of the Cadbury's Flake woman – I had let Stu get his argument in first, so I was duty bound to oppose him.

'It might work.'

'You're a Muppet.'

The spirit of Oscar Wilde lived. There we were, fifteen-year-old boys sitting on a wall outside a pub on the North Circular Road, kicking our heels against the bricks, when a shocking, strange and powerful sound began. A groan that became a wheezy wail that became a massive, unavoidable scream, making it hard to breathe, blocking out all other noise as if a massive herd of invisible beasts in terrible pain had come charging down the street.

'Damn!' said Stu, sagely.

'What shall we do?'

'Walk.'

So we walked. What else could we do? We knew what it was. The sound was coming from the elderly sea-green air-raid sirens bolted to the streetlamps, high over our heads. The four-minute warning. The end of the world. I wanted my mum. Stu proba-bly wanted his too, but neither of us was going to say so, so we walked. The traffic kept moving too, and the sky didn't flash or darken, but the sirens didn't stop either. Every boy we knew had a fantasy about this. It starred a woman – any woman – who would hear the sirens and realise that what she wanted to do with her remaining four minutes was make furious love to an adolescent boy. She'd tear his trousers off and they'd do it right there on the pavement, not caring who saw. Which would, obviously, leave an awkward post-coital silence lasting three minutes and fifty seconds.

There were no women about. There was nobody on the pavement and the drivers wound down their windows to peer up at the sirens, but they kept going. I was shaking but I managed to put one foot forward, then the other and swing my arms because if I didn't, I would stop and fall down sobbing. I wanted to be held. I wanted to be home. I wanted to hide. What happened now? What happened next? The blinding light, the bleached bones.

Please – the words formed slowly in my head – God.

The gut reaction of a frightened boy. A petition in the face of oblivion, when there was nothing else to do or say. My first prayer.

Help.

Me.

Then the noise stopped. The silence was even more powerful.

'Blimey.'

We were walking, going nowhere.

'Didn't believe it.'

'Nah.'

Just for a moment, though, I had been convinced it was the end. The rise and fall of the siren was exactly like the one we had heard on a public information film called *Protect and Survive*, which advised people to get into fallout shelters built with tables, doors and mattresses. If you were caught out in the open, you were supposed to lie face down with your shirt over your head. Then, as Stu said, 'Bend over, put your head between your legs and kiss yerself goodbye.' We knew there would be no warning, really. All the decisions were being made in briefing rooms, on secure lines, in nuclear submarines off the coast of Sweden. Nowhere visible. The apocalypse would be sudden and ordinary. The sky imploding, just like that. If you thought about it, as we had just been forced to do, it was absolutely terrifying.

I was at the stage described by Lofland and Stark as 'ready to make a change'. Frankly, I was prepared to listen to anyone who said they could save me. I imagined UFOs in the skies above our house, and spoke to ghosts when they rattled the window frame. I burned my hand on the radiator trying to copy shamans who trained their minds to ignore pain, having read that Evel Knievel could do the same. I wished for a near-death experience like the ones nearly everyone in America seemed to have had. I believed in the Loch Ness monster. I was ready to believe in anything.

I kept having a nightmare, the same one again and again. A flat sea, a strip of sand, some trees. The sea boiling and the sky burning, the clouds flying fast in all the colours of fire. Silhouetted against them, bodies passing overhead; hundreds and thousands of them, some looking down. People I knew, staring but not seeing. Whatever had carried them off lifted me too, into the air. All I could hear was the rushing wind and roaring waves and the sounds of earth, metal, glass, groaning, cracking and shattering. The sunset, a nuclear sunset, was slowly overcome by the darkness until it was a black tunnel with a bright light at the end of it. An awesome, peaceful, scary and calming light. Then I woke up.

It was just a dream, until it came true. We were on holiday in Italy, camping in a wood that led to a beach. Striking moody poses, as teenage boys do, I went down by the shore on the first night and realised, to my alarm, that this was the place of my nightmares. It looked almost exactly the same. How could that be? Then I became aware how strange the atmosphere was: the wind was ducking and diving, coming from every direction at once, and the air smelled like a wet electric-bar fire. Spooked, I ran back to the tent and tried to calm down, telling myself not to be daft. I didn't know that out on the horizon, heading for us, was a violent, cloudboiling, sky-shattering storm that would grow and grow in the night until it tore the leaves from the trees and tore the trees down on top of them, turned dust paths into muddy torrents and flattened canvas.

'Come on!' Dad shouted. 'How can you sleep in this? Get out!'

The tent was heavy on our heads. I pushed out into the maelstrom and ran through it behind my father, who forced the door of an empty caravan. In the morning, we looked out like lifeboat survivors floating on a thick, brown sea.

The campsite owners packed us off on a free day trip to the walled town of Porec, down the coast in Yugoslavia. The colours were wild after the storm: the sea more blue than I had ever seen it, the sun sharp. The trip was pleasant and uneventful, until I lost my parents somewhere in the Old Town, deliberately, by stepping through a little wooden door into a church. The air was cool in there, both dusty and damp. There was nobody else around. Sunlight cut through a stained-glass window and on to sandy wall, the colours shifting until they settled. They formed a fixed pattern and held it, just like that . . . and I saw that the pattern was a face. A sweet, simple, friendly face. It made me smile. My heart tripped. I looked at the face. It looked back.

'Hello,' I said.

The face said nothing.

'Can I take a picture?'

Nothing. So I got out the camera, but when I took my eye away from the viewfinder, the face had disappeared. The sun had gone. It was cold in there, suddenly.

The final countdown

Sunlight on sandstone, that's all it was. I know that, of course
I do, but after seeing it I couldn't stop thinking about angels.
They were everywhere: on the television, at the cinema, in the
charts, on gravestones and company logos, sneaking through the
letterbox blowing their trumpets on Christmas cards and wrapping paper, populating the earth in their thousands. They always
had been: winged figures appeared on carvings made by the
Sumerians three thousand years before Christ. Shining visitors
feature in the stories of Judaism, Christianity and Islam, and at
least two of them have the same names in all three major faiths:
the archangels Michael and Gabriel. Michael, the commander of
the armies of the Lord, is identified as the protector of Israel in
the Book of Daniel; he fights Satan for the body of Moses in the
New Testament; and in the Quran he is named as one of the
three angels who visited Abraham. Gabriel visited Daniel himself while the Jews were slaves in Babylon; he told Mary she was
going to give birth to the Son of God; and he revealed the words
of the Quran to Muhammad, later flying alongside as the
Prophet rode his winged horse through the seven spheres of
heaven. They were busy fellows, these angels, and they were just
the superstars.

The word comes from the Greek *angelos*, meaning messenger.
They often create havoc, as with poor Joan of Arc. Christians
were told many times down the centuries to keep their eyes on
God and not the gorgeous ladyboys with the huge white wings,
but the angels kept coming anyway. They were the outriders of
folk faith: unofficial, popular, superstitious, mysterious, improvised beliefs that refuse to die. When the photograph came back
from the developers, I showed it to people back in England and
asked what they saw. Some said nothing but bright, hazy shapes
on a black background. Others said quickly, without much
doubt: 'It's a face.'

They were all believers, the ones who saw the face. The Angel of Porec, as far as I was concerned, had found them for me.

'The end is coming.'

I turned away from the bus and let the doors close.

'What did you say?'

'The end is coming.' The boy at the bus stop hadn't been talking to me, but now he was. 'No doubt about it. We must be prepared. Why? Are you interested?'

'Maybe.'

'I'm Dave, this is Shaun, and this is Chris. We're the Christian Union.'

They weren't *in* the CU at our school, they *were* the CU. They couldn't contain themselves. They were suddenly desperately excited that someone was prepared to hear them out and not just hurl abuse, so we walked home together instead of taking the bus and we met in the playground next day and after school and I started to get to know them. Three boys, raised in church – Sunday school, choir, Scouts, the whole shebang – and rebelling, as every teenager must. In the most unusual way.

'We don't take drugs,' said Dave. That was not a problem, I was too scared myself.

'We don't smoke,' said Shaun. Fine, I hated the taste.

'We don't drink –' Ah. Now then. Here was a stumbling block. '– any more than Jesus did. He was always at a party.'

Was he? Thank God.

'We want a Gospel that is pure, not compromised.'

'We want to bring in the kingdom.'

'We want to believe totally and to commit ourselves to the work of the Lord. He's coming back.'

Right. When?

'Soon,' said Dave, confidently. 'The Bible says so. What's going on in Beirut is a sign. It's in Revelation. Two thousand years after His birth the Lord will return in glory. You want to be ready.'

He sounded so sure. For a moment I thought he was joking, then I wanted to take the mickey, but that instinct was overtaken by another. Maybe, unbelievably, the apocalyptic mess in my head had a form and structure and a story and these boys, even more unbelievably, just boys at school, understood it. If they could, then surely I could. Was he sure?

'The year 2000? Might be sooner. I wouldn't bet against it. Mind you . . .'

They didn't bet?

'Yes. Exactly. Come and see Isaiah. He'll explain everything.'

Isaiah was short and bald, with a clipped beard. He was in his early forties, I guessed, but dressed like the boys in combat trousers. 'The Boys have told me about you,' he said. They were The Boys. That was what they called themselves. Isaiah led the way into his flat, which was only a bedsit. A pillow stuffed down the back of the sofabed was the only thing out of place in a meticulously clean room: stripped wooden floor, spotless blue rug, polished chrome-and-glass coffee table. The records were stacked alphabetically. That was not natural. They started with Abba.

'I believe you expressed an interest in prophecy?' He hadn't offered me tea or anything. We were still standing. Had milk or something gone off in the room? No, those stale wafts were his breath. 'Please, have a seat. We have beanbags only, I'm afraid, apart from the sofa. The Boys like the floor.'

I chose the floor too, and felt the draught. His voice was whiny and mean but insistent. Why did I stay? Why didn't I run for it? Isaiah (which I was already pretty sure was not the name his parents had given him) was creepy, but The Boys had something. They belonged to each other. They had confidence, which was attractive to someone who felt like he was whirling in a washing-machine drum of doubt and fear. They had answers. They told me I had a God-shaped hole in my heart as a result of humanity's separation from the Creator after the Fall. Was it that, or the need to feel accepted by a group of my peers, however strange?

The second stage in the process of conversion described by Lofland and Stark is about having problems and looking for solutions. I had three main problems at this stage of my life: a fear of the end of the world, a lack of mates and a strong desire to leave home. Christianity, as described by Isaiah, offered an apocalyptic world view. The images in my dream had been the Lord's copyright, apparently, since the apostle John sat on the island of Patmos and had his delirious revelations. The moon would turn blood red. The horsemen would ride, the earth would shake. This was not news, it was prophecy, and had been for nearly two thousand years before the splitting of the atom.

Joining The Boys solved the second problem at a stroke and it was also guaranteed to get right up the nose of my father. Maybe that was why I ended up on the floor in Isaiah's tiny flat, repeating the words of a prayer of confession.

'I am truly sorry for my sins.'

'I am truly sorry for my sins.'

I was on my knees, surrounded by The Boys.

'I turn to the Lord.'

'I turn to the Lord.'

'Yes, Lord,' murmured one of The Boys. 'Amen.'

For the first time in my life, I felt the hands of prayer on my back. It would become such a familiar sensation, but here and now it was unsettling and exciting at once. I tried to feel the weight of sin lifting from my shoulders, but kneeling on the floor by the cold radiator there was only cramp in my thighs and Isaiah's hand hot on my neck, on my skin. At the back of my neck. Burning. That was my welcome to the Church. The hot hand of a strange man.

7

When two tribes go to war

The year of George Orwell's dystopia was the year the State turned on the people. 'The long riot shields parted and out rode fourteen mounted police straight into the pickets,' recalls Bernard Jackson, who was at the Battle of Orgreave in 1984, the central confrontation in the year-long dispute between the miners and the government. 'As they did, police in the line beat on their riot shields with truncheons, creating a wall of noise which was meant to intimidate and frighten. It was more than simply a noise, it was a declaration that we were facing an army which had declared war on us.' There were four thousand police officers in fields near the coke works south of Sheffield on 18 June. They had dogs and horses and shields and truncheons with which to face ten thousand miners and their supporters, some of whom pushed against the police lines. 'It made no difference if pickets stood still, raised their hands or ran away; truncheons were used on arms and legs, trunks and shoulders, and particularly on heads and faces,' says Jackson in *Marching to the Fault Line* by Francis Beckett and David Hencke. 'Men lay around unconscious or semi-conscious with vicious wounds on their bodies, more often than not with bloody gashes on the backs of their heads.' Jackson himself was smashed in the face with a riot shield. A policeman dragged him from the field by the neck, threatening to break it. He was in prison for a week, charged with rioting. It took a year before he was acquitted.

The other side of the story was that bricks, rocks, bottles, ball bearings and planks with spikes driven into them were thrown at the police. Cars were rolled downhill to make a barricade and set alight. Officers faced extreme provocation, but then so did the pickets. The arguments still rage on either side, even now, when we are so distant from these events that Sir Elton John can make a West End musical out of a ballet-mad boy from a pit town who watches his striking father burn the family furniture to keep warm.

It seemed so clear cut at the time, but it wasn't really. One side was led by a wild-eyed megalomaniac with weird hair who refused to compromise and was intent on smashing everything the enemy stood for. So was the other side. Margaret Thatcher and Arthur Scargill were both extremists, and proud of it.

The pits closed anyway. The jobs were lost. The communities took years to recover. A few never did. What matters most for our story, though, is that these events polarised the country. You had to decide which side you were on. Margaret Thatcher had turned the police into her private army. Even those of us who had already worked out that Dixon of Dock Green was as fictional as Dr Who were shocked. We knew the police would arrest you for no reason, and beat you up, and maybe throw you down the stairs if you were black. Or Irish. We were lucky enough to have been born the right colour and with the right accent, not to have been bothered by the bully boys in blue – but now we were finding out they could be just as vicious, in massed, shielded ranks, like a Roman cohort, if you happened to have different politics.

Difference was despised. Before the eighties it was possible to believe the police were working for all of us. After Orgreave it was not. The truth had been revealed to those too slow or uninvolved to have seen it before and it would be reinforced in a year's time at the Battle of the Beanfield. The police would use excessive violence to stop a peace festival at Stonehenge, and again at many other demonstrations in the years to come, up to and including the kettling, beating and scything down of passers-by at the G20 summit in London in 2009.

The loss of respect for authority has been one of the defining shifts in English society over the last few decades, and people often blame it for our troubles. They talk as if there was no cause and effect, as if somehow a generation just decided all on its own to turn against those who give orders, and in particular those whose job it is to keep the peace. That is just not true. It is hard to do what your mother taught you and respect a bobby when he is charging at you on horseback and wielding his baton like a demented Cossack.

Over the last thirty years, at various times, police officers have demonstrated with spectacular violence that they don't like black people, they don't like Irish people, they don't like miners or socialists or their sympathisers, they don't like hippies or New Age travellers or ravers or crusties, they don't like Asians (who all seem to be viewed as potential terrorists), they don't like Brazilians (who should never, ever, run away, as the innocent Jean Charles de Menezes did, because they look a bit Asian so might get shot at point-blank range), and they don't even like nice, white, middle-class people if they start shouting about the destruction of the environment or have the temerity to question the capitalist system.

There are always inquiries, reports and promises, and attempts to recruit a more diverse force, usually after a scandal, and it is true that the prejudices have shifted. We need the police, and individual officers are good people doing their best for the right reasons. Yet the historic evidence is overwhelming: on the whole, the police don't like anybody who is different from them. They are tooled up to defend their own, essentially conservative, definition of normality. How can you really respect a police officer when you know he is working for a particular political ideology, and if you dare to protest against it he will smash you in the face?

Fights were crippling the Labour Party in 1984. The moderates had gone off to sip claret with the Social Democrats, so once again the question arose: who was going to oppose the Thatcher revolution? Once again, Robert Runcie felt like he had no choice. This time it would be much more serious than the spat over the Falklands. The Church and the State were ancient allies, collaborators with the Crown in the creation of the English God and the Establishment that served and sustained Him, but they were about to take each other on in the most public way, questioning each other's motives, morality and sanity. They hadn't done such a thing, in such a vicious and public way, since the Civil War. This wasn't just a political argument, it was the breaking of a pact fundamental to Establishment England. Some saw the dangers, but others felt it was inevitable. It was just the right thing to do. You had to decide which side you were on. 'Thatcherism has destroyed the cosy political consensus in which the Church could stay politely on the sidelines,' wrote one religious commentator. 'Thatcher put an end to that. The night she won her second election, a senior Church of England official said to a friend: "Now the Church will have to grow hair on its chest."'

For perhaps the first time in its history, when faced with a choice between the forces of the Establishment and the righteous anger of the people, the Church of England sided with the people. 'For a time,' says the historian Anthony Howard, 'the bench of bishops appeared to supply the sole effective opposition to an administration which, in its Prime Minister's words, wanted to change everything.' One of those bishops was about to become notorious. 'That Durham bloke' would make himself famous in the pubs in a way no other modern bishop could dream of (apart, perhaps, from the dashing David Sheppard of Liverpool, who had captained England at cricket). This Doberman in a dog collar, this Norman Tebbit of the nave, was a most unlikely figure: a donnish fifty-nine-year-old accused by some people of not believing in God at all.

David Jenkins had been happy tutoring students, marking papers and thinking deep thoughts at Leeds University, until a letter landed on his mat in early 1984 asking him to be the next Bishop of Durham. The request came from 10 Downing Street, because the Prime Minister chose bishops. There was nothing to suggest Margaret Thatcher was asking for trouble in appointing a man who was considered quite orthodox until he appeared on television on the Sunday after Easter and said: 'I wouldn't put it past God to arrange a virgin birth if He wanted, but I very much doubt if He would.' There were miracle stories in all religions, he said. These ones were just as mythical, and were meant to express something about the nature of God and Christ. You didn't have to believe in them literally to be a Christian. The press immediately branded Jenkins the 'Unbelieving Bishop' and went big with the story, which shows what different times we live in now. More than fourteen thousand people signed a petition demanding that he be removed from the job, before he had even started.

There were three main tribes in the Church of England, and Jenkins had managed to antagonise two of them. He was a liberal, part of the tradition that stressed the importance of reason, exploring ways to understand God in the context of wider advances in human knowledge. 'To believe is to question,' he said, 'and to have faith is to be under a divine compulsion to explore.' His critics didn't see it that way. Some were members of a second tribe, the Anglo-Catholics, who stressed continuity with the faith and ritual of the Church as it had existed in England before Henry and Elizabeth. The man who organised the protest was the Catholic chaplain of the choir school at Hereford Cathedral, William Ledwich, who thought that allowing the likes of Jenkins to hold high office was proof that his Church had departed from historic truths and was full of heretics. But many of those who signed the petition were members of the third group, the Evangelicals. They stressed the authority of the Bible, the importance of having personal conversion, and Martin Luther's central idea – that we were saved by believing in Jesus and not by any good works we might do.

The argument about what was most true about Christianity had been going on for ever, but it now became personal and public in a new way. The fight that started over David Jenkins would grow fiercer in the years to come, raging over the ordination of women and the treatment of gay priests. Cracks would become fault lines then chasms. The tribes were going to destroy the Church, and the phoney war ended here and now. It was a gathering storm, and the Unbelieving Bishop was the lightning rod. Literally, as it turned out.

On 9 July 1984, three days after David Jenkins had been consecrated there as Bishop of Durham, York Minster caught fire. The blaze in the south transept took a hundred fire fighters three hours to put out. Immediately, the tabloids suggested it had been struck by lightning as an act of vengeance by God, upset at the new man's lack of faith. This mischievous conceit on the part of an editor was taken seriously by some Evangelicals who believed in a God who would do such a thing. Enoch Powell didn't, but the sly old campaigner still used the idea in a debate in the House of Commons, speaking against a proposal that MPs just happened to be considering at the time, to simplify the way bishops were appointed. 'I mean no jocularity whatsoever,' said Powell, who hardly ever did, 'but for 450 years, no transept has been struck by lightning in the continuance of a procedure whereby the Holy Spirit was invoked in the deliberations of the dean and chapter.' It was a naughty bit of speechmaking, but as a consequence the MPs rejected a church proposal. That hadn't happened in half a century.

With typical perversity, David Jenkins now gave a long interview to the magazine *Marxism Today*. The Church ought to be 'more of a disturber', he said, by, for example, 'constantly drawing attention to the obscenity of nuclear weapons'. Or, indeed, to the dangers of Thatcherism – 'drawing attention to the way in which, if you go for nothing but the profit motive, then you are betraying your love for your neighbour'. This was not just politics. 'It is quite clear from the Bible that you are up against this battle between good and evil all the time.' So there it was: Thatcher was evil.

In his consecration sermon Jenkins had said a class war was going on. In parts of his diocese, unemployment was at 50 per cent. 'This government, whatever it says, seems in action to be determined to defeat the miners and thus treat workers as not part of "us".' He was suspicious of Scargill, but used his strongest words against Thatcher and the man she had brought in to run the National Coal Board, Ian MacGregor, 'an imported, elderly American'.

If the Bishop was looking for a fight, he got one. The Energy Secretary, Peter Walker, accused him of preaching 'fiction rather than facts'. Inevitably, Nicholas Fairbairn MP quoted Henry II: 'Who will rid me of this turbulent priest?' Was Jenkins going to retreat gracefully? Like hell. He called the Tory policies 'imprudent and thoughtless'.

Other bishops came out in support of him, particularly if they represented mining areas, but Robert Runcie was not exactly a tower of strength. He sent his chauffeur across London to take a personal, handwritten letter to Ian MacGregor, apologising for the 'hurtful' remark that Jenkins had made. To nobody's surprise but Runcie's, the contents were leaked to the press. Upset by this, the Archbishop finally found the courage to say to *The Times*: 'People won't accept that greed and self-interest are the dynamic of our society.' That really upset Tory backbenchers, who condemned these 'mindless' and 'unprecedented' comments from 'muddled old men'. These bishops had never had to live in the real world and run their own company, what in heaven's name did they know?

Somebody should have told David Jenkins that St George did not take time off from fighting the dragon to ponder the existential truth of his shield. In October he went on the telly again, and talked about the virgin birth again. Maybe he just didn't care that his critics would slaughter him again. 'To believe in a Christian way you don't have to necessarily have a belief that Jesus was born from literally a virgin mother, nor a precise belief that the risen Jesus had a literally physical body,' he said. In a society that didn't yet realise how much faith it had lost, his statements were news yet again. 'A conjuring trick with bones only proves that somebody's clever at a conjuring trick with bones,' he said, meaning that the Resurrection was real in a more significant way, but that was not how it was taken. The phrase would be used against him for ever more. Nicholas Winterton MP denounced it as 'diabolically blasphemous' and urged the Bishop to step down. Lord Hailsham tried to be clever, saying: 'I much prefer the word of Matthew, Mark, Luke and John, because they were there, and David Jenkins wasn't.' That was ridiculous, because nobody with a Sunday school education seriously thought that all four Gospels were eyewitness accounts, but the jibe hit home.

Why had all these Tories suddenly become such enthusiastic theologians? They had always seen the Church as their ally in the protection of traditional values, but now it was acting like a Judas. Could it also have been anything to do with the Bishop's claims that their policies were devastating the country?

Politicians were preaching and preachers were pushing their way into politics. Instead of civility, respect and restraint, the watchwords of Establishment England, there was name-calling, back-biting and utter rudeness. Respect for authority? Whose? David Jenkins had emerged as an unexpected political hero to rebels without a clue, like me, but his spirituality didn't offer much to hold on to. The English God was looking confused. The traditionalists and the radicals had swapped places. Was He supposed to fight injustice and comfort the poor, or pore over His company accounts and wave a wad of cash? Luckily, someone with supreme confidence was coming to the rescue, claiming to know all the answers. Another elderly, imported American . . .

8

Doctor, doctor (can't you see
I'm burning, burning?)

Billy Graham was the most famous preacher in the world and one of the most famous Americans, a man with a face made for Mount Rushmore. As handsome as a lion and just as persuasive, he appeared to be one of the most confident men ever to walk the earth, utterly convinced that the message he was bringing to England in 1984 was right. It was the same message he had preached to at least a hundred million people in his lifetime, making more than a million converts. God loved us all, even though we were sinners who had fallen far short of His glory. He had sent His only son to die on the cross, to take the punishment that should have been ours. We could know God and be sure of a place in heaven by accepting the Lord Jesus Christ as our personal saviour. There was someone waiting to pray with us, if we would only get up out of our seats and come on down to the front of the stage. Right now. The Lord was calling. And that was it.

Life was simple in a Billy Graham world. Believe and you would be saved. There was no need to get your knickers in a twist over something like the virgin birth. Of course it had happened, he said. It was in the Bible. 'Proclaim the message of the

82

Gospel,' Graham advised Jenkins and the other bishops of England on his arrival. 'If you have some doubts, keep them to yourself. Laymen have enough doubts of their own.' His own message was easily understood and eagerly accepted by people who felt confused by the modern world. Here was something you could just accept was true, and live by. Graham preached it in stadiums and on television with the clear-eyed, eloquent charm that had once made him the best door-to-door brush salesman in North Carolina. Unlike other American evangelists, whom we were just beginning to hear about, he didn't seem like a liar or a fraud or someone who would be exposed as secretly paying women for sex. He drew only a relatively modest wage of $50,000 a year or so, never met with women when he was alone and even left the door of his office open when he was talking to his secretary.

When he wasn't on the road, Billy Graham retreated to a farm. He had been born in 1918, the son of a dairy farmer who once made his boy drink beer until he was sick in order to prove the evils of alcohol. The young Billy took it to heart. His first 'crusade', as he named it – with little apparent care of what that word meant outside America – was in Los Angeles in 1949, when some circus tents were put up in a car park. It was supposed to last three weeks but ran for eight, and the press loved him and in reference to his booming voice called him 'God's Machine Gun'. In those days that didn't seem such a loaded phrase.

William Randolph Hearst, the press magnate whose life inspired the film *Citizen Kane*, decided that here was a potentially powerful ally in the fight against his biggest dread: communism. Graham saw the Soviet way of life as a satanic conspiracy. Hearst told his editors, who never disobeyed: 'Puff Graham.' The preacher quickly became an American superstar, granted a personal audience with successive presidents. He tried to keep out of politics, but couldn't really help himself: he refused to speak to segregated audiences, and invited Martin Luther King to share his platform in the fifties, when the minister was despised and feared by many of Graham's fellow white southerners. His contact with Richard Nixon was not quite so admirable. Recordings were released of him apparently going along with the President's forceful anti-Semitism, even though he was very keen on building better relations between Christians and Jews. Graham would make other dubious moves over the years, but in 1984 he was at the peak of his reputation as an honest man of faith.

He came to England from Anchorage, Alaska, on his way to the Soviet Union. He spoke in Birmingham, Bristol, Liverpool, Sunderland and East Anglia, at football stadiums which were usually packed. Graham knew how to stay in tune with the mood music of the country that was hosting him: he appeared in a BBC series talking about the Four Horsemen of the Apocalypse – Deception, War, Famine and Death – and comparing the Book of Revelation with contemporary events in the world, including African drought and the threat of a nuclear holocaust. Naturally, I watched and listened. Here was someone saying the things Isaiah and The Boys had said, only Billy Graham had immense stature. I had heard his name spoken with respect and admiration by people of my father's and grandfather's generations who were not even believers.

Billy Graham had first preached here in 1954. 'Not since the late Victorian period had there been such powerful evidence of a professing Christian people in Britain,' says the historian Callum Brown. The numbers of church members, baptisms and weddings soared that year. 'Accompanying these was a vigorous reassertion of "traditional" values: the role of women as wives and mothers, moral panic over deviancy and "delinquency" and an economic and cultural austerity which applauded "respectability", thrift and sexual restraint.' Dr Graham was in London for three months and spoke to a total audience of nearly two million people, at a time when the population of the capital was eight million. He won relatively few converts (just 36,431) but his influence was great. America was the source of all that was glamorous and modern, and the visiting star preacher carried all that with him. Just his presence in the same city was enough to convince some men that they really had to get their lives together. He was reminding them of something they already knew. 'The mental world which drew in those worshippers was a national culture,' says Callum Brown,

> widely broadcast through books, magazines and radio and deeply ingrained in the rhetoric with which people conversed about each other and about themselves. It was a world profoundly conservative in morals and outlook, and fastidious in its adherence to respectability and moral standards. Many people may have been hypocritical, but that world made them very aware of their hypocrisy.

Billy Graham's message was not alien to England. It was, essentially, the faith of John Wesley; but a version of it that had sailed away to America and come back fortified by the smooth skills of the salesman. His visits pumped up born-again English faith like a Charles Atlas body-building course. Before his first crusade to this country, only 10 per cent of priests had been prepared to call themselves Evangelicals. These are, you recall, people who stress the authority of the Bible above all, and the importance of a personal relationship with God through Jesus. The message that Billy Graham preached was effectively their manifesto.

He made several more visits over the decades, acting as an inspiration, a cheerleader and a point of focus for attempts to win converts. In 1984 he spoke to a million people, and 350,000 watched on television relays elsewhere. The number of people who came forward was 135,000. More than half of them were younger than twenty-five, which gave the Body of Christ, as the believers call it, an unexpected boost. In the crowd at Carrow Road, home of Norwich City, for example, was a fifteen-year-old girl called Sally. 'I can't remember what he actually said, but I remember the atmosphere was electric,' she said many years later. Sally got up and went down to the front, then saw her mother do the same, and her father, and her sister. She is now a priest herself, as is her father.

The impact of these meetings went way beyond the number of converts. Take the song book, which laid out the Graham brand of faith in a combination of traditional hymns and the new, catchy 'worship choruses' that some churches viewed with suspicion. More than two million copies were sold and the Sunday habits of countless congregations were changed. Three years after the 1984 crusade, when the full effect had filtered through, it would be discovered that Evangelicals now accounted for a third of all people in the Church of England's pews, and a mighty 50 per cent of priests. The Baptists also benefited from the Billy Graham bounce.

The faith of England was changing, becoming more direct, simpler and more personal. In the recent past, going to a service had mostly been something you did out of duty, a discipline that would improve the spirit but essentially an ordinary part of life. Now there was an expectation that something extraordinary might happen in church. You could experience God, get a dose of His love. It was something you had to choose to do – 'nominal' Christians who went out of habit or tradition were seen as inferior, possibly not even saved – and your choice would be rewarded with peace, contentment and the certainty of salvation. That was not all down to Billy Graham, of course, but he was

Doctor, doctor (can't you see I'm burning, burning?)

undoubtedly a talisman. 'I have the impression there is a possibility that this country is on the verge of a spiritual revival,' he said in 1984, and that idea would become the driving force, in the run-up to the end of the millennium, for some of the most extraordinary manifestations of Christianity this country has ever seen. The doctor's allies would seek to give the ailing Body some very strong medicine indeed. So strong, they could be accused of killing it off.

I never got to meet Billy Graham, but I was sent to interview one of his protégés in the summer of 1984, at the age of seventeen, while working as a trainee reporter on the local paper. Leaving school had meant leaving The Boys behind and, happily, shaking off Isaiah too. It had all been too creepy, but I was still curious enough to want to see what was happening in the circus tent put up on playing fields behind the Town Hall. This was a series of events held to make up for the fact that Billy Graham had chosen to go somewhere else in England. Instead, we were getting someone I had never heard of, another honorary doctor from across the Atlantic.

I was late for the service, as usual, trying not to get mud on my patent winkle-pickers. The wind was worrying at the walls of the tent, which was crowded with wooden risers. Every space was taken, and nobody wanted to shift up for me, so I stood in the shadows and listened. I couldn't tell you what the doctor said, but it was dull, dull, dull. I do know that when I tried to interview him afterwards, as arranged, I was flanked by two giant men in dark suits, who allowed nothing more than the briefest of exchanges. The evangelist had come out to meet the assembled press and found . . . me, basically. His smile faded for only a second. He was a professional, from his well-polished shoes to his beautifully tailored preaching suit with shot white cuffs. He was

87

handsome, of course, but in a vague sort of way, like one of those actors with good hair, wide smile and cleft chin you see in the background of an old episode of *Battlestar Galactica*. I asked a stupid question; the doctor gave a bland answer. I asked an even more stupid question; he gave a shorter, blander answer. I asked a third; he gave a terse answer, and raised his eyebrows to the bodyguards. That was it. 'I'm sorry, sir, that is all we have time for.'

I know what the doctor thought of the likes of me, because I have seen the video his team produced to describe the long-term results of what they tried to do in London that year. It is smug, patronising and insulting to the whole city, and it nails young people in clothing like mine as symbols of everything that was going wrong. 'A rich heritage of faith has been part of British culture for hundreds of years,' says a voiceover as grand as Tom Baker's in *Little Britain*, as we see the dome of St Paul's Cathedral. 'But, as the mid-twentieth century dawned on Great Britain, signs of spiritual apathy and moral decay began to emerge.' To illustrate this thought, we're shown a couple of boys with punky, spiked hair and black clothes. Bad lads, obviously. The lost. But hang on, what is that one holding on the end of a stick? An American flag, which is burning. And here come two women in dark glasses and baggy white t-shirts, carrying lilies. They're all at some kind of demo. The camera slowly zooms out to reveal CND slogans daubed on to the t-shirts and their faces. Now it becomes clear what we are seeing. The flag is being burned in protest at the siting of American missiles on British soil. Is this a sign of 'moral decay'? To the good doctor, yes. To me, it looks like a sign of young people caring enough about their world to protest against things they consider immoral or wrong. No apathy there, spiritual or otherwise.

'Empty churches became commonplace,' says the sonorous

voice, 'as secularism gained momentum.' He spits out the word 'secularism', like poison. 'The spiritual climate of Greater London was also reflected in the searching and emptiness within individual lives.' So that's all of the seven million people in the capital written off in a sentence. How do they illustrate this? With a shot of two women waiting to cross a road. They're not identified, we're not told anything more about them, they appear to have been chosen at random from the crowd, but the narrator says their lives are empty. One of them is – avert your eyes, it's shocking – smoking. She's clearly going to hell. Send for the doctor, quick. I wish I had seen the video before I met him. Our conversation would have been even shorter, but much less bland. May God have mercy on his well-dressed soul.

I slithered away that night, but the best way of getting a teenage boy interested in anything is to tell him he can't do it. The moment the bodyguards ordered me to get packing, it was inevitable that I would return, if only to ask better questions. When I did go back, a few nights later, I got a surprise: the gorillas had gone. There were no bodyguards, only churchy-looking men and women who smiled and said hello. The American was somewhere else that night. Instead, we were to hear from a youngish English bloke called Eric, who looked like Jim Dale from the *Carry On* films and had a voice like Tony Hancock's. He wasn't smooth, he was funny. 'Who says Jesus was a miserable so-and-so? What kind of killjoy spends all his time going to parties, drinking other people's wine and telling stories to his friends?'

Somebody laughed. Not loudly, just a little. Nervously. This speaker was actually quite interesting. Pacing up and down the stage, jacket off, sleeves rolled up, tie undone, telling stories and using accents like *Monty Python*. 'Oi! Look out! Jesus is at the door. Hide all the grub. No, don't let him at the olives, I'm saving them for me mother.' I remember him saying: 'Maybe we should stop thinking about our pinched, pale, po-faced Christ drifting three inches above the ground in his shining white nightie and think about someone who was very much a real man, the best man who ever lived, and who was very good at having a laugh.'

The laughing Jesus. He had me then. I was ready. His voice became calmer. 'I'm going to ask you to do something. I'm going to ask all of you to stand. But you – you know who you are – I'm going to ask you to make your way along to the end of the row, and down these aisles.' Writing it down, I know it looks corny, but there and then it made sense. I felt like he was talking to me, this reassuring, funny man who made it all make sense. Talking right into my ear. 'Come and stand quietly at the front, facing in this direction. I'm asking you to do it with everything you've got. Body, mind and spirit. Your social being as well as your private being. To say before the world, "Yes, I am willing to admit that I need Jesus Christ, I need the living God, and I'm quite willing to admit too that I'm not what I ought to be." He wants you.'

I was out of my seat, down the unsteady wooden steps and into the semicircle just in front of him, the first one there. It was how I imagined going on stage would be: under the hot lights, with hundreds of strangers watching. If they'd thought it polite to applaud, they would have risen and cheered and yelped. Hallelujah! The preacher looked down at me, winked, then spoke to the rest of the tent, over my head: 'Don't be shy.'

A man stumbled up behind me. He smelled of fags. A woman with a helmet of black hair and a smudge of red lipstick on a pale face came and knelt. I knelt down too, as that seemed the thing to do. The band played 'Just as I Am', Billy Graham's favourite hymn: 'Just as I am, and waiting not, to rid my soul of one dark blot.' There were a dozen volunteers by the time the preacher stopped teasing, pleading, cajoling, asking. 'Lord, come and meet our new friends here,' he said quietly. And all the people said, 'Amen.'

I stood there shivering. My head felt like it was going to burst. I was tired, I wanted to be out of there and down the pub or back in bed, but a man in a rainbow-coloured jumper came and stood by me and prayed with me and gave me a booklet. Then he didn't know what to do. Neither did I. So we shook hands. 'You are a new creation,' the man said. I felt no different. I couldn't just take his word for it, I had to go and see Eric.

The door to his dressing room was half open. He was changing his trousers. I could see his pants, dark blue Y-fronts, and his legs, pale, white and hairy. He smiled, and carried on getting changed. 'Okay? It can be a bit overwhelming.'

'Fine,' I said. 'I'm fine.' I was surprised – to have done it, to be there talking to this man. This nice man. What was I supposed to say?

'Don't worry,' he said. 'You've done your bit. It's up to God now. He'll do His stuff.'

We talked about football. There were other people at the door. We shook hands. 'Take care,' he said. 'Thanks for coming.'

I was happy all the way home. Happy and certain. I was still riding that wave of certainty when the invitation came.

9

This is England

The bells were ringing. The soft, sweet scent of summer hung in the air as I walked along the edge of a village green, past ducks in a pond. What could have been more English? The pub across the way was garlanded with ivy and looked like the sort of place where the landlord pulled his real ale by hand and set out bowls of Cheddar cubes for the regulars on a Sunday. The green was wide and bright, and at its centre was a pitch on which cricketers in white were moving slowly through the golden evening light. A batsman prodded the ground and waited for the bowler to run in. Old men dozed in deckchairs on the boundary. The crack of the bat on the ball jolted them into a smattering of applause. These were Sunday sporting heroes, legends in their own clubhouse, playing a slow, civilised game that embodied England. Their England. The England of the suburbs. Not mine.

My England was half an hour away on the bus, and a million miles. There was nothing bucolic in our tight streets strewn with glass and litter. If we played cricket at all, it was with a tennis ball and a wicket scratched out on a wall. We certainly never wore whites. Nor did we iron our rugby shirts and turn up the collars, like the young men I could see ahead of me on the path, making for church. Here it was different. This was another country. Establishment England, at its soft suburban edges. The girls still had Di fringes, their mothers and fathers climbed out of Mercs and Beamers dressed in sweaters and pearls and collars and ties. I felt very conspicuous, even in a clean black shirt, but they seemed in a trance, drifting to church like particularly sleek zombies. 'How are you?' I heard one ask. 'Fine. How are you?' Then an equally lifeless response. 'Fine.' They had noticed me, of course. Coded whispers were being exchanged, but I didn't hear them. I didn't yet know that manners were everything here, a restraint as tight on the middle-class Christian mouth as a gimp mask on a curate's face.

I was there because the people from the mission had sent an invitation card, suggesting this was a good church. I knew the area by reputation. It was not really a village any more at all, despite having an ancient, picture-postcard (taken from a certain angle, ignoring the main road) village green. The myth was perpetuated by the bankers who lived in large houses here, half an hour from the City on the tube. There were wine bars down by the station, and little boutiques, and an art gallery selling Athena posters, and a florist that tied up the flowers in lengths of ribbon, and lots of other things we didn't have where I lived. In the Edwardian homes beside the railway station I had seen people unloading Marks and Spencer food from their cars, presumably to eat while watching *The Antiques Roadshow*. I had passed a private health clinic and a very minor public school, with gates and a quadrant that mimicked the grander ones. On my way across the green I saw a red setter, a Labrador and a couple of greyhounds. Proper dogs. No mongrels here.

They had to be well trained too, so they didn't scare the cows. The myth of the village, like the price of property, was boosted by the presence of cattle grids on the main roads and the quaint old custom of allowing cattle free rein on the green (except the cricket pitch) in the summer. Never mind if they crashed through garden fences and munched begonias, or that the farmer would demand £5000 from anybody who hit one in their car, regardless of whether a mighty side of beef had smashed the windscreen and crushed the bonnet. Those were risks worth taking for living in a 'village'. And anyway, the farmer would never have confronted anyone face to face. Not around here. His solicitors would be asked to do it all, without fuss. You could charge into one of the Tudorbethan mansions that overlooked the green, pee all over the carpet, skewer the cat, smash the television, make love with the au pair up against the wall and write rude slogans on the mirrors with her lipstick and the most reaction you would ever get would be, 'Look here, this is not really on.' I know, because in later times I tried it. Well, apart from the peeing. And the cat. And the television and the au pair. And the mirrors. They were pretty buttoned-up people, though. Only the very afraid have Laura Ashley curtains.

There were new rules to learn in the suburbs, as I discovered when I entered the church and was met by evasion. Eyes were averted as a hymn book was handed over, weak smiles were offered into mid-air and nobody said a word to me, let alone told me where to sit. The English middle classes are strangers to each other, even when at worship with friends. Then, more than ever. To go to evensong at a parish church in the suburbs is to see the English social disease at its most extreme. Awkward in company at the best of times, we don't know what to say or how to say it, we are afraid of intimacy and of emotion, and usually we cope with this alienation by making a joke, often at our own expense, or by moaning. 'Bloomin' weather. Still, it's going to get worse tomorrow, eh?' The thing is, though, you can't really do that within the ritualised, whispered setting of a Church of England service. This was a relaxed one, in which the priests wore simple robes, the altar was plain and the lighting was relatively good, but still, everything was done according to a set of assumptions and values that was never referred to, let alone explained. Each of us was already bound up in an invisible straitjacket of Englishness and now, on top of that, we wrapped ourselves in the suffocating cloak of religious respectability.

Just by going along to this parish church I had stumbled into a world of mysterious costumes, arcane language and ancient rules that nobody really seemed to know properly, but which, nevertheless, still had to be obeyed. The parish system, the basis on which churches all over the country operated, was very old indeed and intimately bound up with the nationhood of England. To understand it, you have to go back a thousand years, to when the village really was a village and the original All Souls was built, stone by stone, by immigrant Norman wealth. The lord who owned the land, having seized it, paid for a church to boost his status and help him keep control of the people. The clergyman who was hired to look after the church was not much more than a servant, and could be disposed of easily if he said something that did not meet with his lordship's pleasure. Callum Brown says: 'The parish church and the manor house were the twin seats of local power, and the vicar and the lord were the joint holders of that power.' The symbolism of Sunday was all-important.

The English lord sat in his front-row boxed pew, the clergyman was in his pulpit, and parishioners sat in ranked pews allocated, rented or bought according to social and economic status. To attend church was to participate in a parade of power, to submit symbolically to God and to Mammon. The two were not at odds, but in cahoots. Any threat to the one

was a threat to the other, and for this reason the landed elites
had immediate cause to wish their people in obedience to the
church, as they would have them in obedience to themselves.

Priestly positions were often filled by sons, relatives or friends of
the landlords. It was a nice little earner for well-bred boys in need
of cash, because the priest was usually funded by a tax – or tithe –
of 10 per cent of everything produced in his parish. The farmer,
the miller, the baker, they all paid. The nepotism helps explain
how the tough, unsentimental Christianity of the public schools
became such a force in the land; and it accounts for why so many
acclaimed archaeologists, botanists, authors and others in the age
of the gentleman amateur were parish priests. Samuel Taylor
Coleridge said that each parsonage throughout the land was a
'germ of civilisation' to its local community.

The Victorians professionalised the clergy, who were eventually almost all paid from a central pot, but the parish system
endured. The idea behind it was to provide a priest in every
community, to care for every soul. The Elizabethan demand that
everyone attend a service every Sunday had evolved into the
principle that the priest should strive to be available even to those
who didn't bother to turn up. They might yet want to be married, or have their children baptised, or be sent into the next
world with a prayer. He did not work for some exclusive club,
and those who did come to worship could not be turned away
just because they didn't believe the right things. That was all-
important, it made the Anglicans more than just another
squabbling sect. This was the Church of the middle ground,
steadfastly serving the whole nation, whatever people thought of
it. Which was, of course, a lot easier when most people in the
nation had roughly the same culture, lifestyle and skin colour. At
the home of Liverpool Football Club there is a sign that says,

'This is Anfield'. There could have been a sign over the entrance to All Souls saying, 'This is England'. On that first Sunday, and on many Sundays to come, I entered a world of quiet conservatism, caution, modesty, manners, tradition and restraint . . . which made the extraordinary things that were going to happen in that place all the more astonishing.

The service went on and on and on. The vicar told us we were all sinners, led a prayer, then told us we were now forgiven. The usual stuff, which I recognised from my few enforced family visits to churches in the past. There was something odd about the way the three hundred or so worshippers were behaving, though. This wasn't like a wedding, in which the grown-ups mouthed the words and got the churchy bit over quickly so they could start drinking. These people were really trying to mean it. Brows were furrowed, lips pursed, eyes locked shut during the prayers, and they were doing their best to say well-worn prayers as if the thoughts had just occurred to them and God was sitting up there on the altar steps, looking down, nodding approvingly. He wasn't. I checked.

The vicar introduced a 'time of worship'. What had the rest of it been, then? A man with an acoustic guitar led a small band and the rest of us through simple, repetitive songs. Musically, they were like the Eagles mainlining cocoa. Not my thing, but not unpleasant. 'Lord, you are more precious than silver/Lord, you are more costly than gold.' To sing them properly here, evidently, you had to assume the faraway expression of a lead in an amateur production of *Miss Saigon*, all love and longing and devout hope with a soft little catch in the throat. Quite a few people held their hands in the air, palms upturned as if standing under a very big shower. They were nearly all women. Most of the men were looking sheepish. It was actually quite difficult to concentrate on trying to feel all lovey-dovey towards the Lord, because one or two of the women were being swept up in the moment and sounded as if they were having quiet, soft orgasms. 'Oh yes! Hmmm! Amen, yes Lord. Yes!' My focus returned when I realised the loudest of the semi-ecstatic noises was coming from a hefty woman in a twin set with beads of perspiration on her downy upper lip. 'Oh yes, Lord. Yes!'

If it was hard to get into the right frame of mind for the quiet, devotional songs, the loud, celebratory ones were worse. 'Come on and celebrate,' the next one ordered. What if you didn't want to? What if your hamster had died or you were just feeling particularly downright fed up, thank you very much? Tough. 'Come on and celebrate,' they all sang, and not to do so was to disappoint God. It was depressing. We were into the second hour and still no sermon. Looking at the vicar, elegant in his white robes, I somehow knew it wasn't going to be a quickie.

'We will keep a time of silence,' said the worship leader, but then he seemed to panic and it wasn't one at all: it was a time of finger picking on the guitar and ethereal washes on the keyboard. 'We're going to wait on the Lord. If you feel the Lord is giving you a word or a picture, don't be shy, come up to the microphone here or just stand where you are and share it with us.' Nobody did. Nobody spoke, nobody moved. They seemed afraid of giving a false impression, like someone scratching their nose in an auction house. The straitjacket of Englishness was tight. Then a woman strode up to the microphone, very confident of herself, and faced us with her eyes half closed. 'There's somebody here with a leg.' Oh, I thought, that narrows it down. 'A bad leg. Maybe a hip. Something about the way you walk. God wants you to be healed.'

He does what? This was new to me: some kind of spiritualist medium in a church, offering to make you better. 'If that's you, come up and see a member of the ministry team afterwards.' I heard murmurs behind me, a woman saying to her neighbour, in a loud whisper, 'That's you, that is, you should go up.' Could this be for real? The vicar, who I'm going to call Norman, seemed to think so. He was up in the pulpit, laying out a very calm, considered argument and in a few moments I forgot, temporarily, about the woman with the dodgy leg and the promise of healing. He seemed so English, in a good way: cool, reserved, his voice charged with an authority that suggested everything he was saying was self-evidently true. Norman had been called to the ministry young, in the fifties, when everything seemed as if it might be all right with the world if we could just get back to traditional ways. For him, that meant traditional Evangelical ways: believing in what the Bible said. Not always literally, because he was smarter than that, but as what he often called 'a manual for life'.

It's a popular phrase in such circles, and quite a thought. Let's think for a moment about following the lead of a real hero of the book, like King David, for example. Here is a man who had many concubines, who sent his best commander to the front in order to expose him to lethal danger so that he could take the general's wife. She didn't get a choice about it. The King had spotted her when he was being a peeping Tom and watching her bathe, a steamy scene that doesn't feature for long in many sermons. He also slaughtered innocent civilians because they happened to belong to alien tribes, because God had told him to. Taking David as an example to follow from the manual for life would liven up the suburbs no end.

I became very interested in Norman, but not because of his calm authority or what he said. It was his daughter, to be honest. She was lovely, and so were her friends, of whom there were many. They seemed attractive in a shiny, happy, wealthy way to which I could only aspire. The phrase 'Middle England' was just beginning to be used for people like these. For me, beginning to date the vicar's daughter meant being invited into a circle of friends who studied the Bible together, went out for drinks and pizza and even holidayed as a gang. It was all hugely comforting, and I could still play the dangerous stranger – they'd mostly been raised in the belief that Marks and Spencer were the costumiers of the Lord, so even my feeble attempts at Goth style looked a bit rebellious. There was safety in numbers, too. 'Look,' I could say to my parents (in those rare moments when I was hormonally able to say anything to them at all, beyond a hostile grunt), 'these people are normal, the sort of kids you wish I was, so it's okay.'

That was true, up to a point, but there was also something else going on at All Souls. Something intriguing. Unsettling. The Invader and the Upsetter are names used for the Holy Spirit in the Bible, and here in suburbia this ancient, invasive, upsetting, ghostly force was being asked to have its way. Norman was a careful man who measured the world against what he read in the Scriptures, but in doing so he had come to believe in something I found quite alarming at first, called spiritual warfare. Good versus evil, not in a metaphorical sense, but as a fight between real angels and real demons, in the real world. God versus Satan, fighting for control of our lives in a war we couldn't see, except for its effect on us. We could, though, sense it and even take part, by praying. For that reason, Satan attacked us: our minds, our bodies and our lives, trying to make us afraid.

This was not Norman's own private flight of fancy but fairly orthodox teaching for his kind of Christian. Demons or evil spirits could 'take up residence in any part of our personality', he said. 'They express themselves in such ways as uncleanness, lying, distorted speech or physical manifestations.' This was terrifying. I hadn't realised. 'We should not be anxious, however.' That was easy for him to say. He was convinced that Jesus had won 'the decisive battle' by dying on the cross, and that we had the right to claim the victory. We were encouraged to seek help with that by coming to the front of church after the service, where somebody more experienced would be waiting to pray with us.

I was confused, I thought what he was saying was ridiculous, delusional, medieval, but at the same time it made some sort of weird sense. I didn't want to miss out on a possible answer to everything. No wonder the person who sat with me in a pew in the side aisle that first time and listened to my worries come pouring out said gently, 'You're anxious.' Yes, anxious. That was right. It was an intimate encounter, he and I close to each other in a quiet corner, speaking almost in whispers for the sake of confidentiality. He was older, the owner of a small business, but on the way to being ordained. His ordinariness appealed. His manner was methodical, like a doctor asking what seemed to be the trouble, then, when I had talked myself hoarse, saying: 'Do you mind if I pray with you?' His hand was on my shoulder, suddenly, but it didn't feel invasive or strange like the hot hand of Isaiah; it felt reassuring and fraternal. Comforting. 'Father, come in peace by the power of Your Holy Spirit, in the name of Christ, to heal my brother here.' I sat with my eyes closed, head bowed, waiting for something to happen. And waiting. 'Amen,' he said, and then again, to let me know our session was over. He smiled. Was that it? He seemed to think so. We stood up, shook hands and each turned to go. That was when I saw that all hell had broken loose behind us.

The church was strewn with bodies, like a crisis centre after a bomb attack. A woman was doubled up, apparently in pain, crying loudly as two or three concerned people stood over her. A man was face down on the carpet in the aisle, his arms wide, muttering to himself. A woman was sitting on the floor with her back to the end of the pew while two others knelt by her side, their hands on her shin as if she had broken it. And only a few feet away, astonishingly, since I had been oblivious to it for what turned out to have been an hour, a big, hairy man was flat on his back, thrashing about and bellowing, strange animal noises full of pain, while two men and two women attended to him, one at each of his limbs, holding him down. Another stood over him, shouting: 'We rebuke you, Satan!' What was this? 'We command you to leave him in the name of Christ.' Still he thrashed and writhed, and then, all of a sudden, the man whose face was wet with tears and snot and drool let out an enormous sigh and stopped moving.

'Peace, Lord,' someone said. 'The peace of the Lord.'

Was he okay? Was he dead? No. He opened his eyes. He smiled, weakly. They all smiled back, warmly. 'Okay?' He moved his head to say yes. 'Okay. Thank you, Jesus. Amen? Amen.'

Norman had been the sort of vicar who would wear his dog collar to the swimming pool, until the Holy Spirit whispered in his ear that it was time to relax and open up. He knew that fighting demons was playing with brimstone as well as fire, and said repeatedly that none of us should get carried away.

We did, of course. We saw demons everywhere: in coughs and splutters and bad breath and broken marriages; and in the behaviour of people we didn't like. The demons gave us a way of understanding the world, and a reason why God didn't always heal people when we asked Him to. There were others, too: we didn't have sufficient faith; some secret, unconfessed sin was getting in the way; the timing wasn't right; or the person we were praying for just didn't believe enough (which shifted the blame and was the excuse we liked most). None of this was new, we were told. It was in the Bible and still very much alive in parts of the world where sensitivity to the spiritual realm had not been blunted by Enlightenment thinking. It was part of the English psyche to be suspicious of anything that could not be understood rationally or scientifically, but our duty as Christians was to shake off those mental chains.

We were in the Church of England but our pursuit of the Holy Spirit made us part of a movement that went way beyond that, taking its inspiration from a story in the Bible. The Book of Acts tells how the bereaved followers of Jesus had gathered together in one place when they heard a mighty rushing wind and saw 'tongues of fire' hovering over their heads. They began speaking in what sounded like a nonsensical babble to them but was heard by foreigners sitting near by as the languages of their own lands, including Egypt, Libya and Rome. Under the influence of the Spirit, the followers of Jesus behaved so strangely that other people said they must be drunk. After this, they acquired supernatural powers that became known as the 'gifts of the Spirit', including the ability to see or hear images or 'words of knowledge' that revealed hidden truths about the world. They began casting out demons and seeing mental and physical problems healed in the name of the Lord, as Jesus had said they would. So the story goes. We believed it was true and that these miracles were also available to us. Collectively, across the churches, all of us who sought to enjoy the gifts of the Spirit called ourselves after the Greek word for grace, *charis*. We were Charismatics. That was a bit of a laugh, as some of us were as charismatic as a puddle on a hot day, but there were hundreds of millions of us and the numbers were growing all the time, all over the world.

The English will usually only believe in something if we see it for ourselves. Our leaders believed we were rediscovering at first hand the full riches of faith, and it was possible to experience a little of God's glory in the here and now. We could taste God, if we wanted to. The first step was to say the magic words . . .

10

Shecameonahonda!

'She came on a Honda.'

'Faster!' said the youth group leader, grinning.

'Shecameonahonda!'

'Showaddywaddy. Remember them? No, probably not. Say it though, and the other, fast as you can.'

'Shecameonahonda! Showaddywaddy!'

'There you go. Tongues. Nothing to it.'

He was laughing. Me too. Daft as it was, I hoped this might just help. I wanted, desperately, to belong. I wanted to know how to speak in tongues. Some people sounded as if they really were eloquent in another language. You could hear the slurred shushing sounds of Russian among their apparently random syllables, or an Arabic growl in the throat. Others just made the same noises over and over again – dadadadalamalamaram – or elongated recognisable words like shal-oah-omm.

'Tongues are a sign that the Holy Spirit is active in your life,' said the leader, Roddie, who was only about ten years older than me. He worked in a bank, not in the City, a local branch. Part of me wanted to be him; part of me hated him. His wife was like a shadow: I can't recall her ever speaking more than two or three words, even while bringing a hot drink to us in the living room of their very tidy house. They drank barley cup, a foul concoction made from barley, rye and chicory, because the caffeine in coffee was too exciting. They got all the thrills they needed from the Lord. 'Just relax, open your mouth and speak. Let it come.'

'I . . . er . . .'

Spidery lines floated across the backs of my eyelids.

'Father, thank you,' said Roddie, 'for the gift of Your son which my brother has accepted in his heart. Come now, by your Holy Spirit, to lift him up and inspire him. Shicalumredala, inxala micalum ni salamana—'

'Shu . . . schu . . .' My tongue swelled. My throat tightened as if I had swallowed a peanut and found an allergy. It was hot in the room, all of a sudden. 'Schunda chi akai . . .'

That was me. I was making those noises. What were they, Middle Eastern? First century, definitely. It was happening. Roddie babbled on and I joined him, getting louder and more fluent. 'Shilaman chai kilondera shala.' The sounds came faster and faster, rat-a-tat, like machine-gun fire translated into ancient Hebrew or something, and I couldn't stop. I couldn't stop my tongue tripping and my throat clearing and the air popping in my palate and my blood fizzing. The hairs on the back of my neck were like razor wire, my spine was electric, the sweat prickled my scalp and this was like speed, it must be like a speed rush, I thought, I'm flying. And Roddie was flying too, he was laughing and I was laughing, loud. We laughed and laughed, we chuckled and guffawed and snorted and the laughter came up from my belly like sunshine and fireworks and dazzling light and it was all utterly, unaccountably hilarious.

I opened my eyes and Roddie was looking at me, eyes crinkled and creased with pleasure and I just felt abandon, as though the tripping of tongues had loosened my bones and shaken me down. 'Shecameonahonda!' shouted Roddie, and I was off again, weeping with laughter now, ribs hurting. Strange, uncontrollable, hysterical laughter; a muscle-straining laughing fit. When it abated and I came to, laid back on the sofa with my legs wide apart and my t-shirt wet with sweat, I felt almost naked. And elated.

What was going on? Speaking in tongues looks crazy. It can be frightening when you hear it for the first time, all of a sudden, without warning. It can be beautiful, too: when people sing together in different tongues you hear an eerie, goose-bumping rush of sounds that are at once both familiar and unfamiliar. Psychologists used to believe that glossolalia, as it is also called, was associated with schizophrenia and hysteria. That was until a study in the early seventies declared that it might not be a symptom of mental illness after all, but an unusual stress buster. Research also tells us that extroverts are more likely to speak in tongues than introverts, which is not exactly earth-shattering news: it stands to reason that people who are willing to stand up in front of a room full of strangers and spout what sounds like gobbledegook, while claiming the authority of the Lord, might be naturally outgoing.

The favourite theory of the mid-eighties was that it was all a trick. Not a Paul Daniels sleight of mind – 'Now, that's magic!' – but a trick we learned from those around us, as a sort of rite of passage. The pride with which Roddie looked at me and the feelings I had of joining in properly at last would back that up. But I didn't want to think about it. I just wanted to believe it was God.

Linguists insist that people who share a common language in their ordinary lives make similar sounds when they speak in tongues. When a person from England does it, the sounds are identifiably English. The same principle applies to Finnish, Thai,

Indian, Japanese, Maori or Klingon, apparently. Whatever we think we sound like, we usually use the building blocks of our own language. The right notes, as Eric Morecambe would say, but not necessarily in the right order. It's not just a Christian thing: people from many other faiths know what it is like to be swept up in a form of expression they don't fully understand. They talk about losing their sense of self and feeling at one with the cosmos, whether they get there through prayer, chanting, dancing, drumming, or speaking in tongues. One theory is that the brain is overloaded by repetition and shuts part of itself down for protection. Dr Andrew Newberg of the University of Pennsylvania injected radioactive tracers into the bloodstream of an experienced Buddhist as he went into a deep meditative trance. The tracers showed that the parietal lobes – which give the sense of what is you and what is not – were dark and dormant. Under those circumstances, the brain would find it hard to tell where the body ended and everything else began, which would explain the feeling of being bound up with the endless universe. It would not, however, prove it to be just a matter of electrical and chemical reactions. As Professor Vilayanur Ramachandran, a pioneer of this kind of research, says tentatively: 'It may be God's way of putting an antenna in your brain.'

What does it all mean for our big story, about the change in English belief and self-belief? England had seen this sort of behaviour before, notably in the days of John Wesley, but the gifts of the Spirit had been seen as odd shenanigans indulged in by unconventional people in private rooms and rented halls. Or Americans, perhaps. Out on the dusty plains of the Wild West in 1900 a group of men and women began speaking in unintelligible ways, in a little Bible school, and inadvertently began a religious movement that became known as Pentecostalism, which now has 115 million followers across the world. It took its name from Pentecost, the fiftieth day after the Jewish feast of the Passover, the day when the Bible says those tongues of flame originally fell.

Four years after Kansas, closer to home, the Welsh became enthralled with a former blacksmith from Swansea called Evan Roberts who spread around him the feverish touch of the Holy Spirit. Everywhere the preacher went, crowds followed. Postcards of his face sold in great numbers; one biographer has called Roberts 'a spiritual David Beckham'. Half the population of Wales went into a place of worship in 1904. Beer sales plummeted, pit ponies became confused when their operators stopped using bad language, and chapels, choirs and societies were formed that still exist today. David Lloyd George described this national revival as 'rocking Welsh life like a great earthquake'.

None of it was seen as quite the thing for the English. No, this was behaviour best suited to foreigners, like those excitable Celts or the superstitious natives of Africa who believed spiritual warfare to be part of everyday life. One day they would come over here in great numbers and change the nature of Christianity in England, but not quite yet. In the fifties, most parish priests gave short shrift to a West Country man called Arthur Wallis who toured England calling for believers to listen for the voice of God, see visions, speak out prophecies and perform miracles. His was seen as an over-emotional faith, out of tune with the English character. That didn't stop him, though. His ideas gained ground and eventually inspired something called the House Church movement, whose members met in each other's homes. They were looking for a way of doing church that was closer to what they thought Jesus would have known – without robes, altars, vestments, ornaments, liturgy or even buildings of its own – and in which the Spirit could have its way. Their name became absurd during the seventies, as they grew in number and started hiring community halls, schools and even cinemas. By 1984 they were calling themselves simply the New Churches and welcoming about a quarter of a million people to their Sunday services. Their leaders – largely self-elected elders with a fashion for tidy beards – were unapologetic about faith and took membership very seriously: it was impossible to tag along without being questioned as to your beliefs and intentions, and in some congregations there was a deadline. After three months, say, you had to sign up or move on. Doubt was out.

I had been along to a church like this for a while myself, after Isaiah, and briefly fallen in with a group of young men and women who allowed the elders to dictate exactly how they should dress, how they should spend their time and money and even who they should (or should not) fall in love with. This was known as shepherding – or heavy shepherding, to its critics – but while it might have worked for people with chaotic lifestyles who needed to be treated like sheep, it wasn't for me. I declared my rebellion by turning up to a church fancy-dress party – at which everyone else was dressed as a biblical character – in full drag, with a little black cocktail number stolen from my mother. I didn't stay long. I wasn't allowed to. It was tricky, running away in high heels.

Still, the New Churches were successful. Theirs was the only kind of Christianity that was growing at the time, bucking the trend. They were very good at selling a personalised, emotional, hands-on God to the cynical English, even if what they actually did most of the time was take disillusioned Christians out of existing churches rather than make new ones.

There were, however, enough Charismatics left among the Anglicans, Baptists and Roman Catholics to begin making an impact. Their supernatural behaviour, long considered threatening and marginalised, was now being seen in the most respectable places, in the wealthy suburbs and big city churches where the posh people went. It had entered the bloodstream of Middle England. Cautious, conservative, restrained English people like Norman were finding what he called a new reality, an experience that was 'like going from black-and-white to colour television'. The movement was growing and something very big and very exciting was about to happen, Charismatic leaders of every kind agreed. Billy Graham hinted at it, and someone else dug up a prophecy from the fifties that said the momentum for a Welsh-style revival would build up during our times and explode in 1994. Then the churches would be full again. The streets would be crime free. The blind would see, the lame walk, the sick heal. Nobody thought about what a disaster it would be if we all got our hopes up and nothing happened. Revival was on its way and that was our thrilling secret. Shecameonahonda!

To help it come, we needed another imported American. The rest of English culture had already succumbed to the brash charm of the States, falling for the movies, the TV shows, the music, the food and the clothes. We were constantly being told to get loose, get free, lighten up. It was not just okay, it was compulsory to be emotional, angry, happy, to let the tears flow and show feelings in public, in a way that horrified our grandparents. This was not a new message for most of society but now, at last, it was beginning to get through to some of the more uptight members of the Church.

Norman once described the priest and author David Watson as 'a model of the public school, National Service, trustworthy Englishman . . . if David said something or somebody was worth listening to, then it was'. This helps to explain why so many conservative Bible-believers paid attention when Watson, the highly respected vicar of a church in York, invited a man called John Wimber to come and speak in this country. Wimber was going to make a huge impression on modern English Christianity, through his own meetings and the things that his followers did. He was, however, no Billy Graham. He wore Hawaiian shirts, not suits and ties. He had a big, round, friendly face with a white beard, so inevitably he was compared to Santa Claus. Graham had the authority of a president, while Wimber was a keyboard player who had been with the Righteous Brothers and now called himself 'just a fat man going to heaven'.

The story of how he became a Christian is worth watching on YouTube for the skill and humour with which he tells it, even if you don't believe a word of his actual faith. The 'beer-guzzling, drug-abusing pop musician' was twenty-nine, estranged from his wife and playing the midnight shift in the casinos at Vegas, a long way from home. 'I began driving out into the desert at four o'clock every morning to watch the sun come up, because somebody had told me that was a good way to groove on a religious experience.' He pauses. 'Nothing happened.' Then, on his way out to the desert one morning, he started weeping. Unable to drive, he pulled over, got out and started 'cussing and kicking the cactus. I stopped, and I looked up at the heavens and for the first time in my life I saw the stars and constellations as something emanating from someone. I was awestruck and I said, "Oh God, if You're there, help me."' In most testimonies of this kind there would be a well-timed word from the heavens just now, but not in this one. 'I thought, Oh no, now you've really done it, now you're talking to the dark. You've gone over the edge. The only thing left is to go commit myself into the hospital. Then I remembered . . . I had some drugs I'd better put away.' Back at the hotel, the night clerk told him there was a message from his wife. She was willing to give their relationship one more try. 'That was like a blow to my chest. I fell back against the wall and I thought, Wow, I'm in touch with the supernatural.'

Wimber was funny and he made fun of himself. When I heard him in person for the first time, at a conference in London, I felt I had found someone as likeable as Eric, the preacher who had got me into all this, which was a very rare thing. Wimber was the leader of fifteen hundred churches called the Vineyard, and known for emotionally direct worship songs. 'It's your blood that cleanses me,' sang a man with a clear, clean Californian voice. The people around me had their hands in the air. Some of them were weeping and so was I, without wanting to, without understanding why. The music was slow, moving down and into minor chords, like a sad love song full of yearning but rising again, full of strength and hope. It was an expertly written pop ballad, but the beloved was God. 'Whiter than the snow, than the snow . . .' This was the first worship song I had ever heard that had soul.

The air in that huge conference room seemed to have been thickened with essential oils, calming and soothing and overcoming all our natural reserve. Some people got zapped, as we called it. A man in his twenties, living and working in Toxteth, wrote a description of what happened to him during one of Wimber's talks:

I heard about the first three sentences and then POW!! It was incredible, God fell on me, I was utterly broken, my whole life lay before him on the line. I thought he was going to kill me – so much so, I said goodbye to my wife. It was awesome and painful as what felt like high voltage electricity burned through me. Friends around me described it like I was being stretched. There appeared to be a force around me. And this lasted about fifteen minutes, and then I thought I had died because my body seemed filled, transparent with light.

This very un-English form of faith was savaged by people who took offence. Michael Saward, a respected clergyman, said we were

112

being 'towed by the nose by the American fundamentalist style, by extremists like John Wimber. The more you give people this exciting, miracles-guaranteed type of show, the more they get into a kind of drugged state.' He didn't hold back: 'It reminds me of a Nazi rally, of Goebbels-style crowd control. There are too many similarities not to be worried. It's the manipulation of the gullible.' Professor Verna Wright, who combined distinguished work at Leeds University Medical School with duties as a preacher, judged a Wimber show 'a very expert performance containing all the textbook characteristics of the induction of hypnosis'.

Wimber said he was just trying to demonstrate the power of God through miracles and healings, so that people would want to know Him. He blew my young mind, frankly. He told us all to fill up with the Holy Spirit there and then and go back to our churches and give it away. So we did, or at least we tried. Did anyone get healed? That's the big question. Professor Wright, a person of faith with a high medical and scientific reputation, was dismissive of the idea: 'All the detailed analyses which have been made of healing claims over the years have failed to produce evidence of cures, except for the kind of disorders which in medicine we call functional states, in which there is no change to the structure but the illness has a psychological cause.'

Only once did I get close to what might have been a healing, when a man came forward saying he could no longer walk properly, because he was in constant pain. The problem seemed to be that one leg was longer than the other, so he was asked to sit down on the floor at the end of a pew with both legs stretched out, and we laid our hands on his shins. 'Come Holy Spirit, by Your power,' said Roddie, who was there with me and a couple of other members of the ministry team. 'Come in Your healing power.' Under my hand, in a subtle but undeniable way that made my heart hammer, I felt the man's leg move. Maybe he was just adjusting his position. When we opened our eyes, we saw that the soles of his shoes – which had been at least a couple of inches apart – were now level. Was it a healing? Every parent knows there's a trick you can do to make your arm seem to grow, by rolling your shoulder invisibly. It gets the little kids every time. Was this any more than that? Roddie thought so, and was ecstatic: 'Amen, Father, thank you.' I said the same. Was it real? I don't know. The man got up and walked away and I never saw him again.

I went to see Norman, my old vicar, before writing this chapter, to ask if he had any proof that people had been healed. He would have known about every claim, and he was a man with the instinct to test alleged miracles against Scripture and the physical evidence. He thought for a while, then told me of a woman who had asked him to pray about a lump in her breast. Later, her doctor had said the lump was gone. That could have been a major miracle, I said, or it could have been nothing. He agreed. Then he suggested that I read about a well-documented case, the healing of Jennifer Rees Larcombe, who was wheelchair-bound with encephalitis until she was prayed for by a young girl. She walked home that night, pushing her wheelchair. It's not a simple story: one cruel Christian said it was 'such a shame' that Rees Larcombe had wasted so many years in the wheelchair just because she was short on faith. Never mind the healing, it's a near miracle that Rees Larcombe didn't slap that woman in the face. I have never met Jennifer Rees Larcombe, so I can only take her word for what happened. As for Norman, a man I do still know and whose word I trust, the most I can say for sure is that his belief in miracles remains sincere.

'Gaaraaagh! Raralagh!' The voice wasn't mine but it was coming out of my mouth. It started down in the pit of my stomach, like something alive squirming and searching for a way out, burning in my chest, forcing its way up through my throat and choking me, twisting my tongue into sounds like words from an alien language, nothing human. A grunt. A gargle. A yawn and a roar, like somebody – something – crying out loud. Very loud. Bellowing.

'Come out now,' said a man's voice. I heard him as if I were deep underwater and he were calling down to me from the surface. I knew who he was and what he was saying. I knew the words. 'Come out in the name of the Lord.'

Phil, the leader of the ministry team, was praying for me. Casting out a demon. He was leaning over me, pressing a hand against the top of my head and there were other hands on me too, on my shoulders, my arms, in the small of my back. I was aware of slipping down the sofa a little under their soft pressure and I felt dizzy, nauseous. I kept my eyes closed. I had volunteered for this, by asking people to pray for me privately, in someone's parlour. They had come to seek the Lord and act in His power as the disciples did . . . which apparently tonight meant dragging a demonic tapeworm from my guts with the hook of prayer.

'Spirit of anxiety, you do not belong in this young man. Come out now!'

They sang, not a song, but a babble of trills and slurs, all on the same note, or near enough. They were singing in the Spirit, giving notes to the gift of tongues, and as if in response the demon call within me grew louder. Was I doing that, responding somewhere deep inside to the expectation of a performance? Or was I really channelling some bitter force? I was past caring, or even thinking. Blood thundered in my ears. My eyes were shut tight but I could feel the fear of some of the people in the room. I could sense they had taken a step back, as if alarmed at what they were seeing.

'You have no authority here,' said Phil. 'All power belongs to Christ. Go!'

'Amen,' said a voice.

'Amen,' said another. 'Hallelujah!'

The noise stopped. My throat felt as if a tiger had just leapt unexpectedly from it. My breathing grew deeper, calmer.

'Holy Spirit. Bringer of peace. Come upon him now.'

A woman was speaking, softly. Phil's wife, Mary. The only voice in the room now. 'Peace. Deep peace.'

My shoulders dropped. I was not in control of them, any more than I had just been in control of my tongue. My eyes loosened and I opened them through tears: big, fat, hot tears brimming on the rims. When they cleared I saw my girlfriend standing beyond the immediate circle of praying men and women, who were all much older than us. Her eyes were wide with wonder. Or fright.

'Amen,' said Mary, sighing and smiling.

'Amen,' said Phil. 'It's okay. Show's over. Somebody put the kettle on.'

I was sick twenty-six times that night, on my knees in the bathroom at my parents' house. Into the peach-coloured toilet bowl: gag, retch, vomit, shiver, fall back into bed. If my mum heard me calling her, she kept away. Maybe she thought I had drunk too much, like the old days. I roared and gargled again, the blood vessels around my eyes popping every time. The towels were soaked with my sweat. Twenty-six times. I counted, as I lay awake, waiting for it to come again. It was dawn when I passed out. I looked like a panda in the morning. Something had happened. I believed then, with absolute conviction, that a demon had been cast out of me. I couldn't tell you now, for certain, what really happened. I just don't know. All I do know is that it wasn't nothing.

11

Walls come tumbling down

We thought we were the ones to feed the hungry, clothe the naked and free the slaves, because the Bible told us so. In truth, we turned those revolutionary commandments into modest, very occasional donations to charity. Then something happened that put us all to shame. It changed us and it changed the lives of many people around the world, starting with the opening words of a report on the television news: 'Dawn, and as the sun breaks through the piercing chill of night on the plain outside Korem, it lights up a biblical famine. Now, in the twentieth century.'

Michael Buerk was reporting from Ethiopia, where drought had devastated the crops and millions were starving. A baby whose life was as faint as a breath of wind tried to suckle on a mother who had nothing left in her breast. 'This place, say workers here, is the closest thing to hell on earth.' Many people watching were moved to tears. Bob Geldof, a punk singer past his best, didn't just gulp down the lump in his throat and go and make a cup of tea. He did something about it. He didn't set up a committee or join a working party or write a paper. You know that. Instead, he got some mates together to make a record and sold copies of it to raise money to buy food for Africa. Then he got those same mates

117

together again with some others to put on the biggest concert in history, which took place in London and Philadelphia on 13 July 1985 and was watched by a billion people – and which raised, when all was said and done, £150 million.

You can ask questions about where the money went and how it was spent. You can say that the structural problems were not addressed and that famine kept on happening. You can say it was bizarre and excessive for Phil Collins to play on both sides of the Atlantic on the same day; or remember the moment when Simon Le Bon screeched like a tone-deaf owl; or dwell on the shock of seeing Bob Dylan give the worst performance of his life then say, hey, shouldn't we, like, y'know, give some of this money to American farmers? You can say that Live Aid rescued the careers of a few washed-up egomaniacs. You can talk about the 'earthquake in the relief world' that followed, changing the way charities told their stories, the way we responded and the way governments in the rich world understood their obligations to the poor. You can say and do all that, but there are two things that most of the people who watched Live Aid – which was most of us – still remember. One was surreal. The other didn't happen at all.

The first was a video. Putting images of the famine together with a soft-rock song by the Cars was a strange idea. 'Who's gonna drive you home tonight?' Nobody, in the desert. Absurdly, it worked. The image of an emaciated child with flies in her eyes became a cliché, but on that day, with incongruous music, it was immensely moving. It dared you not to respond.

The other memory people have is of Bob Geldof, wild-eyed and gaunt, shouting into the camera, right into the viewer's face: 'Give us your effing money.' He didn't say 'effing', obviously, but some people are offended by the word he did say and I don't want the language to get in the way of the point. What Geldof actually did was interrupt the TV presenter who was trying to give out a postal address for donations. Geldof was exhausted and strung out and thought it was all going too slowly. He wanted us to get the telephone number for credit cards instead so that we could make an instant response, so he cut in and said: '[Never mind] the address, let's get the numbers.' That isn't how people remember it. They recall the moment as something much more dramatic and personal, because that was how it was experienced. It was emotional. It was beyond reason, a direct demand to act on feeling. These days every charity appeal, and every sale of everything from politics to breakfast cereal, is made on that basis, but then it was shocking. It offended people. It worked: after his outburst, donations began pouring in at £300 a second. Geldof had cut through the crap. In the summer of 1985, God was not an Englishman. He was a Dubliner and he wanted, he demanded – and his cause deserved – your effing money.

Now, here's a pop quiz question: which band opened the show at Live Aid and with which song? Most of those who can remember the day say it was Status Quo with 'Rocking All Over the World', but the Quo were actually on second. The first group of musicians to perform at the most famous concert of all time was the Band of the Coldstream Guards. The pips went, the television screen filled with an aerial shot of Wembley Stadium under a blazing sun and the voice of Richard Skinner said: 'It's twelve noon in London, seven a.m. in Philadelphia, and around the world it's time for Live Aid. Wembley welcomes their Royal Highnesses, the Prince and Princess of Wales.' As planetary pop egos sitting in the Royal Box all stood to welcome the guests of honour, down on the wide stage the band began a fanfare, sweltering under bearskins and in scarlet uniforms, before playing 'God Save the Queen'.

That song again. Long to reign over us. They wouldn't do it now. The royals might not even be invited, but it must have seemed essential that day. Princess Diana wanted to see some of the singers she loved, and Charles tried to sway along, but the generational difference between them was never more obvious. What would they have done if they had been in the studio later when Geldof lost it? Diana would have laughed. Charles would presumably have looked embarrassed, hoped his mother wasn't watching and felt a little angry that such a thing should have been said in his presence. God only knows what he made of the Style Council, as Diana danced along. 'The class war's real and not mythologised,' sang a pale, rake-thin Paul Weller, whose band was not the best on that day, nor the most important, but whose choice of song made one thing very clear: the Live Aid genera-tion may have been willing to acknowledge the power of Establishment England in order to get things done, but it was running out of patience. 'You don't have to take this crap/You don't have to sit back and relax/You can actually try changing it,' sang Weller. 'Governments crack and systems fall/'Cause unity is powerful/Lights go out and walls come tumbling down.'

Live Aid changed the way we saw the world. Years before the internet and rolling satellite news, it made the global village feel like a reality. A heartbreaking one. This, in turn, made more people think about the causes of the famine, which were both political and natural. The green movement was still relatively young, but the drought in Ethiopia showed what would happen if we did not prevent an environmental apocalypse. Live Aid also offered a new way of approaching potential supporters on behalf of the poor. Direct, emotional, dramatic. If Bob Geldof had been the Archbishop during the riots in Toxteth and Brixton, he would have stormed up Downing Street and ordered the Prime Minister to seize some effing money from the City and give it to the stricken cities.

Walls come tumbling down

Robert Runcie was a different kind of Bob. He didn't know many chart toppers. Instead of behaving like a Boomtown Rat on a bender, after the riots he had very quietly done what most archbishops do best – he formed a committee and asked it to have a jolly good think. The man he put in charge was Richard O'Brien, former head of the Manpower Services Commission, who met with academics, trade unionists, a deputy council leader, the Bishop of Liverpool and Wilfred Wood, who was soon to become the first black English bishop. They did think about things, for two years. Then, shortly after Live Aid, in the autumn of 1985, they published a report called 'Faith in the City'. One commentator described it as the Church 'appointing itself the conscience of the nation' – which just goes to show how out of touch religious people were, because everyone else in the nation realised that its conscience was now in the hands of the pop stars.

Church reports are read only by the people who write them. Nobody else pays attention. This one, however, was a spectacular exception to that rule, because it was a direct attack on the policy of the government of the day and the morality – or rather lack of it – behind what Margaret Thatcher was doing. The language was moderate but the politics were confrontational. Because the blow came from the Church – long seen as the natural ally of the Tory Party – it was far harder than any the Labour Party could have landed. Even the Iron Lady was rattled. The Home Secretary, the Chancellor and all the other senior cabinet ministers were called to a meeting to discuss the report, and were handed a briefing note containing a word that would come to define their response: 'Marxist'. This new opposition had to be crushed. One cabinet minister, whose name was never made public, broke the rules in talking about the report before it was published and told the *Sunday Times* that the Church had come up with 'pure Marxist theology'.

That was rubbish. The report did quote Marx, saying evil was to be found in social and economic relationships as well as the human heart and that the rich would get richer and the poor poorer unless something was done, but 'Faith in the City' also suggested the founder of communism had got the idea from the Old Testament, and insisted: 'It is a clear duty for the Church to sound a warning that our society may be losing the "compassionate" character which is still desired by the majority of its members.' That sounds mild, but in relative metaphorical terms, considering the intimate history of the Church and the State, it was like a mortar firing shells across the Thames from Lambeth Palace. For the report to ask 'whether some politicians really understand the despair which has become so widespread in many areas of our country' was like the Archbishop kicking down the door of Number 10 and shouting: 'Oi! Maggie! Sort it!'

The Church was also ready with solutions, for a change. No wishy-washy waffle or hand-wringing here. The medicine prescribed was money, applied liberally in all the right places: to regenerate the inner cities; to boost child benefits and the dole; and to help charities care for the needy. Where was it going to come from? Higher taxes for people who had good jobs. Mortgage tax relief – which helped the middle classes – should be abolished and the income used to help homeless people, to build more council houses and to improve bad ones. The Church was daring to challenge one of the commandments of the gospel according to Margaret Thatcher: thou shalt have the right to buy thy council house. The report said she was wrong to promote her idealism so aggressively by subsidising ridiculously low buy-out prices for tenants: 'The right to buy and the growth of owner occupation are effectively carried on the backs of poor people.'

The bishops had accused Mrs Thatcher of robbing the poor to pay the rich, and now 'Faith in the City' said: 'It is the poor who have borne the brunt of the recession, yet it is the poor who are seen by some as "social security scroungers" or a burden on the country preventing economic recovery.' This was 'blaming the victim'. The Church wanted no part in it and from now on would 'proclaim the ethic of altruism against egotism, of community against self-seeking, and of charity against greed'.

Egotism. Self-seeking. Greed. That was close to calling Margaret Thatcher evil. No wonder she unleashed her own attack dogs, led by Norman Tebbit, the party hard man, who fought dirty and accused Richard O'Brien of being a Labour supporter. The Church of England had once been described as the Tory Party at prayer, said Tebbit, but now the Tory Party was praying for the Church. Again, it sounds mild, but at the time Tebbit was like a Rottweiler with a chewed-up dog collar in its bloody jaws.

The most surprising attack came from someone the church leaders might have considered a friend: the Chief Rabbi, Immanuel Jakobovits. He was close to the Prime Minister and lashed the report as placing too much importance on benefits and not enough on self-help. Jewish people had pulled themselves out of deprivation with good hard work, he said. 'Cheap labour is better than a free dole.'

The Thatcher regime then found the chink in the report's armour. None of the proposals had been costed, ministers announced, and some of them must have thanked God for that. The Church was being hopelessly naive, sounding off like a political party but utterly failing to do what parties must and think about how much everything would cost. Now the bishops could be dismissed as unrealistic, unworldly do-gooders, whose opinions were of little consequence in the real world. This was the age of the entrepreneur, and nothing counted more than the bottom line.

St George didn't pause on his way to meet the dragon and purposefully stab his spear into his own foot. The authors of 'Faith in the City' should have learned from that. Not only did they fail to cost their ideas, they included passages which attacked the Church as fully and frankly as the State. This was very humble and quite proper, but a serious error. It would have been much better to put all the self-loathing in a separate report, rather than provide opponents with ready-made ammunition. Instead, just a few pages away from all that feisty talk about the poor was the confession that the Church of England, its leadership, its priests and its people were all so thoroughly middle class that they were unable to connect with those beneath them in any meaningful way.

This part of 'Faith in the City' revealed the Church still to be Establishment to its core, the spiritual equivalent of the old-style All England Tennis Club: a place where the whites shone as brightly as the lawns, the umpire was in charge, and if you didn't have the right ticket or tie, you couldn't come in. The big congregations were all in the suburbs or the countryside. The report said more priests should be sent to the inner cities, to work with other churches and faiths. It also proposed a huge new charitable fund that would give out £80 million over the next two decades. The money would come from rich parishes and from the Church Commissioners, who provided salaries and pensions for priests with the income generated by a bulging property portfolio. Surely that cash would never run out, would it?

One observation was lost in the fire fight, but it would prove to be horribly truthful. The report said that black Christians had been 'frozen out' by patronising attitudes among congregations and their leaders. There were less than a hundred black clergy, one of whom, the Reverend Rajinder Daniel of Smethwick, said black believers had been effectively invisible for years and could not relate to the mainstream denominations. He was right, but nobody who mattered was listening. They didn't know that the colour and culture of England were going to change so dramatically over the coming years. They didn't realise that congregations run by and for black Africans and other immigrant communities were going to become large and boisterous, fighting for attention in the marketplace of faith. They did know, however, absolutely – because they were told this very clearly by the report in 1985 – that black and Asian people did not feel welcome in the Church of England and did not believe it represented them, their faith or their idea of what it meant to be English.

The arrival of so many people from the Caribbean, many of them Christians already, had been a fantastic chance for all the churches to gain and grow, in membership and understanding of the world. They had blown it. Was the problem personal or institutional? Was it subconscious or explicit? All of these, in different ways and different places. Arrogance, stupidity and racism meant the Church of England had turned its back on a generation of new English people and lost for ever the chance to recruit them or their children. It would come to regret that, deeply.

'Faith in the City' revealed a tug of love, to use a phrase adored by the tabloids. The Church and the State were pulling with all their might to take the English God in two directions at once, and He was bound to be ripped apart. Margaret Thatcher believed, sincerely, that her policies were releasing people into a personal freedom at the heart of Christianity. Those who could do so should be free to make serious money, for it was in the creation of wealth that the poor would be helped – through either charitable giving or the trickle-down effect of spending. It was not the State's job to pursue social justice; indeed, that was impossible.

The Church missed just how radical she was, at first, but then it had only relatively recently worked closely with the Conservatives, as well as Labour, to help set up the Welfare State, sacrificing itself for the greater good. Before that, the main source of education, healthcare and alms for the poor had been Christian charity. Then Christians had become some of the most committed campaigners for free, universal schooling, the National Health Service and the social services. By leading those campaigns, as Jeremy Paxman points out in his book *Friends in High Places*, 'they actively promoted the instruments of their own irrelevance'. If you had a calling to serve society in the fifties, there was now no need to be a believer. 'Many who before the war might have joined the ministry because they wanted to act out their Christian beliefs found they could do so more easily working as state-employed teachers, social workers or doctors.'

The Church was left without much of a purpose after that, except to consider the things of God, until the collapse of Her Majesty's official opposition encouraged it to jump back into politics. It wasn't welcome. And actually, on second thoughts, 'Faith in the City' did not reveal a tug of love at all: it was a tug of loathing. The Church hated the State (or, more specifically, the liberal leadership of the Church of England hated the Conservative government, and it was mutual). Each thought the other was betraying the values of God. Each thought the other should keep out of their business.

Understandably, the Prime Minister did not feel like appointing any more bishops who were going to spend their days ripping bits out of her. The bishops saw no reason why she should be allowed to appoint spiritual leaders at all. But if her right to make those appointments was now open to question, then so were all the other intricate ties that bound the Church to the State and vice versa. Both sides were taking the strain. It might take a while yet, but something was definitely going to break.

12

Make way! Make way!

I knew everything. I was one of the Chosen. Walking across a housing estate in the summer of 1987, at the age of twenty, I was at the height of my powers. Tall and skinny, with longish dirty-blond hair, I was wearing ordinary jeans and an ordinary white t-shirt, but I was not ordinary at all. My job was to tell people about Jesus, and give them the answer to all their problems. For some reason, they didn't seem to want to know. They didn't often answer when I knocked on their doors; or they told me to go away in words that a good Christian mind had a duty to forget; or they got their dogs to chase me away, although that was not a problem. I was fearless. I could rebuke the dogs. I shouted at them: 'Get back, in the name of the Lord.' They got back. They stopped and stared, those dogs, never having seen such a thing before.

If I looked like a fool, even to dogs, then that was not a problem. It was good. We were called to be Fools for Christ. I used a lot of capitals in those days, because my life was full of important stuff. The fiery lake of hell was waiting for those who did not repent of their sins. People just had to accept that. Make way, as the song said. 'Make way, make way for Christ the King in splendour arrives.' I was wearing an old, cheap guitar and strumming that song as I walked across that housing estate, on a cold and damp day that deadened the strings and put them out of tune. That didn't matter, the Lord would still be magnified. Beside me walked David, an American who had a posh guitar and played complicated songs really well. I liked David, with his short, neat hairstyle, pressed chinos, check shirt and white t-shirt underneath. He was very preppy, very neat, even now when we were sleeping every night on the floor of a church hall. It was David, me and a dozen fellow members of a missionary organisation for young people, which did not pay any of us. We lived by faith, which was supposed to mean relying on the Lord to provide all we needed for food, clothes and accommodation (but in practice meant being as nice as possible to the people back home, so they would send money). The organisation had been started by Americans but had thousands of members in more than a hundred countries, with teenage recruits supplementing their numbers for summer missions like the one we were now on. Norman, my vicar, had been very keen on my going to the three-month training school, which cost £1000, and then out into the world to spread the word. Thinking about it now, I can see why. I was going far away from his daughter.

So there we were, standing on a triangle of scruffy grass at the end of a terrace, on this housing estate. Two of us were playing while the rest sang. 'Make way! Make way!' It was not much of a sound, but it was attracting attention: two women were standing on the corner with their arms folded, staring at us. Scowling. Behind them, down the street but walking towards us quite quickly, came two men, with shaved heads and flushed faces. They looked like trouble. Maybe now I ought to mention the huge mural that was right in front of us, covering the end of a row of houses. It was intimidating, to be honest, even if the Lord was my shield. The picture showed a man dressed all in black, wearing a balaclava so that his face was hidden. He was cradling an Armalite machine gun. Above his head were written three tall letters: 'IRA'.

I wasn't stupid (although I appreciate that might be hard to believe at this point). I knew we were not welcome in this place. This was, after all, the Bogside. Extraordinary, isn't it? Our leaders had brought us to march around singing Jesus songs in the place where the Troubles began in August 1969, and where the British Army opened fire on a peace march in January 1972 and killed thirteen people. I didn't know it at the time, but I was strumming my guitar and shouting at people to make way for Christ the King on exactly the spot where a seventeen-year-old Catholic boy called Michael Kelly had lain in the street, bleeding to death after being shot by a representative of the English God. Kelly's family still lived there. It is hard to think of what we could have done to be more offensive. Our group included people from Protestant and Catholic churches, and we considered our born-again faith to be above such sectarianism, but to those people who stood watching us in horror and disgust we can only have looked and sounded like arrogant Prods come to shout in their faces. We did believe that our truth was the only truth.

Perhaps the American and Australian accents of our leaders saved us. The people of the Bogside had suffered enough religion, and had a reputation for dealing fiercely with those who tried to impose it on them, but perhaps they just thought we were mad strangers and took pity. There was also the matter of the twenty or so British soldiers who had encircled us, with helmets on and guns out and armoured Land-Rovers waiting. Some of them were smiling, or maybe smirking. It wasn't funny where I was standing. The red-faced men were now shouting, violently, and some kids had appeared with stones and lumps of concrete that they were throwing at us, over the heads of the soldiers. I saw one arc like a rainbow and shatter at my feet. Some of our singers were screaming and one of the girls was sobbing but we were still going on because this was the work of the Lord. 'Make way! Make way!' The sound was feeble now. The soldiers had tightened the circle, with their backs to us, and they were shouting warnings at the kids and the kids were running for it, scattering, but the men were standing their ground and shouting back, and there were more of them now, and a brick came over the troops and smashed into the body of my guitar, splintering the wood, leaving a hole like a wound, and the strings were broken and I stopped playing and the captain turned and said to our leader, loud and clear over the noise: 'That's enough, I think, don't you?'

And I thought, Captain, do you know your trouble? You haven't got enough faith.

The *Guardian* once described that missionary organisation as 'fundamentalist' and I would agree with that. Speaking for myself, I was a teenage fundamentalist. I am using the f-word in the modern sense of someone with unshakeable convictions, who feels the urgent need to press them upon the world. Just this week, in the papers, I have seen mention of Islamic fundamentalists, Sikh fundamentalists, animal rights fundamentalists, eco-fundamentalists, even congestion-charge fundamentalists. The word began to be used in this way in southern California in 1910 when a pair of oil tycoon brothers paid for a series of pamphlets setting out 'The Fundamentals' of faith. In *Fundamentalism* Malise Ruthven lists those beliefs as including:

The inerrancy of the Bible; the direct creation of the world, and humanity, ex nihilo by God (in contrast to Darwinian evolution); the authenticity of miracles; the virgin birth of Jesus, his Crucifixion and bodily resurrection; the substitutory atonement (the doctrine that Christ died to redeem the sins of humanity); and (for some but not all believers) his imminent return to judge and rule over the world.

I would have signed up to most of those while I was with the mission. Of course, as Ruthven says, 'fundamentalist' has become a byword for bigotry. 'For the secular non-believer, or for the liberal believer who takes a sophisticated view of religious discourse, the god of fundamentalism must be mischievous, if not downright evil, a demonic power who delights in setting humans at each other's throats.' We have certainly had enough evidence of that in recent years, and not only from terrorists. The only reason there are no Christian suicide bombers, by the way, is that Christians seldom feel powerless against an overwhelming military force: the invading army is usually theirs. In time, a world view much like ours was used in the White House to justify war. Like us, the born-again George W. Bush saw the world in terms of a fight between good and evil. Once you begin to see it as your divine duty to convert the planet to your way of thinking, even at gunpoint, anything is possible.

As for me and my friends, in the eighties, we were not content with marching all over the Bogside. We were about to play our part in a series of much bigger marches that would stop the traffic in London and make front-page news, helping to turn quiet English Christianity into a noisy, exhibitionist faith and unwittingly connect it to that seemingly irresistible, worldwide phenomenon, the rise of fundamentalism. And that is how I found myself standing in the rain, shouting at the Bank of England.

The doors were locked. There was nobody inside the massive building on Threadneedle Street because it was the weekend.

The rain was falling in bucketfuls and the police officers who had been told to watch us thought we were mad, but we didn't care. We had a job to do, and we didn't need anyone else's help or permission. We had come to fight a demon, a huge and powerful spiritual force hovering over the bank. We couldn't see it, of course. But we knew it was there because our leaders said so, they had named it as a spirit of greed and unrighteous trade and told us that our prayers would enable the angels of the Lord to go into battle against that hideous being. We believed them. There were thousands of us from hundreds of churches, an unarmed army of Christian soldiers in drenched pac-a-macs marching past the bank, yelling beyond the mighty pillars to drive away the unseen spirit, telling it to be gone in the name of the Lord.

The organisers had hoped that five thousand people would come and join us on the march from Smithfield Market to the London Wall, but three times as many turned up on the day. The route was only a mile and a quarter long, passing the Stock Exchange, the Royal Courts of Justice, Lloyd's of London and the newspaper offices in Fleet Street, but it took more than two and a half hours to get everybody through, as they shuffled forward waving banners or singing the same songs we had sung on the Bogside. 'We are not on a ramble,' one of the leaders said. We were seeking to 'effect serious change in the heavenlies' and transform 'the supernatural atmosphere of our country'.

The City March in May 1987 was inspired by the outdoor meetings of the Salvation Army, pilgrimage processions, carnivals and the Anglican custom of beating the bounds of a parish, but the theology was a bit more controversial than that. It was based on what we called principalities and powers: the idea that buildings and communities could be under the control of invisible spirits, but prayer could help the angels defeat them. 'For we wrestle not against flesh and blood,' writes Paul in his letter to the

Ephesians, 'but against principalities, against powers, against the rulers of the darkness of this world, against spiritual wickedness in high places.' You could take that to mean the oppressive structures of human society, or say this is about the mythical dimension to life, the allegorical struggle between the best of life and the worst. Or you could take it literally, as we did.

'Strategic spiritual warfare' was the latest thinking, a bit like a global game of invisible chess played with winged warriors. One woman involved in the organisation had been given a vision of two angels with their swords raised over the cityscape, ready for a fight. A researcher had come up with possible historic origins for the presence of satanic enemies in London, including pagan or Roman gods, Freemasonry, slavery and good old-fashioned greed. Some of the notes prefigured *The Da Vinci Code* by nearly two decades: 'The corrupting spiritual powers which at one time, no doubt, hovered behind the mystic Knights Templar, who met on the site of the Temple and wielded great power, are only an example of the power bases which have swayed the City and its past and still do.' How were we supposed to visualise these evil influences? Was I the only one who saw, in his mind's eye as he looked up and prayed, Godzilla bearing down on the Bank of England?

The organisers believed that being physically present outside buildings that were 'strongholds' of the demonic power would make a difference and that prayer would lift some of the problems of London 'whether it is housing, unemployment or drug addiction'. A prototype march through Soho had apparently been followed a few weeks later by a police raid on unlicensed sex shops and shows. This time our target was the financial centre. 'The economic establishment of the City was at one time considered a citadel of integrity,' said our notes. 'Scandals of recent years have shown how far the enemy's inroads have eaten into our way of life.'

The marchers included Christians who worked as bankers. One of them, near me, spent his time between prayers pointing out the best sandwich shops. This was weird. A book written about the event by its leaders, called *March for Jesus*, quotes a teenage participant as saying: 'At first it seemed strange to be praying at all these huge and ancient buildings in the rain. But we soon began to feel that God really was able to work through our prayers; that we were helping the battle for London by breaking down barriers and repenting of the capital's sin. There was such a feeling of being on the winning side.' That was right. The feelings of rebellion that had led me to join the faith of David Jenkins and John Wimber were rampant that day, as we squelched about in a place where we would not normally be welcome, apparently bossing the powers that held sway.

We sang new songs that had driving rhythms and big, bold choruses, telling the Devil and everyone else to bow down to our God or get out of the way. They sound so gauche now, in this different world. *March for Jesus* claims they worked:

> We were sure that God would answer our prayers, but we didn't know how. Within months the City had experienced Black Monday when shares crashed in London and New York. At a stroke £50 billion was wiped off City stock values and by the end of the week they had dropped nearly £102 billion. We praised God that changes were taking place.

Did my friend the sandwich expert celebrate in the same way? I don't know if he lost his job as many did in that crash, including sandwich makers and office cleaners as well as City boys who had back bonuses to live on. The rest of us, far from the reality, were ecstatic. We were, as Wimber said, in touch with the supernatural. We were part of something big, and it was only going to get bigger.

In the spring of 1988, while still working full time for no pay, I acted as a press officer for the renamed March for Jesus. The plan this time was to assemble on the Embankment and walk through Westminster – 'the political rather than the economic heart of the capital' – to Hyde Park with about thirty thousand people. The police didn't believe we could get that many and neither did the press. Nobody was interested, however many phone calls we made or press releases we sent out. Then the day arrived, and far more marchers turned up than even we had hoped. They filled the Embankment, then stacked up to Waterloo Bridge, then across to the South Bank. Still more kept arriving. Traffic was gridlocked.

The huge mobile phone I was carrying, the size of an over-weight baby, rang and the man from the Press Association was on the line. What was going on? Could he come down? Of course he could, that was what I had been trying to persuade him to do for weeks. He brought a photographer. Neither could quite believe what they were seeing, but then neither could I. The reporter asked who was on the march. People of all denominations, I said. The Salvation Army had taken off their uniforms, to blend in better, although a group of extreme believers in combat gear called the Jesus Army had flooded the front, trying to make the march look like it was theirs. They were sent back. Were there any Catholics? 'Ah, yes,' I said. 'Some.' Not many though, in truth.

The spiritual warfare had been toned down this time. We didn't rebuke demons, we repented for the sins of the past and asked God to raise up believers to make things right. At the Houses of Parliament we thanked Him for MPs but also chanted the second psalm *en masse*: 'Do homage to the Son of God, lest he be angry and you be destroyed in your way, for his anger can flare up in a moment.' The next morning, every national newspaper carried a photograph of the march on its front page. The *Sunday Telegraph* said: 'Clean cut, healthy living and dancing to gospel music, 50,000 evangelicals set out to convert the nation's leaders in a way reminiscent of the Trotskyite demos of the 1960s.' The picture showed a man with his hands in the air and his eyes closed in devotion. One leader was quoted as saying: 'The power of the Holy Spirit will use us as a battering ram.'

That quote chills me now, thinking about what was to come in the Middle East. We sang about the Lord setting the nations on fire, and prayed for Him to smite His enemies, but we meant it metaphysically. Honestly. The language appalled and alarmed other Christians who wanted no part in what appeared to be a call for world domination. We wanted Christ to reign. We said so. How did we think that would look? We wanted every faith and every government to give up their own religious identity and bow the knee to our God. One God, one faith, one world. It was one horrific image, to those who did not believe.

The March for Jesus was the biggest Christian gathering on the streets of England for a generation or more, but we were not the only ones making public protests on behalf of our beliefs. There were others who, like us, were testing the polite consensus that had been essential to the soul of England for so long, and which enabled people who had opposing beliefs to live in peace. The person, for example, who put a flaming rag through the letterbox of a house in the East End of London, starting a fire that killed a child. It was a protest against the arrival of Asians and probably had nothing to do with her faith, but, naturally, her Muslim family sought comfort and support from their mosque.

Muslims, Hindus and Sikhs had begun organising themselves and getting into local politics, because of the need for self-protection but also through a desire for their faith and culture to be taken seriously. The national media took no notice most of the time, until the Islamic reaction to the publication of *The Satanic Verses* by Salman Rushdie suddenly made that impossible.

The critics quite liked his novel about Indian expatriates in London, but some Muslims hated it. The dream sequences were said to blaspheme against the Prophet. The book was banned in India and there were riots in Pakistan. We thought we were above such things until young men appeared in Bradford city centre, doused copies of the book in petrol and set them alight, using coat-hangers to hold them at a distance so they didn't burn their hands. They felt ignored, they said, after going through the proper channels and writing to the publisher and the government to express their disgust and distress. One of them, Ishtiaq Ahmed, later told the BBC that the book burning 'had a symbolic meaning . . . a faith community demonstrating and saying, "We matter, we exist, we are here, our presence matters." This police station, Town Hall, Magistrates' Court . . . they are ours as much as anyone else's'

The stunt wasn't taken very seriously at the time, but it started to look different the following month, when the Ayatollah Khomeini said all good Muslims should be ready to kill Rushdie. The author began a decade of movement from place to place, hiding with members of Special Branch. Some Muslims wanted to sue Rushdie for blasphemy but the House of Lords told them they couldn't, because that law could be used only with respect to Christian beliefs – and, even more specifically than that, only those held by the Church of England. This unjust, anachronistic tie between Church and State was later abolished, but not until 2008.

Inayat Bunglawala, who supported the book burning but later recanted, has called the Rushdie affair 'a seminal moment in British Muslim history'. Ed Husain, author of *The Islamist*, said: 'Many people found a voice then. It was the first time Muslims had engaged with British political society as a united group.' The Ayatollah's fatwa raised questions about what it meant to be English. Did you have to give up other cultural allegiances? Did tolerance and fair play mean allowing someone to insult your prophet? Did you have the right to burn their books? The response to *The Satanic Verses* was part of a wider change, in which believers of all kinds were starting to demand that their faith be taken seriously, much more seriously than the English were accustomed to. No more flippancy or understatement, religion was becoming life and death again. The presence of Islam alarmed the more strident Christians, but to some of us its seriousness was impressive. If they were going to be so aggressive about what they believed in, why couldn't we?

The March for Jesus grew and grew in the years to come, being held first in Britain then abroad. Over the next decade there would be marches in 180 countries, involving 600 million people. Michael Saward, the churchman who had compared Wimber meetings to Nazi rallies, said: 'I find it a chilling sight. The marching, the chanting in unison, the singing, the slogans. It is a very authoritarian style. It has produced what I call a "Jesus, Jesus, über Alles" mentality.' That looks a bit overheated, but some of the language of strategic spiritual warfare was all too easily comparable to Christian fascism. Those words came to mind when George W. Bush got busy. For now, though, Saward warned fellow believers not to get involved in what looked to him like an attempt at corporate exorcism. 'As Anglicans,' he said, 'we are part of a Christian tradition that has never polarised itself

against social institutions in this way. We follow St Paul's declaration that the powers-that-be are ordained of God.'

That was the voice of Establishment England. On the other
hand, nobody represented the iconoclastic, chippy People's
England better than Gerald Coates, a forty-something who had
left the Anglican Church to look for something more 'authentic' after the Holy Spirit had fallen on him while he was cycling
down the road one day. Coates was one of the early leaders of the
House Church movement in England — his church was called
Pioneer. By the time of the first March for Jesus, it had a hundred congregations, many in the parts of Surrey that people were
beginning to call the English Bible Belt. Coates was a friend of
Cliff Richard, who had been a member of his congregation in
Cobham. The pastor's lifestyle wasn't extravagant, his church was
committed to working with the disadvantaged and included a
'non-judgemental' ministry to people with Aids (although
homosexuality was still considered a sin), but Coates was a performer, with silk shirts and sharp suits. I liked him, not least
because he wasn't dull. He did have a bit of a big mouth, though.
'The traditional churches, like the Anglican and Methodist, have
been haemorrhaging members for years,' he said. The likes of
David Jenkins and Robert Runcie 'do not represent the historic,
orthodox Christian faith. They believe anything, provided it's not
in the Bible.'

That was unfair. Runcie believed in an inclusive, humane
Church that did its historic duty in welcoming everyone and
offering help to all those who needed it. A liberal Church that
represented what he saw as the best English values, including tolerance, decency and quiet service. But that wasn't enough for
Spirit-soaked, Bible-believing Christians who had been bolstered
by the visits of Billy Graham and boosted by the signs and wonders of John Wimber. The March for Jesus put faith on display

in a way that had not been seen before in modern England. It was loud, colourful and full of confidence. Many of those who waved banners and danced along the Embankment would have died of embarrassment if they had been asked to do so on their own. This new Christianity was personal but it was also public. Unafraid to be seen crying or laughing, it was in tune with the times. For a decade, Margaret Thatcher had told us we were individuals first and foremost, who had to look after our own. We had a right to choice in all things. We also had the right to be selfish, which combined with the values we had absorbed from America to make us less restrained, less polite and discreet, more demonstrative and stroppy.

The English were learning to show our emotions in public. As we were about to see demonstrated in the most appalling and distressing way.

13

You'll never walk alone

Jon-Paul Gilhooley was standing right behind the goal. The ten-year-old Liverpool fan wanted to be close to the players as they took on Nottingham Forest in the semi-final of the FA Cup. They were at Hillsborough, a neutral ground in Sheffield where the crowd was tightly packed behind metal fencing that had been put up to stop pitch invasions. The referee blew the whistle, the match kicked off, but something was wrong, badly wrong. There was too much pressure. People were jammed up against each other, they couldn't move, they couldn't breathe. There was no way out past that fence and the pushing was coming from behind and not stopping, getting harder and harder. The family friend who was with Jon-Paul, looking out for the lad, couldn't take the crush and passed out. When he came round, he found himself in the middle of the worst footballing disaster Europe had ever known. Bodies everywhere. Children screaming, men and women wailing, panic in everyone's eyes. In his too, because Jon-Paul was nowhere to be seen. He was gone.

The cameras had captured everything. The millions of people who had tuned in to *Grandstand* had watched it happen. The referee stopping the match with only six minutes gone. The players looking confused, afraid. The police lining up, thinking there was going to be a pitch invasion. The people trying to climb out or over, being hauled out of the crush. The hands reaching out, pleading. The ones who went under. The metal fence buckling. The panic. The bodies on the floor, unconscious or dead. The fans who could stand tearing down advertising boards to make stretchers. The one ambulance that could make it through parked by the goal, among the crowds. One. It looked like a massacre. It was unbelievable. It was like Heysel, the terrible crushing of Italian fans at a European final four years earlier, only worse – because this was here, these people suffering, being trapped, being killed, were people we might know.

Back in Liverpool, a nine-year-old boy called Stevie, a cousin of Jon-Paul who was always having a kickabout with him, was watching the television and hearing reports on the radio and getting more and more distressed. Like everyone else in the city, he was 'wondering whether we had anyone we knew at the game', he remembered, years later. That night he was 'thinking about it, lying in bed and praying if you like, keeping your fingers crossed that it didn't get any worse than what we had already heard'. It did. 'We got the dreaded knock the next morning.' Jon-Paul's father had driven over to Sheffield and been shown into the gymnasium in the stadium, where he had identified the child lying dead on the floor as his son. Such pain. Ninety-four people died that day, and two more would eventually die of their injuries. The people who came back to Liverpool that night and early the next morning were described by those who saw them as looking like a beaten army, staggering home, wordless and empty.

The first flowers had already been tied to the gates at Hillsborough. They were like the ones the Italian fans had taken to the home of Juventus after Heysel, and tied to the gates there. Scarves had been hung too, from fans of Liverpool and Forest and the Sheffield teams but also others who had driven across Yorkshire to make some gesture in response to what had happened. And there were notes. 'Goodnight, God bless,' said one, which then referred to the Liverpool club song: 'You'll never walk alone.' That sentimental ballad, written by Rodgers and Hammerstein, sung by the crowds at the royal wedding, sung by the one mighty voice of the Kop before, during and after every match, would be read, written, sung and spoken countless times in the coming days. Something extraordinary was beginning to happen.

There were people at the Anfield Stadium, the famous home of Liverpool Football Club, at dawn on the Sunday morning. Some of them had not slept. They tied their own tributes to the Shankly Gates, the memorial to the club's spiritual father, and then they stayed. More mourners came, then still more. They bought flowers from the stall outside the cemetery in Stanley Park, and brought them across. Some went to pray first, in the great Anglican and Catholic cathedrals or in their usual churches. James Dalrymple, wandering the streets for the *Independent*, found a lifelong Everton fan called Father Tom wearing a Liverpool badge on his vestments, leading a service over the sobs and groans of women and children. 'We are a family; this city is like one big family. And we have more than enough love to cope with this.' Was that true?

The directors of Liverpool FC drove past the disturbingly silent crowds on their way into the ground that Sunday morning for an emergency meeting. Two hours later they opened the gates, just as a *Liverpool Echo* special edition was being handed around, with its black border and shocking pictures of scenes from the day before. 'They caged us in like animals,' one angry man in a pub told Dalrymple, 'and some died like animals.' By now the goalpost and net at one end of Anfield was woven with red scarves, and

143

blue ones from Evertonians, and a third of the pitch was covered in carnations, lilies, crocuses and every kind of flower people could get, giving off a sweet and powerful scent. The team manager, Kenny Dalglish, known until now for being stony, unemotional, said it was the 'saddest and most beautiful sight' he had ever seen. There were flags and football shirts and teddy bears, and messages, some of them poems, to lost friends, brothers, sisters, lovers, mates. The Salvation Army was there playing the twenty-third psalm, the one about walking through the valley of the shadow of death, but mostly the fans stood or walked in absolute silence, except for their tears. 'It was incredibly sad,' said Dalglish, 'yet deeply moving as well. I cried for the umpteenth time. You just can't help it.' He was already a hero to half of Merseyside for his skill as a player and a manager, but he would be respected by the whole city for the way he and his family acted in the days after the tragedy, turning up to funerals, visiting relatives, offering what comfort they could. One tearful person who could not sleep and called the phone number set up for the bereaved at four o'clock in the morning was astonished to realise that the person on the other end of the line, listening patiently and trying to help, was Marina, the wife of Kenny Dalglish.

On that Sunday night, they were together with three thousand others in the Roman Catholic Cathedral for a requiem mass, with nine thousand people outside listening to relays. Services were also held at the city's Anglican Cathedral and at those in Sheffield and Nottingham. 'How did it happen?' asked the Archbishop of Liverpool, Derek Worlock, articulating what so many were wondering. 'Who did what? Who didn't do what? Clearly there will have to be inquiries. Questions to be asked and answered. But not tonight. Tonight we come here to pray. At a time like this there are no easy answers. But Liverpool is a place of great faith and against that seemingly meaningless catastrophe we shall need it all.' The bereaved had been overwhelmed with sympathy, he said. 'It has been as if the rest of the country, and perhaps Europe itself, has combined to sing with us in chorus this night that especially in these dark days, we shall never walk alone.'

Over the next seven days a million people went to Anfield to pay their respects. The spontaneous creation of a people's shrine, and the mass pilgrimage to see it and stand there and mutter things and maybe say a prayer and think about what a terrible waste it all was happened on a scale not seen before. Grace Davie, the leading sociologist of religion, says the events at Anfield 'astonished the world' and were 'totally without precedent . . . what started as a series of spontaneous actions by individual mourners became within twenty-four hours a shared or communal activity. The Anfield Pilgrimage expressed, indeed enacted, the mood of an entire city, a city united in grief, an example surely of effective civil religion.'

Why did it happen like that? The example of the Juventus fans was perhaps the model for the hanging of scarves and laying of flowers, but it was also because of the special culture of Liverpool, which is influenced by Ireland as much as it is by England, and by Catholicism more than any other faith. Outsiders often say that the people of Liverpool are sentimental, they fall so easily for cheap emotion, but there's nothing cheap about the tears of a mother who sends her son out to a football match as a treat and never sees him alive again.

The thing is that this way of death did not end at the municipal borders of Merseyside when the last of the victims was buried. Anfield changed the way the English show their grief. The shrine arose out of a unique event and a unique city, but it provided a new model for mourning that would be taken up with grim enthusiasm, from the death of a princess to the bouquets that are now tied to roadside railings at accident blackspots all over the country. It started there and then. Just think of all the other times we have seen something similar to what Derek Worlock and his Anglican counterpart and friend David Sheppard wrote about seeing on the Anfield pitch, for the first time in their lives: 'On the turf lay a field of flowers, more scarves and caps, mascots and souvenirs, and incredibly, kneeling amidst wreaths and rattles, a plaster Madonna straight from a Christmas crib. Blasphemy, unhealthy superstition, tawdry sentimentality. Or a rich blend of personal mourning, prayerful respect and genuine faith?'

The close friendship of these Anglican and Catholic clergymen was itself breaking new ground in a sectarian city, as they recognised: 'During these days Liverpool has been like a large family in mourning. Supporters from the world of football terraces have felt able to weep unashamedly. There has been a willingness to share deep feelings in a very open way.' This was not the English way at all, some of the more daring commentators began to say. It was more the Irish way. Perhaps the lachrymose Liverpool way. But for better or worse, it was going to spread beyond Merseyside. It was going to become part of the English soul, this public weeping and reaching out for meaning, this improvised ritual and sharing of pain.

Surprisingly, Margaret Thatcher seemed to understand. Although she had shown every sign of loathing football fans, the Prime Minister sounded unusually vulnerable as she toured Hillsborough the day after the disaster, saw the buckled fence and thought of the bereaved. 'In a family you are always thinking of somebody else. Is there food in the fridge? Is the place tidy? Then all of a sudden there is a big hole, an emptiness. Comfort is the least one can offer, but comfort cannot fill the emptiness.'

The cities of Liverpool, Nottingham and Sheffield came to a standstill six days later, as people kept a minute's silence at six minutes past three that was also observed by the teams, referees and fans at almost every football ground (Millwall's Den being the exception, predictably). Half a million supporters took part in the biggest display of public mourning since the funeral of Winston Churchill in 1965. Again, it wouldn't be the last time this was done. We have since become used to marking our grief this way.

Despite the snow falling, crowds turned up to see the coffin containing the body of Jon-Paul Gilhooley, the youngest victim, when he was carried into St Columba's Church in Huyton for his requiem mass. A red and white wreath in the shape of a football lay on the altar. The Liverpool player Steve Nicol was there with his wife. Classmates from Jon-Paul's primary school sat near members of his family, one of whom would not speak publicly about his memories of Hillsborough until twenty years later. By that time the nine-year-old cousin who had lain in bed, worrying and 'praying if you like', was the captain of Liverpool Football Club: Steven Gerrard, one of the greatest players in the history of Anfield. Thinking about Jon-Paul, he said, was what drove him on to play.

Football was rebuilt after Hillsborough. The fences were pulled down. The stadiums were remade as all-seater theatres. The ticket prices went up and the audience changed. It started with the World Cup in 1990, which appealed to women and children and middle-class men who would not have admitted to liking the game before. The Italian setting, the operatic theme tune chosen by the BBC, the first and only decent team song in the history of football, by New Order, all helped with that: 'We're playing for England – In-ger-land – *arrivederci*, it's one on one.' So did the tears of Paul Gascoigne, when the boy genius was booked and realised he wasn't going to play in the final. People were touched.

It would be too trite, too much like sports journalism, to suggest some kind of connection between his childish sobs and the tears of the bereaved. There was none. The indulgence of egos like Gazza's and the obscene wages that would become available to stars like him would spoil the game again soon. For a little while, though, at the turn of the decade, football had soul. England weren't half bad. The remade game was something we could share in, something optimistic. It was part of a shift in the psyche of the playground, as the war stories stopped being told and the games stopped being about Us versus the Hun. They were light-sabre fantasies instead, after *Star Wars* and all its clones, or they were about the safe tribal clashes of football, enacted by children who rarely saw the top-level game in person but used its mythology and famous names for their solitary games on the PlayStation, the ultimate toy for the cult of the individual.

In 1989, that was all still to come.

The service to mark the closing of the gates at Anfield was attended by thirty thousand people. Seven days after that came the grand occasion that the important people evidently felt was needed, perhaps as a way of wrapping up all the unexpected, uncontrollable, unorthodox responses into one officially sanctioned religious act. The Prime Minister and the Queen were invited, to show that the rest of the country understood the scale of Liverpool's grief and was willing to offer support. Mrs Thatcher made it. Unfortunately, Her Majesty did not. She blew it, completely and for ever, as far as much of Liverpool was concerned. She didn't even send Charles in her place, just a wreath. The leader of the city council had written to her twice, saying in one of his letters: 'There is a whole area of Liverpool where people are grieving, and they want to have their grief marked by the people in the nation whose function it is to officially mark such grief.' The respected commentator Gerald Priestland used the *Sunday Times* to urge the Queen to attend because, 'in a way that is almost atavistic, people who cannot tell one archbishop from another regard the monarchy as a kind of tribal high priesthood and the presence of a royal as bestowing a spiritual value, a blessing, on the occasion'. Neither did any good.

The Queen could not have realised the damage she was doing, and not just in Liverpool, by snubbing the people at a time when they were prepared to say they needed her. More than a thousand bereaved relatives were in the Anglican Cathedral but the event itself was tediously religious, according to one eyewitness. 'For fifty-eight minutes it was a service of pomp and procession, of cymbals and trumpets too grand to pierce the private grief of those who most needed to cry.' Then a lone choirboy sang the first verse of 'You'll Never Walk Alone' and when the congregation joined in there were rivers of tears. People didn't want liturgy or readings, they wanted a chance to be emotional.

They also wanted their Queen. They were angry. She ought to have been at such an event, for so many reasons, not least because she was the head of the State Church and this should have been acknowledged as a time of national mourning. The ballad that had been used to serenade the bride and groom at Buckingham Palace on royal wedding day eight years before was now turned against the royal family. Those who heard it knew exactly what was meant at the FA Cup Final in May, when Liverpool played Everton, their rivals from across Stanley Park, who had been so supportive in recent times. The band played the national anthem, 'God Save the Queen'. That song again. A generation earlier it would have been seen as offensive not to stand for it. Not to sing it would have been worse. On Cup Final day, though, the people of Liverpool, who were still so hurt and full of fury, began to sing *over* it. Loudly. As loudly as they could. Drowning it out. They were singing something else in protest. You know what it was:

'When you walk through a storm/Hold your head up high . . .'

14

Love is not a victory march

George Carey was an Arsenal fan, but he had a Bobby Charlton comb-over. The next Archbishop of Canterbury was a big-faced barrow boy from Dagenham who would speak his mind. That was the spin, but it also seemed to be the truth when a row broke out ahead of his enthronement in early 1991. The plan was to have a choir sing an African song – 'We Are Marching in the Light of God' – with a drum and synthesizer accompaniment. Dr Donald Webster, an esteemed fellow of the Royal College of Organists, was horrified. 'When you have this popular music in the service it lowers the tone and atmosphere of the ceremony,' he said. 'So much of the idiom of popular music has unsavoury associations with drugs, unbridled sex and things of this kind.' Gosh. Robert Runcie would have fretted. George Carey laughed it off, saying: 'He obviously doesn't know very much about drugs or unbridled sex.'

The new man had good reason to be confident. Astonishingly, for the first time in two decades, the number of people going to church and the number of registered members had risen. Only by 1 per cent each, but it was enough to prompt the *Independent* to declare: 'A religious revival is undoubtedly under way.' Charismatics were the cause, it said.

Love is not a victory march

That same month there were quite a few people displaying their emotions at All Souls, when I married the vicar's daughter. The service was a full-on Charismatic celebration of certainty, which disturbed some of those who had been expecting a nice sedate do. 'Oh, you have gone up in the world,' my nan said approvingly. 'But why do those people wave their hands about so much, love?'

George Carey knew. He was one of us. He had experienced a second conversion, at the age of thirty-seven.

> One evening I found myself in Toronto submitting to the claims of the Holy Spirit and experiencing a quiet revolution spiritually. A distinct word came echoing into my mind over and over again: '*Shamayim! Shamayim!*' What did it mean? Later it was to dawn on me. Of course! *Shamayim* is the Hebrew word for heaven.

Of course it is. He read the Gospel in Greek for fun, too. 'I am open to the Holy Spirit in all his power and from whatever direction it comes,' he said.

Carey was the son of a hospital porter and had left school at fifteen. He was the first modern Archbishop of Canterbury not to have gone to Oxford or Cambridge, and he was presented to us as a man of the people who watched *Neighbours* while waiting for his wife to come back from her job at a nursing home. The truth was more complicated. Carey was clever, if you could see past the bottle-bottom glasses and the way he pursed his lips, like Les Dawson playing an old biddy, showing the gap in his teeth. And the clumsy statements he made in his first few days, saying that everybody who did not agree with the growing belief that women ought to be ordained as priests was a heretic. 'The idea that only a male can represent Christ at the altar is a most serious

151

heresy,' he said, condemning the Pope and most of the Christians who had ever lived.

Carey's frequent smile was said to be like that of someone who knew a joke had just been told, but didn't quite get it. Asked by the *Reader's Digest* what kind of person the Church of England might be, he said: 'An elderly lady who mutters away to herself in a corner, ignored most of the time.' He felt 'dazed and unworthy' at being promoted from Bishop of Bath and Wells, but there he was, in the job, beaming away.

The enthronement at Canterbury Cathedral had a bit of everything in the end. The choir danced to the African song but Carey swore on a Bible that had belonged to St Augustine, he sat on a chair that was eight hundred years old and he carried a staff that had been made for William Temple during the Second World War. Billy Graham was there as a personal guest, but so was the head of the Roman Catholic Church in this country, Cardinal Hume. George's robes were decorated with gold and crimson flames in a symbol of Pentecost. He was a Charismatic who had been raised an Evangelical, but his instincts were liberal and he loved the Catholic way of worshipping. He was everything to everyone, and in grave danger of disappointing them all.

Outside the oak doors of the cathedral, someone was being burned at the stake. Well, they were pretending to be. This was a recreation of 'the historical persecution of homosexuals by the Christian Church', according to the campaign group OutRage! Their placards read: 'Keep your bigotry off my body' and, a little more breezily, 'Hi Carey, I'm a Fairy'. The orthodoxy at the time – although it was not often spoken out loud – was that you could be a Christian if you were homosexual, but if you wanted to become a priest you were to take a vow of celibacy that was not expected of anyone who was straight. It was hypocritical and unsustainable, but had been useful to Runcie and his predecessors.

George Carey, the straight talker who had been born straight, said: 'The problem is that the Bible is very clearly against practising homosexuality. That is the reality of the thing we have to wrestle with.'

By 1991, Margaret Thatcher had been driven out of Downing Street in tears, but victory was hers in so many ways. Britain had been transformed from a sick nation crippled by the power of the unions into a lean, mean prosperity machine, or so she said. One side-effect was that our sense of community, the feeling that the English could cope with whatever came up as long as we had each other (and a nice cup of tea), had been smashed. Entrepreneurs were the new heroes, innovation and initiative their superpowers. Their mission was to build a great big metaphorical champagne fountain for themselves and let the rest of us fight it out for whatever trickled down to our level, if we were lucky. Money talk – considered vulgar in the past, under the rules of Establishment England – was now compulsory. Lots of people found Harry Enfield funny when he put on a shellsuit and started waving cash around as his Essex wideboy character Loadsamoney – 'Shut your face and look at my wad!' because they knew people like that: not just bankers now, but plasterers, builders and scaffolders who weren't used to this level of wealth but gleefully danced in the fountain, splashing it all over. 'All you need to know about politics,' said Enfield in character on *Friday Night Live*, 'is that Mrs Thatcher done a lot of good for the country . . . but you wouldn't wanna shag it.'

Indeed. But Loadsamoney was adopted as an utterly un-ironic hero by the people he was meant to satirise, who shouted his catchphrases as they chopped up a line with a credit card. The City was having a high old time. So much for all that spiritual warfare, then. It was the Church that was going to feel as if the wrath of God were coming down upon it in the next decade. Margaret Thatcher had set about smashing monopolies in the energy industry, telecommunications, on the railways, in the health service, and the Church of England was going to get it next. The government, still firmly under her spell, was working towards allowing shops and pubs to open on Sundays. Hotels would be allowed to conduct weddings. The Church's grip on funerals would be broken. These were heavy blows, all of them.

For the moment, though, Mrs Thatcher could be satisfied with having put in place an archbishop who believed the right things. George Carey was her man. He seemed uncannily like her chosen successor, John Major, the son of a circus trapeze artist who had also left school early and made it to power without going near Oxbridge. Major declared early that he wanted to 'make the whole of this country a genuinely classless society' and for a moment, looking at him alongside Carey, it was almost believable. That was until you realised how the new Archbishop of Canterbury had been chosen.

A shortlist of candidates had been drawn up by the Crown Appointments Commission, a secretive panel whose members never told anyone where and when they were meeting or what their discussions involved, chaired by the second Viscount Caldecote, Robin Inskip, an Old Etonian with a First from Cambridge who had successfully led a company that made bombers and guided missiles. His father had been Lord Chancellor and Secretary of State for Dominion Affairs. The Establishment was pulling the strings, even if the rumour was that the Prime Minister had picked the wrong puppet. The Commission wanted John Habgood, the fiercely clever Archbishop of York, but was obliged by the rules to put another name forward. That was the man she chose.

Carey was therefore expected to do the job just as Mrs

Thatcher wanted it done. 'The primary task of the Christian Church', Caldecote said, 'is to preach the Gospel, and to proclaim the good news.' That wasn't controversial, but this was:

> There is also a duty to your neighbour. If you are going to be able to support the weak, somebody needs to be relatively wealthy. It is important that the Christian Church should support the concept of wealth-creation and look carefully at the use made of riches acquired and how they are shared. It should comment on social problems and point out what needs to be put right, but should be careful in saying precisely how those problems should be solved.

Pure Thatcherism. There were to be no more nasty moments like 'Faith in the City'. John Gummer, a Tory grandee who had joined in the attack on Runcie, could not have been nicer about Carey: 'For him, the resurrection and the empty tomb are not mere symbols, but glorious realities . . . we shall be led by a man whose view of the Christian faith has not been diminished by the theological minimalists, nor distorted by fashion-conscious liberals.'

Runcie, in retirement, lamented Thatcher's attacks and 'the violence with which a party has felt it necessary to denigrate certain values for which the Church stood – variety, you know, holding opposites together, a readiness to listen sensitively to the damaged parts of the community'. He'd lost. The long fight that began after the Falklands memorial service was over and Margaret Thatcher was the outright winner. All doubt about that was removed when Carey gave his opinion on the war in the Gulf: 'I believe this is a justifiable war. Peace which does not take into account freedom and justice is just empty rhetoric.' Spoken like a member of the war cabinet. Later, in his memoirs, Carey would say of Margaret Thatcher: 'She was, in my opinion, the right person in that historic office at the right time.'

So the old friendliness between Church and State was restored, for the moment, on a personal basis, but the previous tug of loathing had exposed it as untenable in the long run. What right, after all, did a Methodist Prime Minister with a dubious creed of her own have to choose an Anglican archbishop? In the past, religion had been seen as best left out of these things, but that had changed. Some people were taking their faith very seriously indeed, and demanding that everyone else did, too.

English faith was being privatised, just like the Gas Board. We could all buy shares in whatever kind of god we fancied, or not: it was a matter of choice, the golden word of the Thatcher years. Membership of all kinds of groups had plummeted since the sixties, and were falling further still. The Thatcherite version of 'love thy neighbour' was to leave thy neighbour alone to mind his own business. 'The overall pattern of religious life is changing,' wrote Grace Davie during this period. 'For it appears that more and more people within society want to believe, but do not want to involve themselves in religious practice.' Believing but not belonging, that was what most of us were up to.

As our sense of duty towards Christianity had been broken, so we had lost touch with the old stories. A survey showed that a third of people didn't know what Good Friday meant. The Archbishop of York was grumpy: 'The figures disclose an ignorance . . . which makes me wonder what kind of religious education some of these people receive at school. It seems to me extraordinary that people can be so unaware of some of the main factors which have shaped our culture.' Teachers were now treating Christian stories equally with those of other faiths, whether John Habgood liked it or not. The Queen was accused of breaking her coronation vows by allowing Buddhists, Hindus, Sikhs, Muslims and Jews to take part in the annual service to celebrate the Commonwealth at Westminster Abbey. Nearly eighty thousand people signed a petition urging her not to go, but she showed what she thought of their concerns by turning up with her son, the Prince of Wales, who had never bothered attending before. What kind of Defender of the Faith was he going to be, protesters asked? And not for the last time.

There were a million Muslims in England by now, although nobody knew how many of them went to mosque. There were 400,000 Hindus and about the same number of Sikhs. The New Churches had about 300,000 people in their services on a Sunday, while the Baptists had increased to 270,000. The Pentecostals had as many as that and were growing, but the more established churches were still in freefall. Methodists were down to half a million, the Roman Catholics had about 1.5 million at their Sunday services but that was falling towards the 1.2 million who attended Anglican churches. The Archbishop of Canterbury insisted he was serving a community of 27 million people, and at the start of the nineties he still had a point. The Church of England was still the main Church the English chose to stay away from.

A decade earlier, the most visible form of faith in England had been Runcie's mild, highly traditional, monarchy-loving, polite Christianity that sought to include everybody and offend nobody. Now that was being shoved aside – in public and in the pews – by a faith that was demonstrative and needy. It wouldn't shut up. Impressed and threatened by the Muslims, its followers demanded that the English treat their Christian heritage with more respect and let God give the orders. These people were no longer on the fringes of church life, they were at the top. The new Archbishop of Canterbury was very enthusiastic about something called the

Decade of Evangelism, a big effort in the last ten years of the century to bring England back to Christ, as he saw it. Most church leaders were supportive, and the Catholics were involved with the blessing of the Pope. Not surprisingly, some people were appalled.

'The Jewish community is extremely fearful. It is causing a lot of hurt and upset,' said Rabbi Shmuel Arkush, who thought the Churches ought to be going after lapsed Christians: 'There are millions, as I understand.' Some Jews were shocked because this was all so uncharacteristic. With the empire gone and the world wars over, the English God had settled down as an inoffensive chap, reluctant to impose His values. Evangelists had been seen as outsiders, just a little too keen. Now His people were being told to go out on the streets in great numbers. Enterprise culture had given birth to enterprise faith, selling itself without apology.

The product on offer had also changed, dramatically. In the past, when people went to church out of tradition, duty or discipline, it didn't matter if the services were dull. It wasn't a show and it wasn't supposed to be fun. The new deal was that if you committed yourself to faith, God would offer a life-changing experience. You would feel better, in touch with the divine. You'd find peace, if that was what you needed – some churches still promised calm, stillness and sanctuary – or you could get stirred up, dancing, celebrating, waving your hands, praising, praying, speaking in tongues, soaked in the Spirit. Shecameonahonda!

There was, however, a problem with the new offer. If you promise someone a good time but they don't get one, they become angry and walk away. If you deliver the first time, but not the second or third or thirty-third time, they become disappointed and walk away. If they get bored, or someone else offers a new distraction, they walk away. Whatever you do, in the end, a large number of people are going to walk away. For this reason, and for many others involving money, sex and power, the next decade would be an absolute disaster for the faith that had been dominant for so long. The English God was doomed. He was about to die.

FALL

A family with the wrong members in control –
that, perhaps, is as near as one can come to
describing England in a phrase.

George Orwell

15

We both know I'm
not what you need

The fairytale had long been over, but it was not obvious how much distress the main characters were in until the Queen made the most personal speech of her life, at the end of 1992. The newspaper reports said it was emotional, but they forgot that this was Her Majesty: the catch in her throat came from laryngitis. Elegant in peacock green at the Guildhall, where the Lord Mayor was honouring her fortieth year as sovereign, Elizabeth Windsor said it had not been 'a year on which I shall look back with undiluted pleasure'. If the English are masters of understatement, as people say, then she was the mistress of us all that day.

The words people remember from that speech are the ones she used in the following sentence, borrowed from a former courtier who had written to sympathise with her troubles: 'It has turned out to be an annus horribilis.' The Latin was clumsy and its use made her sound evasive. The Queen was the focus of anger, disappointment and fierce criticism from her subjects, some of whom had begun to demand that this immensely wealthy woman should stop living off the state and start paying income tax, like everyone else. That was a small thing, relatively speaking, but a challenge to the established idea of what her family was for and how it should be maintained. As a mother, she was also struggling to cope with the very public failure of the marriages of three of her four children. As Queen, she was aware of the damage their behaviour was doing to the all-important image of the monarchy. On top of all that she had stood in the rain in the early hours of the morning, a few days before, watching a large part of her castle burn. The fire at Windsor, which destroyed the Great Hall and many treasures, was a cause of deep sorrow to a woman who considered it her true home.

The eight-minute speech at the Guildhall was immediately seen as among the most significant of her reign. She admitted that her family had made mistakes. She could hardly do otherwise, but this was new. 'No institution should expect to be free from the scrutiny of those who give it their loyalty and support,' she said, before adding drily, 'Not to mention those who don't.' The tabloids did not have to invent stories. The year had begun with speculation about the heir to the throne and his wife, whose mutual loathing was impossible to ignore. Certainly, Princess Diana did not want it to be ignored. She had grown out of the shyness of her youth and become a mother, a campaigner and a woman well aware of the power of her image, acclaimed as one of the most beautiful on the planet. The strength she had found on that balcony on her wedding day, inhaling the adoration of the crowds, had sustained her despite the aridity of her marriage. Charles had never let Camilla go, and Diana had looked for comfort elsewhere, in ways that hadn't lasted. She had used an inspired act of symbolism to let the world know what was going on: allowing herself to be photographed alone, looking vulnerable, on a bench by a reflecting pool in front of the Taj Mahal, that great monument to enduring love. The visit had been 'very healing'. Asked to explain, she just smiled and said, 'Work it out for yourself.'

The marriages of two of the Queen's other children were also disintegrating. Typically, the one who handled it with the least fuss was Princess Anne, who had once shouted down a man trying to kidnap her at gunpoint. (Escaping from a side door, she yelled, 'Not bloody likely!') Her marriage to Captain Mark Phillips was described as a constitutional experiment by one haughty aristocrat, and it ended in the spring of 1992. As the Queen was making her grim speech, Anne was preparing to marry her lover, Commander Timothy Laurence, in a small family wedding at Crathie Kirk near Balmoral. They went to the Church of Scotland for the ceremony because it had no qualms about remarrying divorcees, which the Church of England would not do at the time. No such discretion was shown by Sarah Ferguson, the flame-haired Duchess of York, whose divorce had not yet been finalised when she was photographed having her toe sucked by the man she called her financial adviser, while she lay topless in the sun. This was the wife of the fourth in line to the throne, and a descendant of Charles II, but Fergie had always seemed too full of life for the Windsors.

While all this was going on, Her Majesty was under pressure to give as well as take. She was perceived to be the richest woman in the world, worth around £50 million, with an annual income of £5 million, but we still gave her nearly £8 million a year from taxes, to help pay for the palace, the castle, the dresses, the yacht and the royal train. We also paid half a million or so each to her mother and her husband, and generous salaries to her children, her sister Margaret and her ninety-year-old aunt, Princess Alice. 'We know she is one of the wealthiest people in the country, if not the richest,' said the Labour spokeswoman on heritage, Ann Clwyd, leading calls for Her Majesty to cough up tax at the 40 per cent rate for high earners. 'I think the swing of public opinion now in this direction is very strong indeed.' Clwyd was right, as the polls showed. Officials from Buckingham Palace and the Treasury began to negotiate and they had reached a private agreement when the Queen awoke to the most horrible of all the horrible things in the annus horribilis.

The heat from a spotlight in the private chapel of Windsor Castle set fire to a curtain, not long before midnight on 20 November. By the time the on-site fire brigade of twenty or so men could get to the blaze, it was way beyond them. Engines from other stations roared into the castle grounds in the following minutes, but it took all night, all the next day and a million gallons of water before the voracious flames were doused. The great roof of St George's Hall collapsed. Castle staff and soldiers formed human chains and braved the heat to pass out paintings, furniture and other treasures, but there was much that could not be saved. The Queen went down to the courtyard to see for herself in the early hours, as the fire dominated the night sky, and she was back again the next morning. The smoke billowing above the largest inhabited castle in the world could be seen for miles across southern England, and television viewers watched the sovereign, gaunt in a drenched mackintosh and headscarf, surveying the damage. 'I could see how upset she was,' said Stephen Matthews, the head coachman, who was beside her and who felt like hugging the Queen at that moment, even though he knew that would be a treasonable breach of etiquette. 'This poor woman is stood there watching her home go up and all of us are feeling what she must be going through and obviously wanting to comfort her, but no one had the courage to do it.' The Earl of Airlie, the Lord Chamberlain, said: 'It was the most terrible thing to watch, but as you would expect, she was stoic. She doesn't like to show her emotions.'

How very English. How very out of step with the way the English were adopting American standards of touchy-feeliness – but not as out of step as the Heritage Secretary, Peter Brooke, who announced immediately that the government would pay for the restoration of the castle to its former glory. 'The heart of the nation has gone out to the Queen,' he said, but that was not entirely true. There was a strident view, finding support in a time of recession, that Her Majesty ought to rebuild her own flaming castle. People were being put out of work and having to give their homes back to the mortgage companies, but this woman had another half-dozen places in which to live. The bolshy East London MP Tony Banks said: 'There is no such thing as a bad year for the Queen, by definition. I know people in my constituency who can genuinely say it has been a bad year. I don't believe she has had her house repossessed.' Banks was a rabble-rouser, but he did reflect a popular opinion so savage that the Prime Minister, John Major, later declared himself shocked: 'I was astonished. Frankly it was a very miserable and mealy-mouthed response. It just seemed so mean-spirited and out of character for the British nation.'

Was it really, though? People were angry. They didn't really believe in Major, even though he had soap-boxed his way to a fourth election victory in a row for the Tories, much to his own surprise. There seemed to be no vision, no inspiration, no hope. Mealy-mouthed was what the politicians were, and miserable was what they made everybody else. Moaning about the Queen was just part of the feeling that nothing was certain any more, nothing was admirable. Everything was broken. So, in the end, did any of it matter? Did the trials of the House of Windsor have any impact at all?

Well, yes. A huge one. They meant a lot of people lost faith, maybe not in the Queen herself but certainly in the whole damn rest of them, including the heir to the throne, and certainly in the idea that these inbred aristocrats were in any way God's choice to lead the nation, blessed by divine providence to be an example to us all. This had been one of the central myths of England, set up long ago by the Crown and the Church. Plenty of kings and queens had made a mockery of it in the past, of course, but Elizabeth was very serious about her calling to be a good and faithful servant of the Lord, and had taken it up as a reason for her rule in an age in which monarchs could no longer make laws or raise armies. Her position as Queen, sovereign over the law-makers in Parliament and Supreme Governor of the Church of England, was reinforced by personal piety. Within her under-standing of Christianity and the way society should be, she had lived up to an ideal for forty years and was widely respected for it, even by republicans. Her personal standards had become part of the point. She had allowed her family to be marketed as the embodiment of all that was great about Britain − in the pomp and pageantry of a spectacle like the royal wedding, but also in terms of tradition and stability, duty and service, discipline and decorum. Regal behaviour was essential to the Windsor brand. Toe sucking wasn't. The family had let her down. The assump-tion that her children would know how to behave, and would marry people able to understand what was required of them, had been proved dismally wrong. Either God was an idiot for choos-ing them, or the whole idea was just a scam for keeping hold of power. That thought could be ignored when they were doing their duties, behaving well. Now, like Fergie's toe, the fallacy was being shoved in our collective face.

The historian David Cannadine wrote of Prince Charles in this year: 'Whatever the reality of his marriage and its breakdown, he is regarded widely as a man who has failed spectacularly to do the one thing which, rightly or wrongly, people still expect the

heir to the throne to do: namely, to live his family life successfully.' If they were not good ambassadors for the country, if they
were nothing we could aspire to, and if they couldn't even give
us decent pageantry but popped off to quiet kirks, what on earth
were they for? The Americans saw the problem clearly from the
outside, which was worrying, because bringing in the tourists
was one of the few claims left to the Windsors. 'Is the monarchy
really necessary?' asked the cover of *Time* magazine, which
declared 'the notion of the family monarchy' to be 'on the brink
of collapse'. That wasn't quite true, of course, but even the loy-
alists saw that the strategy that had kept the Queen in place was
now exhausted. Asked to name the monarchy's main strength,
arch-loyalist and royal biographer Lady Longford said: 'A year
ago, like everybody else, I would have said it stood for the ideal
of the family. It encouraged people to see the country as one
great family, despite their differences. But now the word "family"
has become inappropriate in that archetypal, idealistic sense.'

The monarchy survived for the moment, partly because of
genuine respect for Elizabeth and partly because of good old
apathy. We were – as ever – much more likely to grumble and
moan than actually do something as much as bother to storm the
palace gates. Still, events had made our institutional faith look
pretty ridiculous. How silly that the monarch was forbidden by
law from marrying a Catholic, or a person of any other faith,
when an apparently perfect Anglican candidate from the right
stock had proved such a disastrous match. How daft that the
Church of England was almost certainly going to be led by a
divorcee in the near future, when it refused to marry people for
a second time. How impossible that the future King would be
asked to take a vow to be defender of the one true Protestant
faith, as his mother had done, when everyone knew he didn't
believe in its exclusivity at all. So much, too, for dignity, restraint

and all those other imperial characteristics of Establishment England, and of the stoic Christianity that this family had sought to represent. The kids had trashed them all. Poor Elizabeth. Spiritually and metaphorically, as well as physically, her house was in ruins.

16

Woman like you's
no good for me

Right. So. On with the job. Once you have called the nation back to its historic faith, and announced that you intend to spend the next ten years converting anyone who will listen, what is the next thing to do? That's right, have a really big row. Start it by proposing something that flies in the face of two thousand years of church tradition, alienates some of your natural allies and threatens to drive away a large number of your own people.

A thousand priests would leave, it was said – and they would take their congregations with them – if the governing body of the Church of England approved the ordination of women as priests. The day of the debate was set for 11 November 1992 and the television crews moved into the public gallery that oversaw the circular chamber in Church House, the Victorian building near Westminster Abbey where the vote would take place.

The newspapers called this the most important decision the Church had faced in four hundred years and 'the greatest upheaval in its history', which was overstating the case a bit, but not all that much. For some people, this was a frivolous issue, a distraction at a time when poverty was stalking the streets. For others, it was fundamental to being a Christian in the modern age. For some, it was about the reconciliation of spirituality and sexuality at long last, a move towards a new expression of the divine truth free of patriarchal distortion. For others, it was about 'Vicars in Knickers'.

The *Sun* came up with that one, and the *Daily Mail* countered with a front-page photograph of a young female deacon in a short skirt. Joy Carroll was described as a 'slim and pretty minister, with green eyes, auburn hair and huge gold earrings'. The writer did not tell us what colour Dr Carey's eyes were, or how daintily he filled his clerical shirt. The piece patronised Ms Carroll and underplayed her intelligence, predictably, although she did manage to get in a quote that said the Church could not speak out on any issue of social justice until it gave women the same status as men. This daughter of a vicar said it had been a 'degrading and frustrating' process trying to follow her father's example, but she was now helping to lead a congregation as a deacon and longed for the day when she could do so as a fully fledged member of the clergy. There were many more like her, she said. 'It would be very sad if a thousand priests go, but there are a thousand good women waiting to step into their shoes.'

The Archbishop was on her side, saying that he felt God was calling His Church to ordain women. He didn't give any details of how the Almighty had made this clear. Despite having made his own mind up, George Carey sought to be a fair, moderate presence during the debate, which began in the morning and went on for six hours. Outside the building, in Dean's Yard, there were two camps of supporters, each praying, holding candles and banners, talking to the media and eyeing up each other. Women in dog collars were on one side, some of them deacons with dangly earrings and serious theologians, too; and on the other were intense young men in Gothic black clerical shirts, and older men with the florid faces of medieval bishops. I was there, as a young reporter for the *Church Times*, feeling like a spectator at a moment of history and trying, desperately, to understand what the arguments were all about. From loudspeakers put up in the courtyard we listened to a complex discussion on the nature of headship, centring on the use of the word '*kephale*' in the first letter to the Corinthians. The gist of it, as far as I could gather, was that St Paul had written that a woman could not be in authority over a man. Or maybe he hadn't. It wasn't clear, at least to me. The main argument against female priests was easier to understand, though: it was that Jesus had been a man, God had chosen to come to earth in a male body, and the tradition of the Universal Church was that the person who represented the Christ and the godhead at the altar, and in particular at mass or holy communion, should be a man. Simple. Except to those who disagreed. This issue exposed, powerfully and painfully, the differences in the beliefs held so sincerely by members of the three main tribes in the Anglican Church.

Stay with me on this. The liberals, who had been dominant under Robert Runcie, believed that God taught humanity through experience, rational thought and the advances in knowledge in the wider world as much as through church tradition or the words of the Bible. To them, it was offensive and outdated not to allow women the same rights and privileges and opportunities to serve as men. More than that, a female priesthood could broaden and deepen understanding of God.

The Evangelicals, now in the ascendancy with George Carey, wanted to stick with what was written in Scripture, above all else; but they argued with each other about what that was, and whether it allowed women priests or not. Some said yes, others said no and threatened to walk away. They were not prepared to give up their historic faith, they said, an attitude they had in common with many Anglo-Catholics, who put equal store in both the Bible and tradition. To them, the Church of England was seen as the continuation of the holy Church that had been established by Christ, led by Peter and was represented on a worldwide stage by the Pope. Some Anglo-Catholics were seriously distressed that a governing body of 563 people drawn from the bishops, the clergy and elected church members was about to put them so far out of step with long-held Roman and Orthodox faith. 'I do not regard the Church as having the right to rewrite the scriptures to suit modern conveniences,' wrote Lady Olga Maitland in *The Times*. The recently retired Bishop of London said: 'It is no more appropriate for a woman to be a priest than for a woman to be portrayed as presiding at the Last Supper or a man as the Blessed Virgin Mary in a nativity play.' As usual, David Jenkins had another view. There were tears in his eyes when he told the chamber it was 'shameful to be quarrelling about women when the world was torn by poverty and strife'.

George Carey closed the debate, led a prayer in his bland, reasonable tones and asked that there should be silence when the result came. 'Divide,' said the legal secretary and the members rose, shuffling to doors marked 'ayes' and 'noes'. Looking down on their bald patches and haunted faces from the press gallery, it was impossible to tell which side was going to win. A little less than twenty minutes later, with the Synod assembled again in the hall, the reporters poised with their pens, the cameras running, the campaigners who had managed to find a way into the packed public gallery willing themselves not to scream with the stress, the Archbishop was handed the results. The supporters of women priests needed a two-thirds majority. They had it, by just two votes.

'I pronounce the motion passed.'

There was silence. Stunned, uneasy silence, apart from a single, stifled shriek in the gallery. Down where the Synod sat, a woman who had opposed the motion and felt that the Church she loved had just been taken from her, began to weep. Others, around her, tried to contain their smiles and even put on sympathetic faces. Out in Dean's Yard there were bellows, cheers, hugs and tears among the deacons, one of whom declared herself staggered at the victory. This had been a bitter fight. The Reverend Nerissa Jones, who had been threatened with decapitation by one fanatic, said: 'It is a day of liberation and emancipation long overdue.' But the Reverend Francis Bown, chairman of the Anglo-Catholic group Ecclesia, said: 'Swamped by modernism, liberalism and feminism, the Church of England will soon be no more than a rotting carcass.'

The motion passed by Synod still had to be ratified by the House of Commons, because that was the law, and there was some talk that MPs might not do it this time. In truth, the idea was ridiculous. Few cared much what the Church did, and they certainly didn't feel they should interfere, as the Labour veteran Roy Hattersley explained: 'The Church of England's conduct is none of my business. I shall vote in apology for the House of Commons' impertinent belief that it is entitled, at the end of a brief debate, to veto a decision which bishops, clergy and laity have taken after years of agonised deliberation. The more I think about it, the more preposterous my involvement seems.' Hattersley couldn't even justify getting involved on behalf of his constituents. 'That would be a difficult obligation to fulfil. I suspect that a majority of residents in my constituency are Muslims.'

There was no place in a multicultural society for an Established Church, Hattersley said, and he was absolutely and prophetically right. Picking faith out of the grand and complex machinery of State would take decades yet, but the argument was essentially over. This was the year in which it became unavoidably obvious that allowing politicians to approve or deny what the Church wanted to do was about as anachronistic as Virgin Atlantic using a Sopwith Camel.

As for the apocalypse, it never came. Not for this reason, anyway. The ordination of women slowed the decline of the Church, by providing new people and new energy to an exhausted body of believers. A thousand priests did not leave; it was only 430 in the end. There was, however, a major shift in the balance of power within the Church. The Anglo–Catholics were weakened and the liberals were brushed aside by the Evangelicals, who were described by one horrified onlooker as 'global asset strippers interested only in driving out the enemy and taking vacant possession of the property and the structures'.

All this was not just obscure in-house wrangling; it had a big effect on how the main Christian group in the country related to the rest of us. The Evangelicals defined themselves by exclusion. They were sure of what they believed, confident that it was right and faithful to the Bible, and suspicious of anyone who was not so sure. The historic mission of the C of E, and its main claim to be the national Church of the country, was that it offered a welcome to all and a prayer for every soul, regardless of personal belief. Now, though, many parish churches were acting like religion clubs, requiring their members to sign up to a clearly defined set of beliefs. Instead of being inclusive, they were becoming exclusive, which was directly against what the Church had been for so long.

They did it because they wanted to feel faithful and strong. Afraid of the changes going on around them, they didn't want to become infected by the fancy new ways of the world. They were the ones with the most members and the most money, so felt they could hold everyone else up to ransom by threatening to leave. Ironically, some of their strength came from women priests. The first was ordained in 1994, and in the next decade 2400 more followed suit. So, Joy Carroll had been right.

As for the priest in the miniskirt herself, she caught the eye of a scriptwriter who was watching the debates while thinking about making a new sitcom. His name was Richard Curtis and the show he was writing was called *The Vicar of Dibley*. The star would be Dawn French, who turned up at Carroll's vicarage on a fact finding mission with a box of éclairs, saying she couldn't possibly work without chocolate. That was the moment when the priest knew everything would be okay. Meanwhile, French and Curtis knew they had found their muse when they saw a mug in the kitchen that said: 'Lead me not into temptation; I can find it myself'. French sat in on services, wearing a big floppy hat so as not to be recognised, and once described seeing Carroll step down from the pulpit and take the hand of a man whose wife had recently died, and sit with him for a while. 'I knew something was undeniably true,' she said. 'Women are good at this job. Providing spiritual guidance and succour comes naturally to us. We do it all the time in our everyday lives and, what's more, we like doing it. I could finally see how Geraldine might work.'

The Vicar of Dibley arrived on the BBC shortly after the first woman was ordained, and announced herself to her startled screen flock with the words: 'You were expecting a bloke with a beard, a Bible and bad breath. You've got a babe with a bob cut and a magnificent bosom.' The first series was full of jokes about the shock of seeing a bird in a dog collar, but by the time it reached its tenth anniversary, having won Emmys and Baftas and picked up fifteen million viewers, there was nothing novel about that at all. Instead, the humour had shifted to make more of its soft-focus, nostalgic view of English country life. Geraldine Grainger had become the nation's favourite comedy vicar, but we weren't laughing at how wet she was, as we had the parson in *Dad's Army*. We were laughing with this feisty, funny woman who seemed like the sort of priest who would make anyone go to church, and we were watching because it made us feel part of a gentler, more generous kind of England we knew no longer existed. Something we had lost, although we were not sure how, just like our faith.

The row over the ordination of women seems like a quaint little episode now, but a look back at the way it was reported reveals what an enormous change there has been in the status of the Church of England and how relevant it was perceived to be. The debate in 1992 was seen as of universal interest, a major evolution in society and a sign that even the crusty old Establishment was beginning to understand the need for equality. The first female chief constable had yet to be appointed, the first female air commodore was still getting her wings, the first woman to be chief executive of a FTSE Top 100 company was still banging her head against the glass ceiling. I went on to work for the first woman to edit a broadsheet national newspaper, Rosie Boycott at the *Independent on Sunday*, but that was not until 1997. The Church was leading the way, reflecting the changes happening all around it and seeming at that moment like a vital part of the evolving new England. By the time the governing body considered allowing women to become bishops, in the summer of 2008, all that had gone. This time the coverage, such as it was, focused on whether the argument – in tandem with another, even more vicious one about the treatment of gay priests – might be the final nail in the coffin of an institution that had obviously already climbed inside and pulled the lid over itself.

Christians were now perceived as a fringe group, a small gathering of hardcore nostalgics arguing among themselves in a side room. Some of them were painfully aware of this. Canon Lucy

Winkett of St Paul's Cathedral declared herself embarrassed by her Church's preoccupation with sex: 'While acute suffering continues for ordinary people in conflict zones around the globe, what greater humiliation could there be for the Church than groups of Christians gathering to argue over one another's identity or lifestyle?' Her article expressed the dismay that many of her fellow believers felt. 'Fiddling while Rome's burning, rearranging deck chairs on the *Titanic*; pick your metaphor and weep.'

Tears were also evoked by the new Archbishop of York, John Sentamu. Born in Uganda, the first black man to hold high office in the Church of England had long been seen as an individual who was unusually and impressively engaged with wider society, particularly because of his involvement with the inquiries into the deaths of Stephen Lawrence and Damilola Taylor. He told the Synod in 2008 that it was 'navel gazing' in debating women bishops at a time when everybody else was horrified and fearful of the violence taking place in the cities of England. That year there had been a sudden rise in the number of young men killing each other with knives. Sentamu was sad and angry and said so: 'Jesus Christ is weeping in the streets.'

17

The love of money

I magine that you are Archbishop of Canterbury. It is a Saturday morning in July 1992 and you are sitting down to breakfast. Somebody hands you the *Financial Times*. You know times are tight, but your money men say it's just because of the high inflation rate. It'll fall again in time. You have been working on a speech that will say so, reassuring people and asking them to put just a little more in the collection plate. Then you read the paper. The headline is hard to take in. You read it again. And again.

'Unholy Saga of the Church's Missing Millions' is what the headline says. The story underneath says the men who hold the Church's purse strings have lost £500 million in two years. That is an astonishing amount. It's a complete disaster. Never mind all the fussing and fighting over women, this is a real crisis, a massive one that could bring down the whole thing. The Church bankrupt. Unable to pay its people. Unable to put priests into parishes and care for souls in the way it has done for centuries. Is this the end?

I don't know what went through George Carey's mind when he read the paper that day, or what he was having on the toast that must have turned to dust in his mouth, or if he was even eating toast, in Lambeth Palace or anywhere else. I do know that

180

the report was said to have come as a total shock to him. And it actually underestimated the losses, which were closer to £800 million. Assets had fallen to £2.1 billion from nearly £3 billion at the beginning of 1990. The financial experts and former civil servants whose job it was to manage investments on behalf of the Church had put all their eggs in one basket, which was property – but that basket had been smashed by a worldwide crash. There was egg on the Archbishop's face. What would he say to people? He must have asked himself the question that was soon being asked on every news bulletin and was first posed by the *FT*: 'How did this august body, which ranks a number of distinguished City figures on its assets committee, get into such a mess?'

The money was supposed to be managed by the Church Commissioners. This was the collective name for the members of an institution set up by Parliament in 1948 to look after historic assets including churches and cathedrals but also farms and homes on hundreds of thousands of acres of land. Some of it had come to the Church of England after being seized from monasteries by Henry VIII in the sixteenth century. The Commissioners owned more land and property than almost anyone else in the country, collecting rents and providing stability to families that had held farms for generations, all across England's rolling landscape; but also renting mansion flats to dukes and duchesses. In Maida Vale, for example, there were homes built on estates that had belonged to the bishops of London since the Middle Ages. Their apartments just by Hyde Park were worth a fortune.

Nobody knew more than the Church Commissioners about the intimate ties binding the Church to the State. They included among their number the Archbishops of York and Canterbury, some bishops, priests and churchgoers elected from Synod, a couple of deans or provosts and a number of other people appointed directly by the Crown; plus three Estates Commissioners, one of whose job it was to liaise with MPs (which was not too difficult as he was one himself). Parliament scrutinised the Commissioners, just as it had to give the final approval for anything the Synod wanted to do (although in return, the Church had a special charitable status, an influence on law-making and the ear of some very important people). There were also ex officio Commissioners such as the Prime Minister, the Lord Chancellor, the Home Secretary and the Speaker of the House, who held the title but had no say in policy.

Not all of these grand characters concerned themselves with the detail of what was going on. The investment and property portfolios were handled by an assets committee of eight or nine people, chosen by the Archbishop of Canterbury, who oversaw but also took their lead from full-time staff hired for their expertise. For years, those staff went about their business with nobody paying them much attention at all, trusted to work quietly away in rather grand offices at 1 Millbank in Westminster, doing impenetrable things with figures. The committee reported to the wider group of Church Commissioners, and once a year, the staff tootled along to the Palace of Westminster and laid out their books for MPs to see. They answered a few questions, went for lunch and perhaps a good bottle of claret at their club, then dozed away the afternoon back at the office. It was all a question of maintaining the status quo, and using the vast capital wealth of the Church to make enough money every year to pay something substantial towards the salaries and homes of priests and bishops, and the whole cost of pensions for retired clergy.

Robert Runcie had no talent for business, so stayed away from their committee meetings as much as he could during his time as Archbishop. All was well, until two things happened. One was the realisation that the clergy were getting older and living longer, the cost of pensions and homes was rising, and all this needed to be funded. The second was Thatcher fever. Increasing demands were being put upon the previously restrained money men who advised the assets committee and their response was to transform themselves, secretly at first, into profit-hungry, market-riding City wideboys who took a series of huge gambles, and lost.

That had not looked at all likely when Sir Douglas Lovelock became the First Estates Commissioner, the paid figurehead of the operation, in 1983. He was a career civil servant, a man of quiet efficiency who had come from running Customs and Excise. An upright Christian fellow, active in his local church. His secretary and right-hand man was an Old Etonian called James Shelley, the son of a vice-admiral, who had been with the Commissioners for thirty years after joining straight from university. They had to take the assets committee with them, but those two would be described as the 'architects' of all that was to come. Their property portfolio manager was Michael Hutchings, known as a bigger, bolder, more flamboyant fellow with a taste for fine wine and big cigars, who had also joined the Commissioners after university. He worked closely with his property adviser William Wells, managing director of a company called Chesterton. A good, solid team, you would think: mostly privately educated, cool heads capable of discretion and pragmatism. What mattered was getting the right return in order to pay the bills. Nothing else was within their parameters. Very Establishment. Very English. What were they to do, though, in answer to the looming problem of pensions?

They found their answer in the siren call of Thatcherism. Their job was to maximise revenue. Mrs Thatcher wanted it to be easier for citizens to buy shares and play the markets, and make money, money, money. The crack staff of the Church

Commissioners saw the wisdom of this. They would invest. To do that, they had to have some cash, so they began to sell off some of those assets. Some of the flats, some of the farms, chunks of the estates, here and there, with the money going into stocks and shares and new building developments. It worked. They did well. They got a taste for it. They began to search for new opportunities, and, for the first time in the history of their august institution, they looked overseas.

America was stable. America was rich. America promised high returns. They set up an American company called Deansbank and started to invest the money they had made in England. A stake in a development here, a shopping mall there, and soon the cash was all used up. So now they did another new thing, and borrowed some more. This was very unusual for a pension fund, and risky, but the money men persuaded the assets committee that it was a good idea. The market was strong, the value of the properties would go up, they would pay back the loans and make a profit for the pensioners. There was no problem. You can see where this is going, can't you?

When Michael Hutchings wanted to see the US property, he didn't fly the flag with British Airways' economy class. Not at all. A friend had died in an aeroplane accident, and as one colleague put it, he was subsequently 'temperamentally disinclined' to fly. So Mr Hutchings did what any other high-roller would do (forgetting, perhaps, for a moment, that he was notionally a servant of priests on wages of less than £12,000 a year). He sailed to America on the *QE2*. He told a reporter he had made it stop in the Hudson River one time, after failing to get off in New York. To make himself more comfortable, as he crossed the Atlantic on the world's most famous ocean liner, then traversed America by train and automobile, he had some of the contents of his wine cellar at home sent on ahead of him. By 1985, the Commissioners had invested about £60 million in America and another £40 million in Japan and other parts of the Far East. At that stage, most of this was the Church's own money: the loans amounted to less than £5 million. But let's keep an eye on that figure.

The new, rampant materialism was beginning to bother church leaders, who worried that the rising tide of opinion would lead to new laws allowing shops to trade on a Sunday. That would threaten the existence of church services altogether, they said. So what did the Church Commissioners do, in the face of Mammon's onslaught? They built shops. And not just ordinary shops but huge shopping malls. The first was the eight-acre St Enoch Centre in Glasgow, a futuristic glass palace with a department store and ice rink. They invested £52 million, enough to make any saint blush. James Shelley said in his review of policy in 1985: 'I hope we do not pay too much attention to the current prophets of doom regarding the prospects for property.'

The next investment was a share in the building of the biggest shopping centre of its kind in Europe, the MetroCentre in Gateshead, which was to stretch out over 1.5 million square feet. When the project was launched in September 1985 the Commissioners 'deliberately minimised' their role in it, presumably for fear of alarming people in the pews, but this was still the largest single investment they had ever made, at (an initial) £130 million. The Synod knew about it, of course. Worried members urged the Commissioners to use their influence with the retailers, to fight against the idea of Sunday opening. The Commissioners seemed to think that was none of their business, even though half of their commercial property portfolio was now made up of supermarkets and shopping centres. In 1986, they pumped another £55 million into the MetroCentre.

Meanwhile, in America, they were allowed to invest up to $230 million, and much of that now came from loans. This was

very risky indeed, but they were in deep. Eventually they would
be found to have set up thirty-seven companies in the States, but
the trouble was that America now seemed to be in recession and
the dollar was weak. It wasn't working out as planned. They
would have to hold their nerve.

The MetroCentre required another £36 million investment in
1987, the year of Black Monday and the stock market crash.
Confidence in Thatcherism may have been draining away elsewhere, suddenly, but not inside 1 Millbank, the magnificent
home of the Church Commissioners. The company chairmen
and bankers on the assets committee had been joined by the
Conservative MP Michael Alison, formerly parliamentary private
secretary to Margaret Thatcher but recently appointed as Second
Estates Commissioner. Sir Douglas Lovelock was also a member,
even though a large part of the committee's job was to oversee
what he and his team were doing. They remained true believers,
who insisted the Commissioners' money would be okay. The
property bubble had not burst, they said. It wasn't a bubble, it was
long-term growth, just wait and see. They had assets worth £2.5
billion by now, and used them to take out yet more loans.

I am in debt here myself, to Dr Andrew Chandler's detailed
account of these events in his book *The Church of England in the
Twentieth Century: The Church Commissioners and the Politics of
Reform, 1948–1998*. As he says, the finances were now, for the
first time, 'founded in no small measure upon debt'. The portfolio was overloaded with investments in shopping centres and
other commercial property that had yet to be finished. These, in
turn, were hugely dependent on loans. Not the nice, shake-on-
it, never-mind-the-interest sort of loans that the Commissioners
made to people they wanted to work with, but proper, hard loans
from banks with no other incentive but to make money. The
whole house of cards was getting very wobbly indeed, standing

as it was on a trembling jelly of debt. The money men told themselves that everything would be paid off when the shopping malls
that were still being built (with another £46 million going into
the St Enoch Centre) started to make money. The assets committee even chartered an aeroplane to take members (without Mr
Hutchings as a guest, presumably) to the sites in Gateshead and
Glasgow, to show how real it all was. Of course, it was still possible, as Chandler says, that 'the whole chain would collapse,
possibly almost at once'.

It was in 1988 that they made their most wonderful, spectacular, monumental and shameful mistake: spending £80 million on
a couple of marshy sheep fields in Kent that would be revealed in
time to be worth less than a million. The two thousand acres were
right next to the M20, near the forthcoming Channel Tunnel ter-
minal, and were going to be the site of a major new retail and
housing development, a 'mini-town' called Ashford Great Park.
Great. The only snag was that there was no planning permission.
They bought into the development without getting the green
light from the authorities, who subsequently shocked them by
saying no. They appealed. No was still the answer. They applied
again. No, for a third time. Their partners in the project went
bust, despite being financed with loans from the Commissioners
themselves. A Commons inquiry into the whole fiasco would
later conclude: 'The best interpretation we can put on these activities is that they display unbelievable naivety.' The next Archbishop
of Canterbury would call it a 'deeply troubling, sorry episode'.

Still, the assets kept rising, up to £3 billion by the end of 1989.
The MetroCentre was opened by Margaret Thatcher, who could
see beyond the woolly bishops to the kindred spirits in the suits.
They paid another £30 million for the land surrounding it, and
spent more on shopping centres elsewhere. Investments were
now being powered primarily by a £250 million loan from the

NatWest, and the interest was beginning to bite. The Commissioners were paying out as much in interest as they paid for pensions and wages, the financing of which had been the whole point of the game in the first place. Sheepishly, Shelley wondered whether it might be time to cash in. But they couldn't. Not until the developments they had invested in were finished, and could be sold. He may, he admitted to his bosses, have 'overdone the optimism'.

By this stage, the Commissioners were getting no return from the £90 million they had sunk into Japan. Deansbank was in dire trouble, because there was just too much property on the market in the States and nobody wanted to pay the prices they needed. In this country, too, the earth now started to shake. They had not negotiated fixed rates on their loans, and in view of the turmoil going on around them, the banks demanded double. The numbers were huge: in five years, the loans taken out by the Church Commissioners – or more correctly their staff, with the approval of the assets committee – had risen from £4.7 million to £518 million.

Needing to raise £300 million by the end of the year, they tried to sell a share in the MetroCentre. It didn't work. They tried to sell the last of their properties in Maida Vale and Hyde Park. That didn't work, either. Meanwhile, the Bishop of Oxford was taking the Commissioners to the High Court over their investment policy, trying to get the judges to say that it was not enough for them simply to be motivated by profit.

There was fat chance of any profit now. Three-quarters of their property portfolio was made up of just six shopping developments, most of which were not finished and not earning. Their chief accountant broke the news they didn't want to hear: their income was exceeded by their outgoings. They were paying out more than they were getting in. It couldn't go on. 'When the crash did come it was so sudden, and so severe, that it allowed almost no room for manoeuvre,' says Andrew Chandler. The loans now 'tightened around them like a vice'. Incredibly, at this moment, James Shelley was made a CBE. 'Like honouring an admiral whose fleet was sinking around him.'

There was no alternative: they would have to tell the rest of the Commissioners, the bishops, the Synod and the wider Church what a mess they were in. They would have to ask for help, but how to do it? Sir Douglas Lovelock, still maintaining the calm exterior of an English missionary stepping towards a cannibal's pot, went to the House of Bishops in January 1991 to 'sound a warning note'. The economy was in trouble, he said, the boom time was over and property prices were falling. All of that was true. He didn't mention that they had gambled the family silver on risky investments, for high stakes, and blown it big time. He did say the Commissioners could no longer be relied upon to pay for homes and wages as well as pensions (which was, actually, their job). They would certainly have to cut the £1 million annual payment to the Church Urban Fund, set up as a response to 'Faith in the City'.

Michael Hutchings left his job and sailed off into the sunset. He is unlikely to have taken the QE2. The expansion of investment in property had been brought to a halt. The new Archbishop of Canterbury came in, but he was as overawed and trusting of the financial experts as his predecessor had been. George Carey went around blaming inflation, because that was what he had been told. Then the FT report appeared and he realised that things were far, far worse than they seemed. After struggling to come to terms with the news all through Sunday, he still had to appear at the General Synod on the Monday and make the speech asking for more from the parishioners. 'We call for sacrificial giving,' he said, 'in order to swell the stream of Christian generosity to the wider world.'

What a cheek, his old muckers in the East End of London must have thought. Why hadn't he stopped that muppet Lovelock and his cronies blowing all the moolah on a bunch of schemes that were clearly barking?

There was no punishment. Quite the opposite. Sir Douglas went off to a comfortable retirement in 1993. And none of the old gang was in place when a committee of MPs belatedly investigated the disaster, which they said had 'done more than any other single act to destroy the parish system of the national Church'. The Commissioners had been 'ethically suspect', 'reckless' and 'foolish'. Frank Field denounced the 'incredible arrogance' of the new staff as well as the old ones, raging: 'The historic resources of the Church of England were contributed to directly by the monarch and by taxpayers, and granted privileges of an exempt charity by Parliament. These historic resources belong not to the Church but the nation as a whole.' Sir Michael Colman, the new First Estates Commissioner, was told by another angry MP that what had happened was 'crazy'. He replied calmly: 'I am not disagreeing with you.' Why had it been done, then? 'I have no idea.'

The Commissioners did eventually find a way out of the crisis: they made the people in the pews pay for all their mistakes. There were reforms, new rules and new structures, but essentially the parishes were left to fund the work of the Church. This had an enormous impact, beyond money. The rich parishes were the ones with priests who expressed their beliefs powerfully and clearly, and attracted followers. They belonged either to the Evangelical or the Anglo–Catholic tribe, both of which had very strong views on the battles to come, over women bishops and gay priests. After the financial crisis they could say, 'Hang on, if you want more of our money in the pot, then you have to give us more of a say.' They could even say, 'We could walk away. If we don't like the way this goes, we could go it alone.' So the incompetence and greed of the Commissioners and their staff created ammunition for the coming war; but it also presented an even more serious threat to the core of the whole enterprise.

The Church of England exists to serve everyone in every community. That is the basis of its claim to be the national Church. Now it was running out of money, and the ideal of a priest in every parish was beginning to look impossible. The only way to keep it going was for congregations to provide the clergy with pay and pensions in a way they had not done before. But they didn't like it, as one churchwarden from Berkshire told a newspaper: 'At some stage there will be a revolt.' If the Anglicans of Royal Berkshire were revolting, there was clearly a serious problem. Every week, the churchwarden said, the people in the pews put their money in the collecting plate in the understanding that they would be provided with a priest. They were now being asked to give more, but at the same time being told the central pot could no longer afford to hire a man or woman to serve them. So where was the money going? To pay off the debts? Trouble was brewing, all over the country. Rural parishes were getting used to sharing a vicar with three or four others. He ran through the door during the opening hymn and rushed out again after shaking everyone's hand. Sometimes, he was doing the job for free.

When the Commissioners went on their mad spending spree at the beginning of the nineties there were twelve thousand full-time priests. After they had blown the cash the figure began falling fast. It was down to eight thousand at the last count; not because of a lack of volunteers, but because there was not enough money to pay for any more. Much of their work was taken over by what are called non-stipendiaries – men and women who have trained as priests but are not paid for carrying out church duties, and have other jobs as well. Recent reports suggest that plans are being drawn up for vicars to oversee 'clusters' of twenty or more parishes at a time, with unpaid people doing the daily work. Which is fine, as long as there are enough Christians with enough energy; but congregations are shrinking and growing older.

Meanwhile, bizarrely, the Church spends £7 million a year on maintaining the houses and palaces in which its bishops live, and £14 million paying their staff, including drivers. 'The crisis, in my view, has now reached an acute form,' said the retired Bishop David Jenkins. 'If it were any form of ordinary institution, it would be on the verge of bankruptcy.' It still has historic buildings with great art and furniture in them, and cathedrals, and sixteen thousand churches across the country, including some of our greatest architectural treasures. Some are being sold off to keep the Church solvent, but some never could be. The question is: who will pay to keep those beautiful ancient buildings from falling to the ground when the congregations no longer can? That day is not far off.

The bottom line, as the accountants say, is that the system is breaking down. If you happen to be in need of spiritual succour these days, you may well find the parish church locked and barred, with security alarms to deter the silver thieves, and the local priest away doing the day job for which he is paid, while oversight is notionally provided by someone twenty miles away, whose number is nowhere to be found. What kind of national Church is that?

The Commissioners are much more closely monitored now, by a panel that will not allow money to be invested in companies involved in pornography or arms dealing, or whose main business is in gambling, tobacco or alcohol. They still have 120,000 acres in rural areas, and more in cathedral cities, out-of-town shopping centres and the West End. They also still have a 10 per cent share of the MetroCentre, having sold the rest for £325 million in 1995. They made a moderate profit on that, but also sold the Marlowes in Hemel Hempstead for £45 million after spending £130 million on it, which was less good. The sorry saga of Ashford Great Park rumbles on: the land is still owned by the Commissioners, who hope development plans will make it worth something after all. They are still waiting for permission to build a thousand homes there.

What has all this taught them? Not much, it would appear. Nobody with any influence seems to have questioned the system of investing in stocks and shares and property, exploiting the markets to pay for priestly work. That sort of rigorous ethical examination of finance is left to Muslims, who more strictly follow the exhortation – found in the Bible as well as the Quran – not to indulge in usury. Instead, the Commissioners carried on as before but cut down on the big projects and spread their cash a little more widely. By 2008, their assets had grown to £5.67 billion and their secretary, Andrew Brown, was able to say: 'We are well positioned to weather difficult financial conditions.' But the money was still in offices and shops; and, what do you know, it happened again. A crash came and a huge portion of the Church's wealth was wiped out. One year later they revealed that they had lost £1 billion. It was, said Brown, 'a very difficult financial situation'. Did he realise how much he sounded like Sir Douglas Lovelock?

Everyone lost money in the global financial crisis, so the Church's losses did not receive much attention. But they were still staggering. The Church also showed a breathtaking lack of self-awareness in its reaction to the crash. The Archbishops of York and Canterbury waded into hedge-fund managers and called debt traders 'bank robbers and asset strippers' and they must have thought they were speaking for the people. That was indeed how many of us felt. But the traders quickly pointed out that the Church itself had invested £13 million in the largest listed hedge-fund manager of them all, Man Group, and had sold some of its own mortgage debts at a profit.

Once more, church leaders appeared to have no idea what their money men were doing. Their ability to speak out against greed had yet again been fatally undermined by their own Commissioners. On the anniversary of the fall of Lehman Brothers, the Archbishop of Canterbury, Rowan Williams, lamented that within the financial world there had been none of 'what I would, as a Christian, call repentance. We haven't heard people saying, "Well, actually, we got it wrong, and the whole fundamental principle on which we worked was unreal, was empty."' When asked whether he felt that people like him should have spoken up sooner, he said: 'I guess I do; but I suppose, like most people, we felt intimidated by expertise, and that's a very dangerous place for the Church to be.' As it turned out, the so-called experts 'didn't know particularly what they were talking about. There was an enormous confidence trick going on.'

How did he not realise that those things could equally have been said about the Commissioners and about his own Church's calamitous inability to handle money? If the Church of England does ever go bust, nobody need be surprised. It may even already have happened. Some people never learn.

18

Every day is like Sunday

Enough religion, already. We didn't stop going to church because of spiritual apathy, or a rejection of the ways of God, or any of those things the preachers like to accuse us of. Well, maybe some of us did; but mostly people just found better things to do. Remember those endless, listless, desperately dull Sundays we all endured as recently as the eighties? No shops open, except for the newsagent who went home at one o'clock for his roast. No pubs open, except for a few hours at lunchtime and in the early evening. Nothing on the telly, except for farming or Thora Hird. Nothing to do, nowhere to go, except along to church, where at least there were people to fancy. And after that, hours and hours enforced 'rest' on the Sabbath afternoon, which in practice meant being dragged out for improving walks or staying in staring at the rain, trying not to overturn the family Monopoly board in sheer frustration. It couldn't go on. It had to stop.

It did, in 1994. By then, the major stores like B&Q had realised that people were desperate to buy Rawlplugs on a Sunday, if only for the sheer thrill of handing over money on a forbidden day. Everything feels more exciting when you're not allowed to do it, even the purchase of moderately priced DIY items. So the stores had begun to flout the law and open up, and challenge it in the courts and in Europe, and the government led by John Major was beginning to see this was a tide whose rise they could not stop, even if they wanted to. Margaret Thatcher's attempt to allow shops to open all hours, as a good grocer's daughter ought to, had been defeated in the Commons in 1986, by an alliance of church leaders, trade unions and MPs who feared that people would be forced to work more hours or prevented from going to their place of worship. The religious argument against it was based on the idea that God had created the world in six days and rested on the seventh, and the direction given in the Book of Exodus: 'Six days thou shalt do thy work, and on the seventh day thou shalt rest: that thine ox and thine ass may rest, and the son of thy handmaid, and the stranger, may be refreshed.' Even in the Bible, the argument was that the people at the bottom of the pile – the sons of slaves in those days, shop workers in ours – needed a rest.

By 1994, though, the Keep Sunday Special campaign had lost ground. The unions had started to believe the promise that workers would be paid a premium wage for these unsociable hours. Everyone knew the existing laws were a mess – remember, you could buy a plant but not a pot – and needed changing, but the questions thrown up by the debate were profound. This was about who we were. Our elected representatives had to decide whether this was still a Christian nation that wished to go on observing and enforcing the biblical instruction to rest, or whether there had been such a shift in the national identity that Christianity was now a minority sport, and most people wanted the freedom – a buzzword of the times – to shop and shop and shop until they dropped. Such votes are a surprisingly good indication of the way things stand: after all, politicians want to stay in their jobs. Given a free vote, they will usually do whatever they consider most popular.

Every day is like Sunday

So it was that the Sunday Trading Bill was passed by seventy-five votes, and the shops started opening immediately (although the ones with a floor space bigger than a tennis court were restricted to six hours). The cause-and-effect was subtle. There had to be enough support for the change, and, yes, lots of people had given up on church already so were glad of something else to do; but there were still more than 4.5 million in worship services on a Sunday, and the big push for recruits was on, don't forget. There was a genuine expectation among church leaders that the numbers might rise again, like the Lord, if the message was put across clearly. Instead, for some strange reason, people started to believe that looking at nice things in pleasantly lit, warm shops, and getting an instant buzz from buying them, and sitting down for a coffee and cake with their companions before looking at some more nice things were more attractive than sitting in a cold and gloomy stone barn being shouted at by a fish-faced man who called you a sinner. Fancy that.

The Church of England contained many people who were not happy at all about the change, but it was not exactly in a position to complain. Ninety thousand people turned up on the first Sunday of opening at the MetroCentre in Gateshead, which was soon declared to be the second-busiest shopping centre in the country on the Sabbath – and by far the most profitable overall, pushing Oxford Street into a distant second place. It was owned, of course, by the Church Commissioners. Prophets were out, profits were in. No priest whose salary or pension was paid with the help of the Commissioners could speak out against materialism with any credibility at all. A full-time chaplain was on duty at the MetroCentre, but he was not about to overturn the tables in this grand temple of Mammon. Indeed, he failed to see much of a difference between preaching the word and flogging jeans. 'I've traded on Sundays for all these years,' he told the papers, 'so why should others not?'

This was presented as a fight between fun-loving people who wanted freedom and miserable Christians who wanted to sing hymns and spend the day motionless on hard-backed chairs, having as little fun as possible. In truth, there had been a running argument for three centuries about whether godly men and women should be able to play sport, take the air and absorb a little culture on the Sabbath as well as attending to their devotions. The Puritans were the ones who insisted on trying to ban such fleshly pleasures, as pointed out by the Catholic commentator Dr William Oddie. Writing in response to a report that the number of people going to stately homes, theme parks and other places for family outings had recently increased dramatically, he rejoiced. The habit of 'highly regulated inactivity' had been imposed on a resentful population during the late Victorian period by busybody killjoys, including the Archbishop of Canterbury. 'After a prolonged and unnatural period in which the Puritan tradition determined the relevant legislation, the British Sunday has now changed back to something more nearly approaching its normal and natural condition. We have not lost the traditional Sunday at all: actually we have regained it.' So we were escaping the cultural straitjacket sewn for us by the Church of England at the height of its imperial influence, something we will see repeated across English society as this story unfolds.

The former day of rest was transformed in the nineties. The licensing laws were relaxed, allowing pubs to open all day. Race meetings were held, and betting shops were open. One and a half million people found themselves working on a Sunday (although the premium rate so prized by the unions soon dropped to not much more than normal pay). Many of those willing to do it were mothers who found it easier to get someone else to look after the kids at weekends. The number of mums at work rose to 71 per cent over the next ten years, and the number of single parents with jobs went up to nearly 56 per cent. The British responded to the recession by working longer hours than the people of any other country in Europe, which had an impact on the weekend: we were too tired, too frantic catching up with essential chores or too occupied with work that had to be brought home to think much about eating, let alone going out to church. The Sunday roast fell out of favour. So did the habit of staying together in one place all day. A decade after the shopping and drinking laws were changed, researchers found that 80 per cent of adults took a trip on a Sunday to visit friends, family, museums, gardens, parks, galleries, cinemas, shopping centres, sports events . . . almost anywhere except a place of worship.

If anything, Saturday had become a day of rest and Sunday was for hunting down pleasurable, cultural or family activities with the ruthlessness of the workaholics many of us had become. Holidays and days out were advertised as if they were life projects to be completed, or trophies to be collected. It was all about having experiences, which was good news at least for those churches that offered mind-blowing warm baths in the Holy Spirit on a Sunday morning (but bad news if they didn't live up to the hype).

Within ten years or so, the old Sunday had gone. Then the writer Blake Morrison described what his had become:

I'm running in the park. A parent now, with three children, I know I'll have no time to myself for the rest of the day. My older son is playing for his football team; my daughter has riding lessons; my younger son has been invited to a birthday party – all these mean my wife or me acting as chauffeurs. We don't bother with Sunday lunch; it cuts into the day too much. If there's no supermarket shop to do, we might drag the kids to an exhibition or for a walk or go swimming at the local sports centre. When they're in bed, we'll probably check our emails and spend some time catching up on work. That's what Sunday evenings are for.

We don't all have such frantically privileged middle-class lives as that, of course, but you get the point. Morrison mentions football, which perhaps did more to end the old-fashioned Sunday than any other force, apart from Thatcherism. The single biggest change in the sporting life of England in modern times had taken place in 1992, irrevocably changing Sundays for millions of people.

The FA Premier League, the breakaway championship formed by the biggest football clubs, attracted the cameras and, more importantly, the vast wealth of Rupert Murdoch. Sky paid £191 million over five years for the rights to televise the new league, topping it up with even more astronomical figures later on, and marketed the games fiercely. Subscriptions became almost obligatory for pubs and clubs, many of which changed their style and menus to cater for families who came to watch the football together if they couldn't afford Sky at home. Actually, it was a more enjoyable experience watching Wimbledon rattle into Coventry with a pint in your hand and your mates all around you than it was sitting there alone on the sofa. The Sky money sent common sense and fair play out of the window along with old-fashioned English football (which was no loss) as the Premiership became the richest league in the world, attracting the very best players. The way they were fêted, indulged and worshipped for being good at running about and kicking a synthetic pig's bladder became a driving force in the rise of celebrity culture, in which flash and cash and bling and a spread in OK! magazine became measures of success and worth. As the money swilled around, every club was possessed by greed and the need for a

Carlos Kickaball, as Alan Sugar so memorably called the merce-
naries who followed the money. Bradford City, for example, paid
the Italian Benito Carbone £30,000 a week to play for them,
more than the price of a house in the shadow of their main stand.
I was there for his debut, writing about it for a national newspaper, unable to believe the madness. And right from the start,
Sky aimed to come in hard on the old-style Sunday like a
twenty-stone centre-back smashing into Michael Owen's knee.

The first match it ever televised was between Nottingham
Forest and Liverpool in August 1992, on a Sunday. Soon it would
be showing matches back to back, all day, giving subscribers a
reason to stay home but also making football glamorous in a way
that led to a boom in people playing the game, both as adults and
children, most often on a Sunday morning. All over the country
now, as Blake Morrison said, bleary-eyed parents ferry their sons
and daughters to matches and back home again, or lace up their
own boots, where once they might have followed the family tradition and gone along to a church service. Some churches have
responded by putting on services on Sunday afternoons, or week-
day evenings, but it hasn't really worked. The connection has
been broken.

We still think of church as a Sunday thing, but really, there is
so much else going on now, isn't there? Walking up to St Gabriel
and All Angels on that morning when I decided to go back, just
to see what it was like, I could have chosen instead to go swimming, or to the library, or to buy a pizza or a fry up, a stereo or
a mobile phone, or have an eye test, or see a film, or watch a
band play in the street, or pop into a pub to watch the match. I
wish I had.

Even if the pews were emptying of young footballers, their
fathers and their shopping mothers on a Sunday morning, at least

the parish church could still uphold its historic claim to be the place where people went to be hatched, matched and dispatched, couldn't it? Er, no.

Baby-naming, weddings and funerals were monopolised by Christians when this story began back in 1981, but in the mid-nineties that began to change. Again, the reason was not spiritual at all, but rather the worldly, enduring claims of Thatcherism. Why should the churches have a monopoly on matrimony? Why shouldn't the people be free to choose where they tie the knot? The teddy bear collector turned Tory MP Gyles Brandreth managed to get the Marriage Act through Parliament in 1994, allowing hotels and stately homes and museums and football clubs and anywhere else with a licence to hold weddings.

The setting had to be dignified, but that was interpreted loosely. (It included both the Kerry Dixon Suite at Chelsea Football Club and the bloody wax nightmares of the London Dungeon.) The law change was actually a recognition of what some people were doing already, like Samantha, an advertising manager who hadn't been able to wait for the new legislation. 'We wrote our own ceremony and held it privately in our garden – then we sneaked off to the registrar to make it legal on our way to Sainsbury's.'

The first of the official new-style weddings took place against the much more romantic backdrop of the dragon wallpaper in the Red Drawing Room of the Royal Pavilion in Brighton in May 1995. The groom was a landscape gardener, the bride a trainee teacher, who said: 'I don't believe in God so I would never have got married in church. I don't want to be a hypocrite but a register office is boring and doesn't match the occasion.' There was a special deal for those who wanted to hire the room next door for the reception, which cut out the fuss and expense of getting Auntie Gladys and her dodgy knees to a hotel. I mean, who was going to give her a lift?

Here's another question: would you get married in your local parish church if the socially awkward vicar insisted on making you sit through an embarrassing talk on sex at his compulsory marriage preparation evening, made you come to services for weeks just to hear your banns read, imposed the hymns you were allowed to have, banned the wedding video cameraman from the service and treated you as if it were the greatest privilege in the world to use his crumbling old barn of a building? No, of course not. Not if there was a choice. Why do all that when the manager of the local hotel said you could exchange your vows in one beautiful room, hold the reception in another, have your photos taken under a willow tree with glasses of chilled champagne, and asked when would you like it and if there was anything else he could do for you, sir and madam. For couples without religious affiliations, which was now the majority, there was no real choice at all.

The change in the law seemed a slight thing at the time, a frivolity even, but it turned out to be an enormous blow – think demolition ball on a long chain smashing the side of a house into tiny bits – to the status of the national faith. In 1981 there had been 351,973 weddings in England and Wales, more than half of them involving religious ceremonies. The slide happened fast after the change in the law. In 2007 there were 231,450 weddings, but only a third of them were conducted by a minister of religion. It's not hard to see where all those couples went instead: that year, the hotels and stately homes and other licensed venues got through 100,000 services. On average, men and women were being married nearly a decade older than they had before, in their thirties, so they knew what they wanted. Not to be in church. It was more convenient, sometimes cheaper, and usually more fun to go elsewhere. The staff were paid to serve them, after all, not convert them.

When one thing led to another, baptisms were out of fashion. Once ubiquitous, the splash was endured by only 30 per cent of all babies by the mid-nineties, and that is expected to fall below 10 per cent some time soon. Lots of people who wanted to have a nice do thought they would go for a non-religious naming ceremony, without a vicar to ask awkward questions and without having to rub up against the strangers in a Sunday morning congregation. They could have it at the nice hotel where they got married: some managers even offered a two-for-the-price-of-one deal, if you did your baby on the same day as you made the little darling legal.

Funerals were still in the grip of the Church at this time, just about, but the end was nigh. There was a growing demand for services that had no religious content at all, or that were tailored to the beliefs of the grieving families. It was readily met by retired clergy who would conduct a quickie at the crematorium with no intrusive religious bits for a few quid; but also by people who were ideologically opposed to bringing God into death, such as the members of the British Humanist Society. The proportion of funerals being hosted by the Church of England dropped and dropped and is now around 40 per cent. Only half of those are actually in church, and burials are rare. Three-quarters of us prefer to be cremated. Slowly, funeral by funeral, we have asserted our desire not to be put in the ground by a vicar who has only just been told our name and knows nothing of our lives, but to be burned after a service in which people we love have been able to say what they want to say, and in which the words and the songs and whatever else have been a reflection of our own beliefs, not somebody else's. It's not much to ask, really.

19

Everything you know is wrong

There have always been vicars with their hands in other people's knickers. I write this with stories from recent newspapers spread around me. There's a priest who sent filthy texts to a teenager, another who left his wife to run away with a man, and a woman who resigned after it was revealed that she liked to take holidays in the South of France with dozens of other free-loving swingers. In the land of the *Carry On* there is nothing we love more than seeing a self-appointed guardian of moral values fall flat on his or her face. Or back, more often.

All this is terribly sad for the people whose relationships are destroyed, but jolly good fun for the rest of us – unless, of course, the people involved are not all consenting adults. There is nothing funny or jolly to say about the hundreds of cases of paedophilic sexual abuse by Catholic priests that began to surface in Ireland and America during the mid-nineties. The suffering involved was horrendous. The Roman authorities took much too long to treat them seriously, even in this country, where they had far fewer claims to investigate.

Authority figures of every kind were letting us down in the mid-nineties. The royal family was no longer even pretending to be a model of morality. John Major called for a move 'back to basics' and almost immediately discovered his cabinet was full of sleazy monkeys who lied and cheated and paraded their wives like grim trophies one minute, then rushed back to Parliament to bonk their researchers (or their colleagues) the next. The papers were full of stories about teachers who touched up their pupils and doctors who put their stethoscopes where they had no place to be. Perhaps these things were not happening any more often than before, but it did feel like they were.

Sexual shenanigans were far from the only way in which our trust was being violated. The police were found to have fabricated evidence or beaten confessions out of the Guildford Four, the Birmingham Six and the Maguire Seven. We already knew they would act as state stormtroopers, but their attitude to the death of Stephen Lawrence confirmed they were institutionally racist, too. There seemed to be nobody you could trust. No wonder the deference essential to the power structures of Establishment England was now crumbling faster than a curate's resolve.

Given all this, the discovery that yet another clergyman was having trouble keeping his pants on might have seemed like a summer season silly story. It was not. The scandal had a significant impact on Christianity in this country. The Reverend Chris Brain was seen as a pioneer and an inspiration as leader of the Nine O'clock Service, or NOS, a radical community in Sheffield that staged worship services using the über-cool music of club culture along with avant-garde art images and spectacular staging, doing church in a way that had never been seen before. They were the future, as far as the Archbishop of Canterbury was concerned, and many of us believed he was right. NOS services articulated the way we felt about things that the rest of the Church didn't seem to understand, and they did it with dazzling images, newly imagined ritual and pulsating rhythms. In future, everyone would do it like this. There were around two hundred groups across the country who took inspiration from NOS in taking over church buildings and filling them with projectors, computers and sound systems. The alternative worship movement, as we called ourselves, was broad enough to include people who wanted to experiment with candles, silence and video icons as well as those who were seeking to put on bombastic, ear-splitting holy gigs. NOS was the most authentically part of club culture, and its members received the most attention — so much so that in the summer of 1995, while renting space at the Ponds Forge Centre, they were officially declared to have formed the first non-geographical parish in the history of the Church of England. They were special, they were outside the system and yet right at the heart of it as the chosen favourites of the Archbishop. So it was startling when we heard in late August that it was all over.

Chris Brain was accused of manipulating, abusing and getting sexual relief from dozens of women in the NOS community. The services stopped, the victims were offered counselling and Brain entered a psychiatric hospital. Within weeks he was admitting that he had done wrong in an exclusive interview with the *Mail on Sunday*. 'I have wronged those who trusted me. I feel very guilty about it now, and I would have killed myself had it not been for my daughter.' She was five years old. Soaked in self-pity, Brain called himself 'an evil bastard'. Those of us who had admired and supported his work found it hard to disagree. We didn't really trust the tabloid reports, though, and it was a while before a more reliable account of events was published by the author Roland Howard. Members of the original core group of well-meaning, committed and passionate people told him how they had been led into a life totally dominated by Brain, who decided what sort of clothes they wore, what food they ate, whether they could take particular jobs and even whether individual women were allowed to have a baby. Brain used mind games, flattery, humiliation, intimacy and secrecy to control the group. It was heavy shepherding of the kind I had seen for myself, taken to new and frightening levels of intensity by a deeply charismatic leader who looked like Jesus with his long, curly hair, dazzled with his new theology and justified what they were doing in a way that was so eloquent and persuasive that members spent years and fortunes in pursuit of it. Women were chosen to act as 'postmodern nuns', which meant cooking and cleaning and caring for Brain, often even putting him to bed. 'The very least that this meant was massaging him as he lay (often naked) in bed,' writes Howard. 'What started as kissing and cuddling soon became heavy petting and by the time the NOS scandal broke, some members felt he had complete control over their bodies.' There was talk of becoming liberated from the possessive, appearance-obsessed sexuality of the times, but as one woman involved with NOS later put it: 'All the stuff about sexual ethics was just clever language; basically, it was about one bloke getting his rocks off with about forty women.'

This was not a saucy vicar, it was a cult.

Even before the scandal, there were people who hated what we did. That was mainly because they didn't understand it. Many of us were in our teens or twenties and our thinking was full of ideas that the Church did not seem to have encountered before, let alone engaged with properly (at least not in a way that had filtered down from theological colleges to the local parish). The most exciting, at the time, was postmodernity, that gathering sense in art, architecture, literature, academia and the media that after all the seismic shocks of the century, it was no longer possible to trust the old narratives upon which history had been built. There was said to be no such thing as objective truth: everything was subjective, having been shaped by personality and culture and power games. Everything was broken. The best we could do was pick among the ruins, treating all claims with the same scepticism and telling our own, self-assembled stories with vigilant irony. Artists were exploring postmodernism all around us, in films, on television, in books and music, where the most obvious example was the transformation of the band U2 from a group of super-earnest, overtly Christian flag wavers into shiny subversives who began their shows with slogans like 'Everything You Know Is Wrong'. Bono, once the most serious man in music, now stood under lights made from Trabant cars and made prank calls to the White House, dressed in a gold lamé suit and a pair of little red horns, calling himself MacPhisto.

The question was – and still is – what did Christianity look like when people had stopped believing in absolute truth and all stories were considered to have equal weight? Our response was to raid traditions and cultures, taking a fragment of liturgy from South America, a Latin chant, a slice of footage from the Gulf War, a white-label remix, a reading from the Torah, another from Noam Chomsky, a clip from the *Magic Roundabout*, some Catholicism, some Calvinism, a shot of liberation theology . . . and put it all together in what some people called pick-and-mix spirituality. It wasn't a tribute to Woolworths, and they weren't being nice.

Some people in our suburban Anglican church got upset when we brought in a full-on Gothic rock band with a drummer playing fashionably baggy beats, lots of dry ice, theatrical spotlights, strobes and booming speakers, and made people walk around in the half darkness as if they were following the stations of the cross. Others trusted us, and liked the sight of four hundred young people in there who would otherwise have been somewhere else.

That bought us some time, but it was extraordinary how quickly we and other groups like ours went from being allowed to put on a show to remaking services to rethinking all that church was. We emerged with the thought that everything we did, from humping the gear into the building to putting it back in the van again, should be seen as an act of worship. Still, we were not nearly as radical as NOS, where people had given up their jobs to work full time on the project, lived together in a community and handed over money from the sales of their houses to buy equipment.

We were in awe of them, from a distance. We were certainly slow to realise the full implications of what they were saying in their services about our responsibility to the planet. 'Denial of that responsibility means denial of the saving work of Christ and collusion with the growth of pollution, oppression and biocide.' Clearly, this was about more than a performance to hook in the youngsters. Meanwhile, Swampy was digging himself into tunnels to stop roads being built, people were tying themselves to trees at Twyford Down, and only a couple of miles down the road from us men and women were taking their responsibility to the earth very seriously and barricading themselves into condemned houses to protest against the construction of the M11 link road.

Wars were being fought for oil, the natural environment was being raped, and these were the moral issues that occupied the people we went to school with, studied alongside at college, spoke to at work or saw down the pub – not questions about whether it was right to have sex before marriage. The sin of destroying the planet was far greater than the sin of sleeping with someone you were not supposed to. That was self-evidently true. We didn't realise quite how far Chris Brain was going with the thought, but then how could we have done? When the rest of us

met together, to discuss ideas and mistakes we had made, some-
times under the guidance of a patient, wizardly man called
Graham Cray, who later became a bishop, the members of the
Nine O'clock Service didn't come.

They kept themselves aloof, even when they appeared on what
many of us considered our home turf – the Greenbelt Festival of
'arts, justice and faith'. This event attracts 25,000 every year and
is a refuge and inspiration for people who might have questions
about the behaviour of the Church but can't quite give up on the
divine. In 1992, NOS took over the Glastonbury-size main stage
to perform a spectacular multimedia event called *Passion in Global
Chaos*. Images of climate destruction were projected on to huge
screens, but what upset some people in the audience was the sight
of women dancing on stage in lycra bikinis. That and the use of
erotic imagery in the liturgy. Some of the criticism felt hysterical
at the time, but perhaps we should have seen what was coming.
I would love to say that I saw through Chris Brain as soon as we
met, face to face, in Sheffield a few months after Greenbelt, but
I didn't. Like so many others, I did not have a clue.

The room in the basement was dimly lit in lilac and ultravio-
let and looked like a druid temple reimagined by the *Star Trek*
designers. The altar at the centre resembled a sun and crescent
moon but was meant to be an eclipse, a symbol of the new
emerging from the old. In a circle around it were ten pillars with
large screens on them, as well as smaller monitors, showing
images of space, nature and humanity. Behind those, on the
curved walls, were more projections: a baby moving slowly, the
exquisite detail of a leaf in the rainforest, that sort of thing. We
sat on crash mats on the floor, taking it all in. The intention,
according to the flyer, was to produce 'a sea of paradox, high tech
but with the ambience of a crypt . . . a place where beat, medi-
tation, dance and light can reconnect people with God,

transforming their vision of the world'. Stars appeared all around us to accompany words from the Book of Isaiah, then gave way to swaying corn in wide fields, before we were invited to remember a time when we had felt that God was present.

Chris Brain appeared, robed completely in white with a large silver pectoral cross, and led a confession and absolution straight from the Anglican liturgy. Bells were rung for the reading of the Gospel as they might be at the highest Catholic service. The pace of the music rose as attendants brought bread and wine to the table. They also brought money, and asked God to give us the courage to share; they brought soil, 'from which life comes'; and they brought a Big Mac, praying for integrity at a time when the McLibel trial was running in the law courts of London. Having each taken wafers and wine, the celebrants walked around the table and then around the circle of pillars with increasing speed, some clockwise, some anticlockwise, apparently to reflect the NOS view of the sacraments as being at the epicentre of a new Big Bang, 'with ripples of life force spreading out like shockwaves'.

Brain broke the bread, holding it above his head as the music became intense. After eating and drinking, we sang simple chants to the dance rhythms, and a few danced. Before the end, some were making for the soft drinks bar in one corner of the room, or moving sheepishly towards members of the ministry team, identifiable by laminated badges bearing that eclipse symbol. By this time, NOS was influenced by the theologian Matthew Fox, who had been dismissed from the Dominicans; but the ministry team was evidence of its earlier inspiration, the signs and wonders of John Wimber. 'The whole community got blasted,' said one of the members in the early days, after a Wimber meeting. Back then they were speaking in tongues, casting out demons and laying hands on each other for healing; all things that Brain would use for his own ends. New members were required to read Wimber's books and Brain went to see him in America. In 1993 Wimber was still one of the names on a council of reference for NOS, which gave it credibility, although the council had very little influence, if any, over what went on.

Brain allowed me an audience after the service, upstairs in an empty café. Members of his team were with him, but they kept a distance that seemed only slightly odd at the time, as if they were respectful bodyguards. I wish I could say he was creepy and evasive and sinister and that I knew something was profoundly wrong, but he wasn't and I didn't. He was self-important and far less eloquent than he clearly thought he was, but I had learned by now that the same could be said of quite a few church leaders. 'I used to feel torn apart, because I had no place to worship, no real sense of any place in the Church which was not culturally hostile to us, and yet we had experiences of God and Christ in various places,' he said. 'To hold that together was very difficult.'

Rave culture is important to this story, on a wider scale, because it took away the old idea of a band on a stage at a gig and replaced the musicians with DJ shamans who helped people participate in a mutual celebration. Ravers were not being sung to, they were dancing for themselves, with their friends, feeling part of a collective, organic experience. The drugs helped, of course, but the big idea was to become part of the whole. To participate, not just consume – a call taken up in computer games, mobile technology and the internet in subsequent years, but which was still just developing in the mid-nineties. The old church model of sitting and listening to a man telling you what to think, when to stand and when to sit suddenly looked wrong, and offensive. We had to find a new, liberating, communal way of doing it and Brain seemed to offer a model. Ironic, really, given that he was a secret dictator.

Fast-tracked into the priesthood, he had not been given the usual apprenticeship. The local archdeacon was doing his valiant best to oversee what was going on, but Brain was evasive and manipulative. It gives me chills to remember him talking about the pain of people who had been hurt by the Church, and those whose lives had been 'wrecked by the hard end of modern culture'. Some of the women standing around us when he said that, dressed identically in black and waiting there like mute servants, were having their lives wrecked by him.

It was everyone else's fault. He made that clear in the *Mail*. 'It seems utterly ridiculous that I was made a priest. I was the breakthrough for the Church but it changed everything for me. Everyone became dependent on me.' That level of denial was disturbing, but the attitude of the Bishop of Sheffield, David Lunn, was almost as bad. He said he couldn't be held accountable for everything his priests did, and complained: 'I still find it difficult to understand why the BBC and the media in general have managed to convince themselves that the problems of a single congregation in a single diocese have represented a management crisis of mega-proportions for the Church of England.'

The Bishop just didn't get it. There had been so much hype, and so much hope pinned on NOS, that this was about more, far more, than an errant priest. The rest of the alternative worship movement was all but crushed by the scandal. Suddenly, every group was seen as a potential cult. It took a very long time for that to change, and for people on all sides to get over their various feelings of betrayal. The revolution was postponed, although intriguing things have begun to happen again in recent years under the new title of 'emerging church' (or 'fresh expressions', which sounds like a cheap instant coffee). One example is in Brighton, where a congregation calling itself Beyond stages a very public, very arty and very popular advent calendar on the seafront in December, by opening up and decorating a different beach hut every day.

Back in Sheffield, nobody seems to know where Chris Brain is now. He was last heard of working for a production company in America. After his departure the NOS community was put under the care of a clergyman in his fifties who had expertise in helping people to overcome trauma. For a while there were meetings in a chapel on a remote hillside outside the city. The survivors sought privacy as they tried to recover and they have rarely spoken out about what happened, but one of them did use his own website to publish a short description of how they tried to bring things to an end. His name is Neil. When I asked him for permission to include those words in this book he agreed, as long as I also allowed him to put NOS in context. I am more than happy to do so, as what he told me gives some indication of the seriousness with which people took what they were doing, and the loss it was to them:

> With the benefit of hindsight, it is clear to me now that while NOS was a powerful artistic expression of feeling it was only possible because of the manipulative structure that persuaded hundreds of people to donate considerable time and money into putting it on. Ultimately it was an empty vessel that rang hollow because of the cynicism at its core. It is very easy to get caught up in the enthusiasm and excitement of organising something on that scale that was so different to anything else happening at the time. I think that somebody once described it as 'the best night out in Sheffield' and it was certainly well ahead of the clubs and raves of the late eighties. However, linking that to a religious message that tapped into the desires of a large number of vulnerable young people was a dangerous and in the end destructive combination.

One night, long after the scandal had broken, a group of twenty survivors held a ritual to close the story of NOS. They made a bonfire and set tables around it with objects that reminded them of what they had been through. They paused to meditate and think over each one. Neil writes:

> This allowed us to celebrate the good things (the worship, dance, and community), as well as the painful negative emotions. The fire served as a focus, symbolising energy as well as destruction. One of my meditations was to read through the membership list, calling to mind each person that I knew out of the several hundred listed, before burning the list. Somebody else had brought along a file, containing such things as instructions for the feeding of Chris Brain's dog! It was good to be able to laugh about such things.

They joined hands around the fire, shared a blessing and listened to an extract from a speech by Nelson Mandela. Remarkably, they hadn't given up on faith completely: 'The last act was to set off some rockets, to symbolise our reaching out to the cosmic otherness of God. The last one was a monster burst of stars, and one person's comment was, "And that's how you create a universe." I couldn't put it any better.'

20

Everything changes

People were nervous. They knew what was coming. They hoped they did, anyway. God was coming to be with them in this place, in a new and thrilling way. The vicar had come down from the pulpit and taken off his white robes, so he stood there in his shiny grey suit, pale grey shirt and dog collar. 'We are going to listen to a tape,' he said. We knew that. We knew what we were going to hear: a woman talking about a visit she had made to Toronto, and what she had seen there. That sounds impossibly dull, but it wasn't. Not there and then. The woman had seen and experienced something extraordinary, and the rumour was that when people listened to the tape, the same extraordinary things happened to them. God came. He over-powered them.

In Toronto, in a little church at the end of the airport runway, they had been holding services every single day for more than six months, every one of them full, and the leaders of thousands of other churches from all over the world had flown there to see what was going on for themselves, to grab a piece of the action, to reach out and touch the presence of God and maybe bring it home with them, in their heads, in their luggage, on their skin, in their hair, however it worked. It did work. We'd heard.

I was not in my own church. I happened to be visiting another one on the day they played the tape, but that was not surprising because it was being passed on from place to place as quickly as possible, for all to hear.

The woman's voice spoke, in a very normal, unaffected way, of how she had seen 'the power of God poured out in incredible measure' in Toronto. She had seen people break down in tears. She had seen them tremble and shake, unable to speak. She had seen them fall down in a heap to the floor and lay there, apparently unconscious, with big smiles over their faces. These were not new things for some of us, we had seen them before, but she spoke of something new: laughter. Wild laughter, throaty laughter, belly laughter, head back and laugh your head off laughter, chuckle 'til you chuck, double up, guffawing, uncontrollable laughter, from people who had never laughed so much in their lives, who weren't the laughing type, who had more self-control than that. Usually. They had no self-control when they were in that church in Toronto. They were overcome. Men roared, too, like lions. What a thing that must have been to hear. A bishop had gone there, a respectable Anglican from a Home County suburb, and had found himself writhing on the floor, roaring like the head of a pride with a freshly caught wildebeest at his feet. It was all about release, an end to repression, a fresh outpouring of the Spirit that made upstanding men and women fall down and roll about like they were drunk, just as it had on the day of Pentecost.

When the tape finished, there was silence. The vicar did not move from his seat. He had his eyes closed. The worship leader, a man called Dave, pulled his guitar strap over his shoulder, stood up and went to the microphone. 'Well . . .' That was all he said. He folded his arms across his guitar and looked to the back of the church, as though confused. Somebody was laughing, loudly. A woman. Bronzed face, pink lipstick, several fillings at the back of her mouth, which you could see because now her head was back and she was braying like a donkey, as if she had just been told the funniest joke in the world. The women standing closest to her, both past retirement age, started to giggle. The pitter-patter, hickle-hackle sound spread from the back to the front very quickly: embarrassed smiles turned to grins, then chuckles and for some then laughs and louder belly laughs and roars of laughter. Eyes watered, hands went up to faces. In front of me, a man I knew they called the Major, a straight-backed, stone-faced churchwarden in a dark blue blazer, sat down suddenly, with a shudder, and his head snapped back and forth as he tried to understand what was happening. Next to him, the other churchwarden, a broad, tweedy vision they called the Matron, was shaking at the shoulders but holding her hands tightly together across her middle to keep it all in. Then she fell down. She just deflated like a balloon, her shoulders slumped forward, her legs went, her backside hit the pew then slid off and she rolled forward into the narrow space between the seat and the kneeler, half upright and half on her side, her considerable bosom trapped. The Major went to help her up: he put his arm under her armpit and pulled but she didn't move. Instead, he fell on top of her. She didn't seem to care, she was beaming, and even the Major's flinty eyes began to glitter. As he regained his feet and his composure and came to terms with the spectacle of his colleague wedged like a beanbag in the pew, and as he saw that others who had never been known even to raise their voices at the PCC were falling and laughing and weeping, the look on his face went from anger and humiliation to a kind of bemused joy. This was new. Quite new.

Was it the revival? Was it the glorious moment we had been promised, when people would have no choice but to look and hear and kneel? Some said it was, that this was how it would begin, with a new thing happening in the churches that would spread on to the streets, into the workplaces, on to the radio, the television, everywhere. It had been predicted. Fifty years earlier, a Baptist pastor had seen a vision and prophesied that 1994 was the year when the revival would come to England, as mightily as in the days of Wesley. This was that year.

The church in Toronto where the laughter started was part of the Vineyard Movement, led by John Wimber, as was the woman on the tape, whose name was Eli Mumford. She lived in London and had been recorded speaking at one of the biggest, richest Anglican churches in the capital, Holy Trinity, Brompton. The first time she spoke there was at eleven in the morning on 29 May. That was when the phenomenon that would be known as the Toronto Blessing first became public in this country. Just as in our church, the end of that original talk was met with silence. Then someone started to cry. When Mumford invited people to come forward to be prayed for, some of them fell down. Some of them were overtaken by laughter. When she spoke again that evening, so many people ended up on the floor that the chairs had to be taken away, and the following week there was standing room only at the evening service. The next edition of the *Church of England Newspaper* appeared with the astonishing headline: 'Revival Breaks out in London Churches'.

The *Daily Telegraph* picked up the story immediately, quoting 'speculation about a world-wide miraculous revival'. *The Times* thought it was a 'religious craze' from across the Atlantic and had fun with how posh the church was. Those laughing, shaking and falling down were 'MPs and young, wealthy people from the Chelsea and Fulham areas'. In truth, it was not all that different from what we had known for years, under the influence of Wimber, but the fact that it was at Holy Trinity made it a big story. Samantha Fox, the page-three model, had recently been converted. More importantly, the congregation was full of the sort of people who knew national newspaper editors and BBC producers socially.

The Mumford tape and the attention it was getting helped the phenomenon spread like a virus: within a few months around four thousand churches were said to have experienced it in some way, including Roman Catholic ones. The Toronto Blessing was the most intense manifestation yet of the shift towards faith as an experience, a participatory show, something that would take you to new heights of emotion. For that reason, among others, it quickly attracted hostility: one Baptist pastor in Derbyshire distributed 33,000 leaflets denouncing 'a supernatural tide of evil' that would leave people 'shipwrecked on the rocks of ignorance'. The sociologist of religion Dr Andrew Walker put it down to pre-millennial tension: 'We're counting up to the year 2000 and there's a strong apocalyptical anxiety.' He was not wrong about that.

Even though rational people knew the year 2000 was just a mark on a calendar and nothing to do with the life of Christ, there was still a nagging thought that it might be significant. I had been part of a missionary organisation that actively sought to convert people by the end of the millennium, with an unspoken understanding that it might be time for the Lord to come back. I'd grown out of that, but all around us, inside and outside the Church, with plans for celebrations and new funds and monuments, the message was being reinforced that this was a significant time. The imminent end of the century played a part in the intensity of those days. 'I have never seen so many confessions of sin, letters of apology and witnessed acts of reconciliation as I have in the last few months,' said Gerald Coates, who was still involved in March for Jesus.

As the weeks passed the hype around the Toronto Blessing intensified, and by September admission to services at Holy Trinity was by ticket only. Dr Simon Wessley, a senior lecturer at King's College School of Medicine, thought the Blessing was not doing any harm: 'This religious experience appears to be cathartic. It is not mass hysteria or any form of mental disorder – it may be rather un-English, but there is nothing sinister about it at all.' Every newspaper sent a writer to investigate and some found themselves overcome, even if they had no faith at all. The agnostic Mick Brown described what happened to him: 'I could feel a palpable shock running through me, then I was falling backwards, as if my legs had been kicked away from underneath me. I hit the floor – I swear this is the truth – laughing like a drain.' He wasn't converted, but he couldn't deny that something had happened. But what?

Students of past revivals asked why it was not spreading beyond the churches and inspiring people to go out and help the poor. Frankly, by the following spring, it was all looking a bit self-indulgent, a fashionable way for middle-class English people to shake off their inhibitions on a Sunday night. Even Gerald Coates was now doubtful: 'If these are meant to be times of refreshment, how come many of the leaders I have spoken to are already exhausted? Something must be wrong.' Slowly, but within a year or two, the Toronto Blessing petered out. The behaviour associated with it became part of the repertoire for some churches, alongside speaking in tongues, casting out demons and praying for the healing of the sick, but as far as most of those involved were concerned, the promised revival never came.

There is a caveat to that, which we will discuss in a later chapter, but as the millennium approached, Middle England remained resolutely unconverted, even by the spectacle of clean-cut Sloanes in rugby shirts with turned-up collars barking like dogs or giggling like laughing gnomes. There was no great surprise when John Wimber announced that he could no longer endorse what was happening in Toronto and asked the congregation to leave the Vineyard. But he remained close to the leadership of Holy Trinity, a church which had experienced remarkable, sudden growth and was not about to slip easily out of the limelight. Sandy Millar, the clubbable vicar, said: 'We are hearing testimony after testimony of this and of many new Christians coming to faith through the Alpha courses and elsewhere too.'

Ah, yes. Alpha. A crash course in Holy Trinity's very English brand of Charismatic spirituality. Packaged up for use by other churches, promoted with sophisticated billboard advertising (you may have seen one of Alpha's posters at a bus stop near you) and television commercials, the subject of a documentary series presented by Sir David Frost, it grew and grew and grew. According to Holy Trinity, by the summer of 2009 the Alpha course had been run 42,350 times in 163 countries, reaching 13 million people. It is the most successful campaign in the history of English Christianity, and God only knows how bad things would have been for the Church without it.

The format is very simple: a series of two-hour sessions, held over ten weeks, each of which begins with a meal or a drink before a short talk and a discussion in groups of a dozen or so people. There's a day or a weekend away, too, but, basically, that's it. Each session is based on a single question, and they get thornier as the weeks progress. The first one, according to the most recent literature, asks, 'Who is Jesus?' By week seven, it's 'How can I resist evil?' Week nine asks, 'Does God heal today?' And the weekend away is an introduction to the Holy Spirit, which is asked to come and do its work. Alpha is a very friendly, very successful way of selling traditional Evangelical faith with a double-shot of Wimberism. Through this and his own work, the self-effacing Californian has arguably had as much influence on English faith as Billy Graham did in his day. You can see his mark on Alpha; on Holy Trinity, the richest parish church in the country; and on countless other congregations that aspire to be relaxed, informal and open to the Holy Spirit, as he used to say, doing the business.

Why did I put that in the past tense? Because John Wimber, the man who taught that God could heal the sick, died. The last time I saw him was in a private room at Holy Trinity in September 1994, when the Toronto Blessing was a new thing. But there was something else to talk about: his cancer. Father Christmas had lost eight stones. He was pale and frail and kept pausing in mid-sentence to spray synthetic saliva into his mouth, to compensate for the removal of his glands. Treatment had left him with constant heartburn and stomach aches. 'For much of my life I assumed that the avoidance of pain was one of the blessings of being a Christian,' he said. 'I've found just the opposite: that the embracing of pain is one of the blessings.'

Seeing him like that was shattering. It undermined everything he had taught, as far as I could see. If there was no healing for him, there was no healing for any of us. I just couldn't handle it. Wimber had always known he was not immune: he had seen his close friend David Watson, another believer in the healing power of the Spirit, die prematurely from cancer. Wimber seemed to know what was coming. He had a stroke the following year, triple-bypass heart surgery the year after that, and in the autumn of 1997 he fell and suffered a brain haemorrhage.

'I lost my very best friend two years ago,' Wimber told me in 1994. 'I've lost my mother and my father. I've lost colleagues. Heaven is becoming more and more attractive. I want to go and visit my friends.'

21

Seven ways to love

The Toronto Blessing looked like a vicarage tea party compared to what was going on in the black churches, which were growing fast. The congregations led and populated by people from Africa and the Caribbean had brought and held on to their own spectacular versions of Christianity, in which demons and angels flew and the Spirit knocked you over like a steam train and singing and praying and speaking in tongues could go on for hour after ecstatic hour, and all of it behind closed doors. Men and women were visible in their finery – the suits, the polished shoes, the tie-dyed fabrics and headdresses – on Sunday mornings in the cities, but nobody much outside their communities knew what went on when the services began. They thought they did, but that was mostly prejudice. The rest of the Church treated them like ignorant infants, to be indulged or ignored, but these people were here to stay. Their children would be English, and play a big part in changing what that meant, in time. First, it took a white man to get their faith noticed – and a loud, obnoxious white man at that.

Morris Cerullo was an American stadium evangelist who had been coming to Britain for years without receiving much attention, until the summer of 1992. That was when he put up posters on the London Underground making outrageous claims. One showed a wheelchair on its side. Another was a broken hearing aid. A third was a snapped white stick and a pair of discarded dark glasses with the words: 'Some will see miracles for the first time.' Londoners were offended, disability rights campaigners started spraying slogans over the posters, and the Advertising Standards Authority upheld a complaint. Cerullo's organisation announced that, according to its own survey, 56 per cent of people present at Earl's Court had received a miracle. That seemed remarkable, until you looked at the details. Only 9 per cent said their miracle was physical. The overwhelming majority, two-thirds, said it was simply in the form of 'a spiritual blessing'. That's not quite the same as getting out of a wheelchair to walk. Dr Peter May, a Christian GP from Southampton who was concerned about Cerullo and his team, said: 'They have been unable to verify one single miracle to my satisfaction. I think that "spiritual blessing" in this context needn't mean any more than that people enjoyed the show.'

The following year, I heard Morris Cerullo suggest from the stage at Earl's Court that people with Aids would be healed. 'How many of you believe God can heal Aids and HIV? Bring them on Saturday.' The guest preacher was Benny Hinn, an American in a dazzling white suit with a voice like Bela Lugosi's Dracula, who paced the stage with a microphone in his hand, telling us what God was whispering in his ear. 'There's a man here . . . the devil of Aids in breaking in your life . . . Another man with Aids is also being healed, a young man is being set free . . .' We were to take his word for it, apparently. People did. They whooped and cheered and applauded and shouted, 'Amen!' Hinn picked up steam, pacing faster, speaking more quickly, more urgently now: 'Somebody's ear has just popped open . . . Somebody's heart condition has just been healed . . . A woman with diabetes has just been healed . . . An alcoholic has just been set free. I give you praise, Jesus. The words of knowledge are coming so fast.'

Hinn was giving us the show we had been waiting for, over three soporific hours. We'd listened to various big-voiced American singers, and heard countless men in suits we didn't know say how much they loved and respected Morris Cerullo and appreciated his love of the Lord and his ministry. One turned out to be the Reverend Wynne Lewis, general superintendent of the Elim Pentecostal Church, who urged us all to support Cerullo's work and give until 'it frightens the flesh'. We were not to worry that there might be bills to pay next week. 'The flesh gets scared. It recoils at what is beyond reason. Reason can be open to satanic influence . . . I want you to make an offering that is substantial.'

After all that, here was Benny Hinn with the incantation of healings that God was telling him about, asking those who felt it was them he was describing to come up on the stage. 'Quickly, come up and tell me what's happened. Don't stay in your seat or you could lose your healing.' Up they went, too. Scores of them. Young people, old people. Someone who said she had come in a wheelchair but who now tottered across in front of Hinn. Someone who said her daughter was a deaf–mute, but seemed suddenly to be able to hear. Others who testified to a burning, numbing sensation in their bodies, like electricity, that had healed their asthma, their arthritis, their cancer. Just now. Just like that. Hinn pushed his palm against their foreheads or just waved his hand in front of their faces and they fell backwards instantly, almost all of them, apparently slain in the Spirit, into the arms of catchers who were waiting behind them. The bulky men who had shepherded them on stage caught them halfway towards the floor, helped them to their feet and showed them backstage. After a while, people were falling in threes and fours around the preacher, as Hinn spun around.

Then he stopped. He looked out at us all and said: 'If you want God to transform your life, you'd better get down here quick.' There was a stampede. Grannies with sharp elbows, mothers with massive backsides, bright-eyed little girls with pigtails flying, it was mostly women pushing past to get out of the rows of seats, down the aisles, down the stairs and near that stage. 'It feels like my right hand has been plugged into electricity: the Lord's anointing,' shouted Hinn. 'Touch them, Jesus!' He flung out his arm and it was like a wave of energy pulsing across the audience, pushing people backwards. An elderly woman went down right in front of me. I stood there, unmoved, as this reverse Mexican wave swept away to the other side of the auditorium. Had I missed some kind of cue?

The audiences were black. Almost exclusively, on the nights I was there. Thousands of believers came from all over London and the South of England to a series of events that provided a focus and a rallying point they had never had before. Cerullo's shows were not representative of the black churches, most of whose pastors were not making the same outrageous public claims or using the same aggressive advertising tactics. However, his meetings were to many new English Christians from Africa, Asia and the Caribbean what the Billy Graham rallies had been to the white English in the fifties: someone coming from outside, providing an inspiration and an encouragement and a place where they could be together and draw strength simply from how many of them were there. White commentators who talked about the 'new supernaturalism' were missing the point, at least in relation to Cerullo. This was about cultural identity. There was little new about waving and wailing and falling and laughing to people who had been brought up to worship God and fight the Devil in that way back home.

Ron Nathan, of the African Caribbean Evangelical Alliance, said the white church leadership didn't understand what was going on with Cerullo because his 'messages, style and format' were more compatible with 'our cultural heritage'. It wasn't that black people were more gullible, it was that Africans had a more holistic world view than Europeans and 'within black belief systems the natural world and the supernatural act in unison within the lives of ordinary people'. Spirituality was not a private affair but a public one, to be celebrated. Writing in the *Weekly Journal*, Nathan said the emotive approach taken by Cerullo, prompting ecstasy and tears and promising miracles, appealed to people who were used to that way of relating to God, but also explained why 'his name sticks in the craw of so many white Christians'.

Missionaries from this country had taken the faith to Africa and now, a century or so later, it was returning in a supercharged form to challenge the nature of Christianity here, uninhibited by the Enlightenment distinction between the material and spiritual worlds. Dr Kwabena Aasmoah-Gyadu, a theologian from Ghana, said the way Pentecostal Christians confronted the Devil was 'continuous with traditional religious ideas, in which evil is believed to be mystically caused'. In that context, it was natural that 'when evangelism takes place it often includes praying for the sick and casting out demons in order to affirm the power and viability of the message'.

Morris Cerullo's meetings appeared to offer living proof to those who sought it that Christians were deluded miracle chasers. On the other hand, they gave encouragement to people who had been rejected and misunderstood by established churches in this country. Their ease with emotions and willingness to admit the supernatural would influence the English in future, as they became more of a substantial presence and gave birth to children familiar with both cultures. But not yet. In the mid-nineties, black and white Christians were more or less divided. The popularity of Morris Cerullo – embraced by so many black believers, rejected by most whites – made that impossible to ignore.

The view of life as a spiritual battle between good and evil chimed, of course, with the view of Charismatics like Wimber and churches that followed him, whose leaders were praying for and expecting revival. Few of them saw Cerullo and his rallies as part of their God's plan, though. Was this because the people taking part were from a culture they viewed with suspicion and didn't understand? Probably. But it was also because Cerullo himself went way too far.

In the autumn of 1994 he began sending out a series of seven letters to his supporters, one a week. They promised seven miracles 'to break Satan's hold on your life'. The person who wanted those miracles had to do what Cerullo asked, seven times, but he warned: 'Partial obedience is disobedience.' The first request was for a 'family memorial offering' of £7 or £77, in return for which he promised to pray personally over the names or photographs of any loved ones that he received. The second letter warned that the Devil had 'set a special strategy to DESTROY you'. It asked for a 'gift of sacrifice', such as the money followers might have saved for a new refrigerator, car or holiday. This would apparently plant a seed for personal deliverance. 'Partner, the Devil will never, ever defeat you again.' In the third week, Cerullo asked each supporter to give him the equivalent of a day's earnings. In return they could have a vial of 'anointing oil' along with 'physical healing, supernatural strength, energy and divine health'. Each of the following three letters also included a request for money, and messages like 'Obey the Word of God's servant.' All this was in response to what Cerullo described as a satanic attack on his ministry, which had led to a debt of £2 million. 'God knows how this happened,' he wrote. 'This is not a financial problem – it is a spiritual battle against the enemy.' When I asked his public relations man for a quote, before reporting the fundraising campaign on the front page of the *Church Times,* he said the amount given in response to them had been 'very substantial'.

The advertising for the 1995 Mission to London was just as outrageous. One poster featured a boy with a football in his hands, standing over two discarded crutches, and the caption: 'They said I'd never stand on my own two feet. I did . . . at a Morris Cerullo mission.' These were stories from real life, apparently, of people who had experienced miracles and could back up the claims with affidavits and documentary evidence. But one was withdrawn before the campaign began, when the healing turned out to have been only partial. Then there was Sue. To be fair, she really did believe she had experienced a miracle. Unfortunately, as I found out when I spoke to her, it was the wrong miracle.

The poster was very clear about what had happened, and was obviously going to command the attention of all those caught up in the desperate business of trying to have a child (which, as it happened, included me). 'I couldn't have a baby,' said the headline over a photograph of a model mother and child, beaming with happiness. 'Miracles happen.' The second part was true, as far as Sue was concerned, but the poster missed the point, either mistakenly or in order to deceive. She took me by surprise with this announcement when I went to see her in Northampton, having been told by the Cerullo people that here was a proper, verifiable miracle.

Sue already had three children. Her husband, a security guard, was out of work. The last thing they were thinking about when she went to a Morris Cerullo meeting in 1993 was adding to the family. Her husband had just applied for a vasectomy. She had a cyst on one of her ovaries, but that was a side issue. The real problem was that doctors at her local hospital in Northampton had diagnosed a pulmonary embolism, or a blood clot on the lung. They gave her Warfarin to thin the blood and prevent more clots, and told her to avoid smoking, drinking alcohol or eating fatty foods. Under no circumstances was she to get pregnant, the doctors said. That was fine by Sue.

She went to Earl's Court as a believer, hoping for healing in her lungs, and did what she was told when members of the audience were instructed to put their hands on the part of the body where they needed God's help. 'Suddenly I felt a heat passing from my fingers into my chest and to my back,' she said. 'I thought I wasn't going to breathe again and I could feel burning inside me. The immense heat was coming over me and I was sweating and gasping for air. I thought I was going to have another attack. Then, suddenly, I knew I had been healed.' How did she know? 'I heard God say to me, "You've been healed. Claim your healing." It wasn't like I'm speaking to you now; it was deep within me. To tell you the truth, I was gobsmacked.'

Back home, she stopped taking the Warfarin, much to the irritation and dismay of her doctors: 'They said I was taking a big risk and I could drop down dead if this blood clot flew off and hit my heart.' Sue went back to work but was taken ill and rushed to hospital. After scans and blood tests a doctor came to tell her the good news. There was no sign of the pulmonary embolism. The bad news was that she was, somehow, pregnant.

It could be fatal, the doctor said. She ought to think about abortion, because if she didn't die then the drugs she had taken could leave the baby seriously deformed. She refused. 'The doctor hit the roof. He thought I was being very stupid.' Nevertheless, a healthy daughter was born in March 1994. The clots had gone. When I met her she was waiting for the doctor to put down in writing what had happened, and said she would send me a copy. I left her terraced house in Northampton wondering what had happened. No letter ever arrived. Perhaps the doctor wrote one, but Sue just forgot to send it on to me.

On the doorstep, she told me what she thought of the people who had devised the Cerullo poster. 'I was quite angry. They had pumped it up. I said, "This is wrong. Very wrong."'

Morris Cerullo was an easy target. A short guy with suspiciously dark hair and a squawky voice who always dressed immaculately and habitually referred to himself in the third person, he had a public image that was somewhere between a showman preacher, a quack-remedy salesman and a pantomime villain. I met him on neutral ground, at a hotel, after waiting around with the suited, stone-faced men of his entourage. Close up, he seemed even more like a living caricature. Did he regret the decision to be so bold in his advertising? 'I don't know. It gave us incredible opportunity to witness. I could have been twenty-four hours a day on television, radio, everywhere.' That was true. For a while, Cerullo had been the face of Christianity in this country, if a highly unattractive one. He made me wish I was an atheist. 'The positive part was that it shook the nation: it made people more aware of the message of healing than ever before. The negative was that "Some will hear for the first time" was taken to mean that some will hear physically.'

Was he really surprised by that? With all those pictures of overturned wheelchairs and discarded canes? 'Oh, of course.' Was it all a trick then, to get people into the meetings? 'I'm not the advertising people, I didn't develop the campaign.' He laughed but he had approved it, I supposed. He had still not provided a single enduring healing in this country that could be verified by doctors. 'But that's not true. We have. We can present dozens of them. But the problem is that you present them to a group of doctors who are incredibly . . .' Suddenly, he swerved away from confrontation. 'Er, I don't call them sceptical, I just do not engage in the discussion, because Jesus didn't. What He did was constantly under attack, but He let the works speak for themselves.'

Cerullo promised miracles, but when challenged he defined them in a way that was wide beyond reason. A miracle was 'something that cannot happen by human beings. Whether it be the transformation of a life, the change of a mental attitude, a physical act or sins being forgiven.' A change of mental attitude? So, if you went into a bar, ordered a beer and changed your mind, made it a Babycham, was that a miracle in Cerullo's mind? No wonder so many of his people claimed to have experienced them.

He was sixty-four when we met, but there was no prospect of him retiring. God had told him to reach a billion souls by the end of the century. 'Morris is called to the world. You understand what a burden that is?' Barely. Not at all, actually. I asked if he realised he was more appealing to some cultures than others. 'I would say that is fair.' He blamed the leaders, saying that if they got behind him, 'we would have as many people from the Church of England out there as we do blacks and as we do Asians'. Why did he think they didn't like him? 'I don't think they understand me. The communication, for some reason . . . and the style.'

The tone of the fundraising letters had been wrong for this country, he admitted. They would be different in future. 'With the fury . . . with what you, yourself, are expressing, that's enough for us to say: "Look, where are we? Let's try to understand, Cole, in the light of what God is telling us to do."' It was just a question of presentation, then; there was nothing fundamentally wrong with the methods? 'Absolutely.' He challenged

me to come up with a moment in his meetings when an offering had been taken inappropriately, so I told him about the leader
who had urged us all to 'give until it frightens your flesh'. If he
had been on stage at the time he would have corrected that, he
said. Then he laughed. 'I take my challenge back.'

He told me he was trying to be reasonable. He was trying to
be transparent. People misunderstood him. The money he raised
went straight to the ministry. 'We publish accounts. We publish
'em with the IRS.' Could I see those accounts? 'Sure. Absolutely.
You'd be shocked at the deficit.' The figures would be sent to me,
he said, then he rose and swept from the room with his
entourage, this man who seemed so unlikeable and yet whose
huge meetings were inadvertently providing a rallying point for
the beginning of a new kind of Englishness.

The accounts never came, of course. If either they or the letter
from Sue's doctor had ever arrived, it would have felt like a miracle.

22

Goodbye, England's rose

The Princess died. You knew that, of course. There could be no happy ending. The details of her death have become so familiar: the high-speed chase through the streets of Paris; the photographers on scooters, zigzagging behind; the drunk driver; the loving couple in the back of the Mercedes, not wearing seat belts. Diana, not royal any more but seemingly happier, stronger and more sure of the power of her image than ever before; and Dodi Fayed, the playboy, possibly reformed. The Muslim. You know all about the conspiracy theories: how Diana was pregnant, how MI6 was ordered to kill her, how the Establishment could not bear to see the mother of the future King in love with a person of another faith, how angels bore her up to heaven to sit alongside Jesus and Mary and so on and so on, and all the nonsense, all the sound and fury that smother the reality of a chauffeur high on adrenaline and drink driving into an underpass at nearly one hundred miles an hour and hitting a concrete post.

We woke to solemn music where there should have been voices. The radio woke us to unbelief on that Sunday morning in August 1997, and on the television there was a report that seemed like a bad dream: a doctor opening his mouth and closing it, gulping like a fish, telling the presenter how the medics wriggling into the twisted wreck of the car might have cut open the Princess's chest and reached in to hold her heart in one hand and squeeze, manipulating the organ to keep it going. They went to an ad break. When we were taken back to the studio, the doctor had gone. We didn't want that sort of thing. We wanted the beautiful face, the cornflower eyes, the seductive smile, the images of her in a flak jacket in an Angolan minefield looking so damned sexy. Never more so. We wanted fantasy. The fairytale, one last time.

We got it. Farewell Princess of Wales, hello St Diana. The canonisation began almost immediately. The flowers and cards and votive candles started to appear by the gates of Kensington Palace that Sunday morning. Tony Blair was fast, the new Prime Minister was slick, he was at the height of his powers, on his way to church in his constituency, wearing a black tie, pausing in the churchyard to speak to the cameras, his hands clasped, his head tilted. 'She touched the lives of so many . . . People kept faith with Princess Diana. They liked her, they loved her, they regarded her as one of the people. She was the People's Princess, and that is how she will stay.' The faraway look, the hesitant, sincere voice, the magical phrase. Tony Blair was the father of the nation that morning, the shaman, the witch doctor, the Archbishop of Canterbury, the tribal elder, the man in tune with the national soul.

He had arrived on a landslide at a time when we had lost faith in authority figures, and in the beliefs they claimed to represent, as one by one they had let us down with their vanities, their greed, their lies and distortions. Blair seemed to be different, a source of hope. There was relief, and more than a little euphoria, that someone so young, modern and apparently highly principled had swept away the exhausted and sleazy Major regime. He promised to bring official life more into line with the way we actually lived, and he had plans for reforms that would make Britain better. There would be more money for schools and hospitals, and more doctors and nurses; there would be devolution for Scotland and Wales and self-governing peace at last for Northern Ireland; there would be new laws to strengthen human rights, race relations and freedom of information; there would be a lifting of the ban on gays and lesbians in the military and the introduction of civil partnerships. All this would reflect the desire for a less rigid, more inclusive society, shrugging off the straitjacket of Establishment England.

But those who believed in Blair would also have to face the inevitable, crushing disappointment when he turned out to be as flawed as he had seemed perfect. Could they have known he would fall under the prayerful spell of a White House fundamentalist and go to war on a lie, discrediting both his country and his faith? Did he look like a new crusader, prepared to smite the heathen? No. He looked like the straight kinda guy he said he was, all teeth and charm and sincerity. Particularly that morning, as he channelled the spirit of Diana, the arch communicator. While archbishops and monarchs floundered, unable to understand or match the feeling of their people, the Prime Minister was pitch perfect. He pulled off the trick that Diana had learned and the Queen had forgotten: that of acting as a magical mirror to society, showing us what we thought was best about ourselves.

Diana's skill at doing so had grown along with her distance from the royal family and her freedom to do things that people like her had never done before. She had been way ahead of the general ignorance and fear when she shook the hand of a man with Aids in 1987, and when she later picked up a baby with the disease in Harlem and gave it a cuddle. Away from the cameras, there were private visits to refuges for women who had been victims of abuse, to hospital wards for the terminally ill and to hostels for the homeless. One of the early tributes to be laid at the gates of her palace was a plaque made by a security guard called Vincent, aged twenty-seven, who had been sleeping in a doorway in central London when he met Diana. She saved his life, he had written:

> I was homeless. You came to me and asked how long I had been on the streets. You then went and got me something to eat and drink. It was very cold and wet on that night. The next time I saw you, I remember you saying, 'I will get you somewhere to live.' And you did. You asked me about my life and I told you about the abuse I went through when I was a kid, and I could see you had tears in your eyes. You have a very caring heart, and I will never forget you. Love from Vincent.

For acts like that, she was forgiven her trespasses. Her fans were blind to the wealth, the extravagance, the indiscreet lovers, the yachts and the £6000-a-night room at the Ritz where she had spent her last evening. They somehow saw her as ordinary. One of them. If she was fame-hungry, manipulative and unstable, she was also visibly more open, more accepting and more demonstrative than any member of the family that had rejected her. The BBC broadcaster George Alagiah, born in Sri Lanka and raised in Ghana, said after her death that she had been the first member of the Establishment to shake the hand of a black person – or even give them a hug – and not look like she wanted to take a shower immediately afterwards. In death, even more clearly than in life, she challenged the assumptions and behaviour of the royal family. Andrew Morton, the biographer with whom Diana had secretly collaborated, wrote: 'Those few days after her death captured for ever the contrast between the Princess and the House of Windsor: her openness, their distance; her affection, their frigidity; her spontaneity, their inflexibility; her glamour, their dullness; her modernity, their stale ritual; her emotional generosity, their aloofness; her rainbow coalition, their court of aristocrats.' His view was biased and sentimental, but it was also widely held that week. The newspapers promoted it, beginning with concern at the way in which the Queen treated Diana's sons.

Up in Balmoral, in splendid Highland isolation, they were woken at seven in the morning and told the terrible news. Harry asked if there had been a mistake. Then, astonishingly, the whole family went off to church and took part in a service in which no mention was made of what had happened and no prayers were said for Diana, whose name was not even spoken. William and Harry, aged fifteen and twelve, had been offered the chance to stay behind, but they had not wanted to be left alone. There seems to have been no suggestion that their father or grand-mother might remain with them. We cannot know the reason why Charles allowed that to happen, or the pressure he was under, and we can only assume that he was trying to do the best for his sons, but to make them sit there and stare at the altar or mouth the words of hymns that must have turned to dust in their mouths, while people stared and the cameras waited outside, just seemed inhuman. It still does.

Much has been made of the Queen's refusal to go down to London in the next few days, as the crowds and the floral mounds kept growing. In a biography informed by confidential interviews with palace staff, Ben Pimlott says that the Queen was 'caught between the private and the public' and her response was 'to fall back on what had always been her defence in times of stress: rou-tine and protocol. There should be no departure from how things had always been, no abandonment of custom.' So there was no personal statement (Diana no longer being a member of the royal family, since her banishment), no flag at half mast at Buckingham Palace (which really outraged the tabloids), and the Queen stayed at Balmoral, keeping the boys safe. 'The royal family were like rabbits in the glare of a headlight,' one former aide told Pimlott. 'The family had no conceivable idea of how the whole thing was being perceived.' Another courtier said the Queen refused to see why a century of tradition should be overturned: 'They thought they knew the British public, thought they had a rapport with it, but that had suddenly deserted them.' The monarch got it wrong, and for a few days people who would never have called themselves republicans displayed real anger and revolt. It was stoked up by the press, of course, but the Windsors had played that game themselves and knew what power there was in a front page, so it must have been chilling to read the *Sun*'s demand: 'Where is the Queen when the country needs her?'

She got away with it, just in time, by finally coming down to London, flying the flag, walking among the tributes and showing herself to the people at the gates, before making a live broadcast on the *Six O'clock News*. The dignity and precision of the state elements of the funeral helped too, demonstrating once again that Establishment England could still put on a show. Unexpected support came from Ian Hislop, the editor of the satirical magazine *Private Eye*:

You couldn't make it up. Here were people kicking the paparazzi on the one hand, and on the other lining up in their thousands to take pictures of the coffin with their Instamatics. Here were people tut-tutting about invasions of privacy on the one hand, and on the other demanding that the royal family line up and weep for the TV cameras. There was just so much rubbish, so much brain-out-of-window stuff, written and spoken. We kept being told that the crowds showed how

> Britain had changed, no more stiff upper lip, we were all hug-
> gers and weepers now. But how could that be when the most
> impressive thing about the funeral was two boys walking
> behind their mother's coffin and not crying?

Actually, both things were true. We *had* changed – there were
open displays of emotion on an unprecedented scale, but also dignity and restraint. As people waited to lay down flowers or sign
books of condolence, they did what the English do better than
anyone else: they formed a nice, orderly queue. Then, when the
funeral cortège emerged from the gates of Kensington Palace,
there were shrieks and wails from one or two women, but otherwise nothing. Silence. Respectful, sorrowful silence
maintained all the way along the four-mile route. The sounds
were from the muffled bell of Westminster Abbey, tolling every
sixty seconds, and the six horses of the King's Troop of the Royal
Artillery, hooves clopping and bridles jangling as they pulled a
gun carriage. The coffin it was carrying was draped in a Royal
Standard, on top of which lay three white wreaths: one from her
brother, Earl Spencer, and one each from her sons, Harry and
William. The cameras zoomed in on the card that was attached
to the front wreath and focused on a single, jolting word:
'Mummy'. The Queen showed herself still capable of powerful
symbolism when she led her family down to stand outside the
gates of Buckingham Palace to see the cortège pass, and bowed
her head. It was brief, but significant, the sovereign acknowledging the power of a woman she had made a commoner.

William and Harry walked behind the coffin for part of the
way, heads bowed for most of the time, between their grandfather, their father and their uncle. The funeral service to which
they walked was, in the words of a palace statement, 'a unique
service for a unique person'. The guests included heads of state

but also fashion designers, television presenters, and performers such as Tom Cruise and Luciano Pavarotti, who entered on the arms of two beautiful young women. The Archbishop of Canterbury was, for once, ideally suited to his part in it, with his comfortingly common voice. He wore simple robes, and left his head bare. This was not a state occasion, and the modesty suited it. The service lurched from formal to informal, from epic to inane. When the choir sang a piece of magnificent intensity by John Tavener, 'Song for Athene', it was as if distressed angels were clinging to the walls of the cathedral. The Queen looked as if she wanted to do the same when Elton John sang his rewritten version of 'Candle in the Wind', a song originally about Marilyn Monroe, in that deep, fake American voice: 'Now you belong to heaven/And the stars spell out your name.' If that was cheesy, Tony Blair's amateur dramatics during his reading from Corinthians were worse. Then Earl Spencer took to the pulpit . . . and nailed the Windsors to the floor. Diana was 'someone with natural nobility who was classless and who proved in the last year that she needed no royal title to continue to generate her particular brand of magic'. That was rich, coming from a member of a family that had served royalty for centuries, but it was overlooked in the acclaim for a great speech.

The applause began outside, among the people, as it had on her wedding day, when that medieval response had made Charles smile. 'I thought it was raining,' said the Dean of Westminster, 'then I looked out at the sky and saw that it was blue.' The doors of the cathedral had been left open on his instruction, so that the people outside could feel part of what was going on. Now their applause rushed in like the Holy Ghost at a revival meeting, slapping together the hands of people who did not feel they could resist, including William and Harry. It stopped when it got to the Queen.

There were 2.5 billion people watching on television, able to see her cold expression in close up. They were also seeing something new – a funeral service that was both liturgical and sentimental, formal and intimate, a clash of cultures that worked because of the depth of feeling for the person who had died and which would turn out to be one of the most enduring things Diana left to the nation. Its echo can be heard in every parish church and crematorium, whenever the bereaved ask a professional to lead them, then slip in a poem or two and a pop song. ('Er, we're thinking "Angels" by Robbie Williams. Mum loved that.') Diana's funeral was not the first of what sociologists call 'mixed economy funerals', but it was the most widely seen, and it was copied. The loosening up of the service was part of the drift away from having a religious send-off at all.

There was one last twist. The guardsmen who carried the coffin did not know how to react to it, and nor did the funeral directors who drove the black Daimler Sovereign hearse slowly through London towards the motorway. They were heading for her final resting place, her family's ancestral home, Althorp in Northamptonshire, where she would be buried on an island in the middle of a lake like the mythical princess she had become. But they had only just left the cathedral when something strange happened. 'The whole crowd started throwing flowers,' said Major Richard Williams, in command of the pall-bearers. 'We really weren't expecting that.' Nobody was. It had not been done before on an occasion like this, as far as anybody could remember. But that was a very selective, very English, very Establishment memory. Because it had been seen before, at funerals in other countries, and the tradition went as far back as humanity: the Romans threw flowers at the dead, the Greeks garlanded them, the Egyptians piled blooms on the corpse. It was ancient, but it was new here in this place in modern times. You could blame it on Elton John for singing about England's rose in such a direct way, or you could compare it with the palms thrown under the feet of the donkey as Christ made His way into Jerusalem. You could evoke the Celtic, pagan tradition of using flowers to ward off evil spirits or bless the dead so that they would not return to haunt the living. Or you could say that people did it because they had flowers to hand, they had bought them and they wanted to be close to her and they wanted to throw them so they did, into the air, on to the roof and the bonnet of the slow-moving Daimler as it passed through the large crowds that lined the roads all the way up to the M1. There, the hearse stopped. Five police outriders were in front, in a line, waiting with their blue lights flashing. Another limousine and a police car were behind. The protection officer sitting in the front of the hearse got out and pulled the flowers from the windscreen, from the wipers, from the hot metal over the engine. There were arm-fuls. He took them across to the hard shoulder and laid them on the ground, watched by the cameras and the crowds who were still there, precarious on the flyovers and bridges. The drivers that were coming south, on the other side of the motorway, stopped in the fast lane to show their respect.

Did we go mad for a while? The flowers, the candles, the pic-tures, the prayers, the weeping in the streets – were these all symptoms of a mass hysteria, as some people said? 'It was like the Nuremberg rallies,' said one who visited the palace gates. Another described it as 'floral fascism'. But that was not what it was really like, to walk among the million bouquets, read the cards and listen in on conversations, in the hot days when the scent of the mulching flowers was heavy; and in the cold nights, when people sat on the grass in the nearby parks, talking quietly, their faces lit by thousands of tiny candles. Andrew Marr, wandering around out of curiosity, as many of us did, saw the pictures hanging in the trees of Kensington Gardens, the candles and the quiet, reflective crowds, and said the place had become 'an outdoor cathedral, its congregation led by no one but themselves'.

Suzanne Moore, not a sentimentalist, wrote: 'I saw dignity and though I saw tears being shed and shed my own, people were not overwhelmed by their feelings but quietly in control of them.' Popular culture had been going this way for years, moving towards 'the subjective, the confessional, the unashamedly emotional' and the official culture of England would have to catch up. David Dimbleby, preparing to narrate coverage of the funeral, wrote: 'I never detected any note of hysteria. My abiding impression was of private grief, thoughtful and articulate . . . as a country we have changed, and Diana's life seems to embody that change. It is no longer thought unmanly for the stiff upper lip to tremble.'

The change did not begin with the death of the Princess of Wales, whatever anyone said. We had seen young men break down and cry before, and crowds gather to make a shrine of flowers, candles and pictures, after Hillsborough. That kind of mourning was repeated in Kensington on a mammoth scale, adopted by hundreds of thousands of people. Some said again that it was an Irish or a Catholic thing, this desire for ritual, for spectacle, and for a collective display of emotion. Perhaps so. The English were Catholics for a thousand years before the Protestant revolution imposed new habits, new ways of seeing the world, new standards of behaviour. The cult of the stiff upper lip was a more recent imposition, a tool of empire promoted by the Victorians and now, after a century or so, apparently being discarded. Perhaps the old ways had only lain dormant, preserved in the working-class Catholic communities of cities such as Liverpool, and were emerging and spreading again, now that the Church of England was in disarray and the God of the Establishment had loosened His grip. Or maybe it was, as others said, a Mediterranean thing, or a Latin thing, or an Asian thing, or something we had picked up from the Caribbean or Africa. Or all of them. All of those cultures were represented among the people who gathered at the gates and in the parks. On her wedding day in 1981, Diana had attracted half a million people on to the streets, almost all of them white. On the day of her funeral, there were three million people along the route and they showed a nation transformed. As the man said, 'a crowd of a different complexion'.

The census of 1991 had recorded three million people who saw themselves as coming from an ethnic minority group. The figure was now approaching five million. The biggest increases were among people from India and Pakistan, as well as the arrival of half a million from Africa, with more to follow. Down in Kensington Gardens, Andrew Marr found black and Asian faces alongside white, gay people alongside straight, middle-aged women with 'tissues balled up into their sleeves' alongside 'the young, tattooed and pierced, who somehow felt Diana, cast out of the royal house, spoke for them' And he wrote, a year later: 'Britain suddenly stared at itself in the mirror and didn't quite recognise the face looking back. No longer was the expression tight lipped, white and drawn with reticence. Diana was the Queen of another country, a multicultural, liberal and emotionally open Britain.'

One of the most memorable photographs of the week was of a man lying on his side on the ground, almost prostrating himself before the flowers and the image of the blonde, blue-eyed Princess. He was big, he was black, he was dressed in what looked like African clothes and he was bawling his eyes out. The image was reproduced in the *Daily Mail*. Some people said this behaviour just wasn't English, just wasn't 'us'. In truth – like it or not – a new England was emerging. There was a new 'us'.

The English God, in the sense of the old, rigid, Establishment figure with a cricket bat in one hand and the Thirty-Nine Articles in the other, had failed us. He had been up there in Balmoral with the Queen, whispering into her ear that what was needed now was discipline, decorum, routine. That was not what the majority of people outside the castle wanted; it was not how we now understood our lives or how we wanted to behave in reaction to this premature death. If Diana were going to be canonised, it would be as a saint of a very different kind of religion, a popular, postmodern spirituality in which every creed was as good as any other. You could take a little from here, a little from there, to make up your own. She was the patron saint of everyone who felt their personal belief system was not taken seriously enough: whether they went in for reading the Tarot or the stars, attending healing services or séances, she had tried it too. People were having visions of her, shimmering in the air, while they waited in line to sign a book of condolence that she would never read. They were tying pictures to the trees that showed her surrounded by cherubs or angels with fluffy wings, or praying for us all beside the Throne of Glory. George Michael, the singer who was a guest at the funeral, said: 'I truly believe that some souls are too special, too beautiful to be kept from heaven.' His words are easily dismissed as sentimental tosh, but the reactions to Diana's funeral suggested he was expressing a widely held folk belief, a loose, inclusive idea of divine justice that would send a shiver down the spine of Dr Billy Graham but said that God was love, and a loving God would surely not deny everlasting life to someone so 'beautiful'. By which I think he meant in thought and deed, rather than physical appearance, which would be breathtakingly shallow.

Diana was at peace, people kept saying. No harm could come to her now. 'You will be carried to heaven on the wings of a million angels,' said one card. Jesus didn't get much of a mention, except in His most inoffensive form, as a baby. Lying there on the pavements outside the palace, the flowers and tributes were a heady, colourful, richly sentimental sign of the new majority faith of this fledgling England. What was it like? Full of contradictions, shot through with common sense and superstition, loving beauty and celebrity, but hating people who were too big for their boots. It was both male and female, but its iconography could be summed up in one, unexpected word: motherhood. This folk faith was culturally post-Christian and essentially English: it still cherished fair play and had a strong sense of justice – both of which were deemed to have been violated by the way the Princess had been treated by the Windsors, and by her unjustly early death – and it still valued restraint, as the behaviour of the crowds proved. Above all, though, it was inclusive. Caring. Religious tolerance had been part of the English way since the first break with Rome, and although it had got a bit lost at times, live and let live was still the abiding principle: do as you would be done by.

Diana was perfectly placed to be the first saint of this new – or very old – feminised faith. At the Hindu temple in Neasden they spent the day before her funeral singing devotional songs for her soul. The Chief Rabbi did not go to her service because it was on the Jewish Sabbath, but equivalent prayers were said at synagogues. She had been married as an Anglican, her mother was a serious convert to Catholicism, she was in love with a Muslim, she believed in reincarnation, and she went to the grave clutching a rosary. Perfect. Even in death, Diana was for everyone. She was anything you wanted her to be.

The idea of this flawed Sloane as a saint didn't last long, but it would be a mistake to say that the faith she inadvertently represented, and which turned out for her on the streets that summer, failed. Consider the population of England, which at the last official estimate in 2009 was 51 million. The surveys suggest that about 33 million of those people believe in God or a higher power. Now take away all those who belong to a distinct faith, including the Muslims, the Hindus and all the Christian regular churchgoers. That leaves about 26 million people who believe, in their own way, but do not belong. They like it that way. I'm not saying they are all the sort of people who laid tributes and wept in the street for Diana, not at all, but I am saying that those were among the first public manifestations of a new, looser, wider way of relating to God that would soon replace Establishment Christianity as the dominant form of faith in this country. It was growing beyond the control of those who saw themselves as keepers of the truth, beyond the boundaries set by archbishops or cardinals, pastors or imams; beyond the formal creeds over which so much blood had been shed; beyond such inconveniences as actually going to church. The English God began to evolve during those intense days in the summer of 1997, to become a more generous, more feminine, more compassionate deity with His – and Her – arms flung wide open to everyone.

Her Majesty changed, too. The Queen said she believed there were 'lessons to be drawn' from Diana's life. Why else would she have taken steps to appear more like the common people in the coming years, cutting back on her spending, visiting McDonald's, even unexpectedly dropping in for a cup of tea in a Glasgow council house? The idea of presenting her family as a model to us all, the best of British, an icon of discipline, duty and faith, had been abandoned because of the behaviour of her sons and daughters, who had made it look ridiculous. The Queen floundered for a while, but found her feet again after the death of her mother in 2002. The Queen Mother had been liked and respected for her wartime resilience and her longevity – as well as her fabled liking for a drop of gin – but her passing made things much easier for her daughter. It gave the younger Elizabeth space to assume the role of national grandmother, whose ways were a bit fuddy-duddy, but hey, that's what grannies are like, isn't it?

The change in her status eased the pressure on Charles, whose reputation was repaired by some skilful public relations work so that he was able to marry Camilla quietly and go on meddling ineffectually in environmental and architectural affairs. The Queen becoming the national granny also helped the boys. Harry's attendance of a fancy-dress party in a Nazi uniform was shocking, but it did not do the damage it would have done a generation earlier. It was more that people felt offended on behalf of his grandmother and her peers. Later, there was pride by proxy at seeing the two young princes get their acts together and make themselves useful, in both charity work and genuinely dangerous service in the military. That was nice for Granny. In 2009 Prince William spoke of becoming more than an ornament 'shaking hands and so on' and said he wanted to make a genuine, demonstrable contribution to society through a newly formed coalition of charities. The Queen may have felt slighted by this implicit public criticism of her style, but she must have known he was the best hope for the future. A modern, informal chap, with his mother's charm, but his grandmother's steel and sense of duty.

When she dies, there will be tributes to the serious, devoted way in which Queen Elizabeth has gone about her job. There will also be questions about whether her son is fit to take her place, just as in any family business. The old-fashioned way of being king or queen – as a model of faith and duty beyond reproach, embodying all that is best about the nation and acting as the head of a single, unified, Christian culture – is gone. Elizabeth did her best to keep it alive, but it's dead. We just don't say so yet, out of respect. It's a bit like a wedding reception: we're content to let Granny sit in the corner, a comforting but irrelevant presence, still holding on to her quaint old views about God and identity while the young people dance to their own tunes, ignoring her.

23

You're gonna reap just
what you sow

The news cameras saw it all: the short, white man to the left, the slightly taller black man to the right, as one tried to cast out demons from the other. 'I deliver you in the name of Jesus,' boomed the Right Reverend Emmanuel Chukwuma, from Nigeria, raising his right hand to bring it down on the other man's head. 'Father, I pray that you deliver him out of homo sexuality, in the name of Jesus.'

The Bishop's hand never reached the forehead of Richard Kirker, leader of the Lesbian and Gay Christian Movement, who put up his own right hand to meet it. For a moment, the two were caught in a semi-embrace, toe to toe before the cameras, their dipped foreheads almost touching, their hands clasped together in the air. The fingers of the Bishop closed around those of his opponent, as if urging a friend to be strong. He wasn't.

'Father, I pray that you make him a devout Christian, in the name of Jesus,' barked Bishop Chukwuma, elongating the two syllables in the name of his Lord: 'Jee-zuss!' The pectoral cross swung on a heavy silver chain across his belly, over his black-and-white-striped waistcoat and purple episcopal shirt. 'Father, I deliver him out of homosexuality!' he yelled, sweating in the sunshine, staring at his opponent through bottle-bottom glasses. 'Out of gay! Because gay is not a Christian, in the name of Jesus! Hallelujah! Hallelujah! Hallelujah!'

Richard Kirker realised he had no chance to put his case, so he just stood there in his checked, short-sleeved shirt, his hand still raised to prevent the Bishop's attempted exorcism, and said, repeatedly: 'Thank you.'

This had all started with an attempt to start a discussion, in front of the media, on the lawn outside the Kent campus buildings where all the Anglican bishops of the world were meeting, in the summer of 1998. Kirker, a priest turned activist, told Chukwuma he believed God created everybody – black and white, homosexual and heterosexual – equal in His sight. 'No, no' was the reply. 'No!' Kirker said that to say otherwise would imply that God had made a mistake, and that would be blasphemous. 'How can God make a mistake?' boomed the Bishop. 'You made a mistake by turning yourself into a homosexual.' Now it was Kirker's turn to raise his voice, becoming shrill: 'There was no button I pressed!' This was a confrontation for the cameras between two opposing sides in an argument that would finish off all pretence of unity within the Church of England and its affiliates.

The worldwide Anglican communion, as they call it, claims to include seventy million people. The Archbishop of Canterbury is the spiritual head of the established English Church, but also fulfils the same role for Anglicans in America, Australia, Latin America, Africa and elsewhere, and all of them have differing views on what the Bible says. Every ten years this intercontinental dysfunctional family sends its bishops to a gathering known as the Lambeth Conference. It is held in Kent, obviously. The reasons are too boring to go into here, as is the history of the conference, but this time it was big news. This time there was going to be a fight, or at least a lot of bishops having a heated row and being rude to each other. The communion had held together for a century because of mutual respect and tolerance, but now it was beginning to fall apart.

George Carey had reacted to his domestic troubles by doing what beleaguered leaders often do – seeking to portray himself as a world statesman. The essential reality was – and still is – that among Anglicans the English had delusions of authority, the North Americans had money, and the Africans had all the people. The Archbishop of Nigeria could claim to represent seventeen million, and those were proper members, not default ticks on a census form. Lambeth in 1998 was the moment for their voices to be heard, the issue was homosexuality, and the faith that shouted loudest was a supercharged version of the one imposed on the people of Africa by missionaries. The sending churches had grown more moderate back at home, but now they were reaping what they had sown. With the support of American conservatives, battling against progressives in their own country, the Africans managed to get the conference to pass a resolution banning same-sex unions and gay priests.

Bishop Chukwuma may have looked like a ranting extremist, but his reading of the Bible was not that different to the one held by English Evangelicals. Up in Watford that summer, a man called Jeremy Marks was running a residential course with the aim of putting gays in at one end and pulling out straights at the other. The Courage Trust was affiliated to one of the leading Anglican churches influenced by John Wimber's teaching and it offered escape from 'the dark cloud of homosexuality'. The seven men who were on the course when I visited lived in a pair of semi-detached Edwardian homes, and their lives were as strictly governed as they would have been in a drug or alcohol detox unit.

They ate meals together, shared bedrooms and attended three evening sessions a week. Church on Sundays was compulsory. Holidays were not allowed. Guests could visit but the bedroom door had to be open at all times. The television had to be off and all the residents indoors by 10.30 p.m. These were grown men, don't forget. They were not allowed to go to London on their own as it was 'a stronghold of Satan where temptation to engage in homosexual activity is likely to be strong'.

The leader of the course, Marks, was a photographer who had once been gay, he said, but struggled with the feeling that it was 'an abomination to God'. He was now married, and claimed his gayness had been caused by 'deep unmet emotional needs' in childhood which had now been satisfied through prayer, counselling and finding some safe, same-sex friendships. 'I don't really believe there is such a thing as a true homosexual,' he told me. 'It's a name we give to an arrested development, or an immature emotional state, where we've got stuck at that phase when we need male or same-sex role models.'

Down at the Lesbian and Gay Christian Movement's offices in Bethnal Green, Richard Kirker was appalled that homosexuality was being equated with the kind of addiction that drove alcoholics. 'No amount of getting on your knees and praying is going to turn a homosexual into a heterosexual.' Kirker was right, as Jeremy Marks later acknowledged. Astonishingly and bravely, in 2001, after reading the Bible again and listening to the Holy Spirit, the man who had claimed to be able to turn gays straight suddenly admitted that his theories were ineffective. More than that, he had been morally wrong. Against the wishes and protests of his supporters, Marks changed his whole approach, and Courage began again as a charity in support of men who were both Christian and gay. 'We have come to recognise that God supports and blesses sincere committed relationships between gay people,' he said. It was a remarkable u-turn, which earned him enemies. Even now, courses are being run by Evangelicals in London and elsewhere that claim to be able to offer a cure for homosexuality.

The traditional teaching of the Church has a terrible clarity about it. The only place for sex is within marriage. That's it, full stop. Christian men and women have to wait until after the wedding. Except they don't, of course, because these days even hardline vicars turn a blind eye to premarital sex. They have no choice, if they want to be heard in a society that has decided it is perfectly all right to cohabit. But Christian men and women attracted to people of the same sex can wait until hell freezes over, because they can't have sex before they get married and they can't get married, so if they want to be faithful, godly human beings, they must deny all fleshly desire, for ever. That is a very demanding thing to ask. How many heterosexual priests can honestly say they would be prepared to give up the intimacy and sustaining pleasure of sex for the whole of their lives, for the sake of their faith?

Catholic priests do it, of course, and the majority keep their vow in a lifelong, sacrificial way – but we have seen how difficult some of them find it, and how attracted to housekeepers and altar boys they become. Importantly, they have made the choice to be celibate as a result of their calling. Christians who are born gay or lesbian do not get to make that choice. Vicars kiss their wives and hug their children and leave their happy homes on a Sunday morning to climb into their pulpits and tell the homosexuals sitting – usually secretly – in their congregations that as far as God is concerned it would be an abominable sin for them to lie down with someone they love. Finding a lifelong companion and lover of the sort that the vicar probably takes for granted is totally out of the question. Being gay or lesbian in a church that takes the traditional line means being condemned to a lonely life of involuntary celibacy. Or you could lie.

This issue, more than any other, shows how much the English and their Church have grown apart. For centuries, sodomy was punishable by death. You could be hanged for it, until the Victorians changed the law. Even when homosexual acts were decriminalised in 1967, it was only if they took place in private between consenting adults of twenty-one years old or more. The Archbishop of Canterbury, Geoffrey Fisher, was in favour of this move. 'There is a sacred realm of privacy for every man and woman where he makes his choices and decisions – a realm of his own essential rights and liberties into which the law, generally speaking, must not intrude.' That was an attitude the Church held for a long time. Gay men were ordained but kept their sexuality to themselves, and the brotherhood of the clergy was sometimes a more supportive place than the rest of society. Call it hypocrisy, call it evasion, but the rule was: don't ask and you won't have to deal with it. It held for just as long as the same hypocrisy, the same evasion, was going on elsewhere in society.

That was certainly the case when our story began, back at the time of the royal wedding in 1981. Homosexuality was legal but widely disapproved of, except for comedy value. John Inman was good for a laugh but real queers kept their sexuality out of sight for fear of a beating. Then came Aids, the so-called gay plague, and the situation grew even worse: blame and demonisation followed. There were a few noble exceptions, but on the whole the Church did not speak out against this persecution. Sometimes it participated. Christian campaign groups supported Section 28, the clause in local government law that stopped schools 'promoting' homosexuality – which meant teachers were forbidden from telling teenage pupils who were already sexually active how to stay safe at a time of hysteria. Conservative believers who had hated the liberal bishops for taking on Thatcher over the miners' strike poured all their strength into fighting over what they saw as bedrock issues of personal morality, such as abortion and gay rights.

Elsewhere, slowly, attitudes changed. The notion that people were born gay, no more able to choose their sexuality than to choose the colour of their eyes, became accepted wisdom. Psychologists had believed it since the early seventies, but, surprisingly, it was not until 1992 that the World Health Organisation removed homosexuality from its list of mental disorders. Creative people took chances and changed opinions: the first gay couple in a soap opera, in *EastEnders*, proved popular; the first lesbian kiss, in *Brookside*, was a ratings winner. (This may have had something to do with the fact that it involved Anna Friel.)

The bishops responded to the changes around them in 1991 with a report called 'Issues in Human Sexuality', but this only made matters worse. They recognised that lifelong, monogamous homosexual relationships could be viewed positively, but said they were absolutely not available to the clergy. No way. Gay priests would still have to be celibate in order to be faithful to God. This created a new category of humanity: the priest not called by God to abstain, in the Catholic way, but forced to stay away from sex because he or she had been born with the wrong genes. It was bizarre and it turned congregations into the sex police. Anyone who didn't like the way the priest treated the ladies on the flower rota wanted to know exactly what he got up to in bed and with whom, so they could complain to the bishop. He could wear a gimp mask and get whipped by his wife and nobody had a right to know – quite rightly – but every gay or lesbian priest's metaphorical bedroom window was crowded with people trying to get a look in.

Andrea and Mary were sick of it, which was why they would talk to me only if I promised not to give their real names or any indication of where they worked. Let's say, then, that we met in the vicarage next to the church where Andrea was a priest, in one of the rougher districts of a great industrial city. They lived there together, these women in their thirties; but if anyone asked, they were just a couple of friends sharing a house for the sake of convenience and companionship. Mary was a priest at a church in the neighbouring parish, so their living arrangements did not seem strange at all.

'We are not out,' said Andrea, a tall woman with long, black hair. She was the more confident of the two. 'In the goldfish bowl of parish life you have to look over your shoulder constantly,' said Mary, who was shorter, quieter and more hesitant. They were both wearing black shirts with their dog collars, indicating that their churchmanship was traditional.

> We are always thinking about where we are in relation to the parish: asking ourselves, 'Is it okay to hold her hand? Can I even look at her in a certain way?' I am only reminded what it is like to be a couple, openly and in public, when we are on holiday. The rest of the time I feel what this is doing to me: it is like lopping an arm off. I feel bereft.

Neither thought much about sexuality or the politics involved when they felt called to the priesthood. One of them knew she was gay, but could not deny what she believed God was saying to her.

> It is a biological fact that I have the feelings and needs that I do. What am I supposed to do, deny part of my God-given humanity? Pretend to change? God made me like this – and

I do not consider it anything other than whole, whatever anyone else says – and he called me to serve Him. Maybe some people feel those things pull in opposite directions. I'm sorry, but I don't.

I think you can guess it was Andrea who said that. Mary had not been sure of herself or what she wanted. 'We met at theological college. We fell in love, just like that. It couldn't be helped, I suppose.'

The first bishop who asked to see them thought otherwise. The job interview was really a diatribe. They would bring the Church into disrepute unless they chose to stop pretending it was biological and asked God to change their sexuality back to 'normal', or – if they were too weak for that – chose celibacy instead. Andrea was still very angry about the meeting, five years later. 'We were both in tears. How dare he?' He was their bishop. They had chosen to serve a church that put him in authority over them. That was how he dared. He had the right. 'Yes,' said Mary with a sigh, 'but that's difficult, you see, when the bishop is so closed.' Andrea snorted, beside her on the sofa. 'You mean offensive.'

When summoned to see another bishop, they steeled themselves for more of the same. They could not have been more surprised. 'It was like a parallel universe. He swung his legs over the arm of the chair and said, "Well, my dears, when did you fall into each other's arms?" Then he smiled and asked, "Have you liturgically consummated your union?"' They had, as it happened. His attitude took away much of the guilt Mary had felt. It turned out that there were more gay priests in his diocese than any other in England and that this was widely known. He arranged for them to be curates at two parishes that were close enough to allow constant contact but distant enough to be discreet. 'People were very sweet,' said Andrea. 'They said things like, "It's lovely that you've got each other as companions, you poor old spinsters.'" She was grateful to their bishop at first, but grew impatient. 'He made us into liars.' That was difficult for women who wanted to follow their callings with truth, respect and integrity. 'It undermines everything that you do, not being able to be yourself.'

St Paul writes that love is the greatest gift of all, greater than faith or hope. Andrea and Mary loved the Church and each other, but they were struggling to find a way to reconcile the two. 'If it came to a choice between the Church or Mary, she would win without a breath,' said Andrea. 'But that is not to say we do not take the priesthood very seriously. I believe, passionately, that it is what God wants me to do. I would not have been through all this crap if I did not.'

It would be wrong to describe all this as a confrontation between homosexuality and Christianity. Tony Blair was a Christian and he led a government that equalised the age of consent, ended the ban on lesbians and gays in the military, abolished Section 28 and introduced civil partnerships that were eventually given the same rights and responsibilities as civil marriages. Blair was influenced by the campaigners at the gay rights organisation Stonewall but also by his own political roots in the Christian socialist movement. It was also a question of fair play. Was it really fair to treat gays and lesbians differently from heterosexuals? No, not if they couldn't help or change their sexuality and if you had no reason for being unfair to them except prejudice. As we became detached from our traditional faith, its attitude to homosexuality looked more and more bigoted – particularly in the light of statements from such groups as the Royal College of Psychiatrists, which says quite simply: 'There is no sound scientific evidence that sexual orientation can be changed.'

There are still injustices and brutalities, there is still ignorance and 'gay' is still a term of abuse in the playground, but for most English people, the argument is over. Gay culture has become so much part of the mainstream that it seems absurd even to write that down. Many of Middle England's favourite performers are openly gay, but it's only an issue if they want to make it one. The freak show is over, too. There is proper respect and affection for Stephen Fry and Sir Ian McKellen, not the snide fascination of the past. The National Survey of Sexual Attitudes and Lifestyles asks men and women how they feel about homosexuality. In 1990 a quarter of men surveyed in Britain said there was nothing wrong with it, but the proportion had risen to nearly half by 2000. Among women it rose from a third to more than half.

These findings are for the whole of Britain, including those with strong religious or moral objections to homosexuality, which suggests that the majority of English people think there is nothing wrong with a man having sex with a man, or a woman with a woman. We have decided through our democratic processes, over time, that same-sex relationships are not just okay but worthy of the same respect in the law as marriages between men and women. That is what we believe. There is no chance of it being overturned. We have changed so much. The Church has not. It used to lead us, but we have turned away from it and run off with God, to define Him for ourselves. For the first time in centuries – and arguably in its history – the Church of England is completely out of step with English morality.

Some people will protest that it's not the Church's job to follow the whims of society, that it has to speak of something more ancient, more substantial and more enduring. That's right, of course. Others will point out that most of Christendom – including the Catholic and Orthodox churches – are nowhere near accepting same-sex relationships as valid, and within that context the Anglicans are actually leading the way. There may be some truth in that, too, depending on which side ultimately wins. But it doesn't remove the problem for the Church, which is simple: when preachers take to the pulpit to denounce homosexuality, they are attacking something the majority of society now sees as perfectly legal and normal, and in some cases admirable.

They may as well preach against baldness.

24

Millennium prayer

Once, when I was a little boy and my parents were having a New Year's Eve party, I crept out of bed and on to the balcony of our flat to see what would happen when midnight came. Inside, they were cheering as the radio relayed the chiming of Big Ben. Outside, I stood and stared. At a van, I seem to remember. A white van. Then, as I watched . . . nothing happened. There was no change. It was a non-event, a hollow moment. And it was just like that inside the Millennium Dome as the year 2000 arrived.

Can any moment have been more hollow? We were gathered together under the massive canopy of a tent erected at great expense which contained nothing of any importance. Ten thousand people, exhausted and irritated by having to wait hours to get on trains to be there because of a logistical disaster. Not just the VIPs who made a fuss but others who were meant to be working, or who had been promised the night of a lifetime after winning a competition, or who were being rewarded for their charitable work. There was no time to look around: we were funnelled into the arena and handed a little brown paper bag containing a warm half-bottle of champagne. Some performers danced, some circus types twirled in the air, some pop stars performed two-minute versions of their hits, but that was all for television, designed to be seen on the screen and not in person. We were cold, we were miserable, but we were still more cheerful than the Queen, who looked as if she would have torn her arms off to be dancing a reel by the fireside in the privacy of Balmoral. Not even the sight of a 203-carat diamond, the appropriately materialistic centrepiece of the celebration, could cheer her up. When they shot laser beams at the thing it looked like a cheap prop from *Star Trek*. Her Royal Highness was forced to hold hands with Tony Blair for 'Auld Lang Syne' (there being no possibility that she would cross or link arms, not with him). It was all so joyless. Oddly quiet, too. From behind us and beyond the edges of the tent, we could hear the people outside in Greenwich and all along the Thames cheering. Someone was having a good time. Out there, it was fun. In here, it was a magnificently staged, beautifully lit, marvellously dressed circus of oblivion. Nothingness as a spectacle. And for what? A turning of the page, a flipping of the calendar.

The Archbishop of Canterbury had said he wouldn't be coming if he wasn't allowed to say a prayer, because this was the anniversary of Christ's birth, after all. Except it wasn't, of course, as every schoolchild knew. Jesus wasn't born in the Year Zero, and he almost certainly wasn't born in December. The date was stolen from a Roman festival. (Some would say he wasn't born at all, but that's a different argument.) The Archbishop made his stand anyway: 'I will not be there and neither will Cardinal Hume.' Hume agreed, saying: 'The crib will always be more important than the Dome. In every age, society all too often loses its way. Ours has. We disagree about the moral values which should guide us.'

The Cardinal, considered godly by all who knew him, would have lent dignity to the occasion. Instead, the leader of the nation's Catholics slipped away to spend Millennium Eve with his Maker. He would have hated it in the Dome. What we experienced that night was all surface shimmer, the New Labour idea of a good time, as empty of ideas and spiritual content as the big tent itself. Time and again we had been told this was the most important moment for a thousand years (which was obviously not true), a moment when the nation could declare its character and what it believed in, boldly, as it gave thanks for the past and prepared itself for the future. To that end, spiritual leaders had spent eighteen months devising a little poem, a form of words that could be spoken as a Millennium Resolution by everybody. It did the job, in that it was a perfect expression of the soul of the nation at that time, a vacuum between the end of Christian England and the start of whatever was to come: 'Let there be respect for the earth. Peace for its people, love in our lives, delight in the good, forgiveness for past wrongs and, from now on, a new start.'

That was it. No mention of God or the supposed birthday boy. No 'amen'. The words had been written to be useful to all in what Tony Blair declared was a 'tolerant, respectful of diversity, multiracial, multicultural society'. A society defined by what it was not, and determined to avoid offence to anyone. The Resolution made clear what we already knew: that there was no point to any of this. No point at all.

No wonder people didn't go out. Event organisers went bust because their tickets didn't sell. Despite having been bombarded with the idea that we should dance with strangers on the streets and have the biggest party in centuries, many of us just didn't feel like it. People stayed at home, or met up with their friends. They wanted intimacy, something warm and genuine. Something real. We had become people who didn't want to be forced to join in, didn't want to be told what to do, didn't want to go along with received wisdom, but wanted to make our own decisions, choose our own paths, find our own truths based on our own experiences.

Going to work at the Dome that night as a reporter felt profoundly wrong. On the other side of London, my little boy was sleeping. What if planes fell out of the sky, as had been predicted? What if the electricity grid went down, the gas stopped flowing, all the computers malfunctioned, as the cyber-seers had said they might, as a result of the so-called Millennium Bug? It's easy to forget how much anxiety there was, but as Damian Thompson wrote in *The Times*:

> What if the computer crisis is actually the fulfilment of Revelation's prophecies? Y2K has closed the gap between traditional fantasies of the End and the complexity of the modern world. Fundamentalist Christians have always believed that society is about to fall apart, but until now the only way to make their prophecies plausible has been to construct elaborate scenarios of nuclear war in the Middle East. Now they need not bother. They have been presented with a ready-made apocalypse which conjures up devastation like a world war, but which is set in train by the tiny dramas of our daily lives: the cashpoint machine that swallows our card, the permanently engaged telephones of a public utility company, the PC that crashes because of a power cut.

The Bug played on our fears because the internet was new, the dependence on electronic packets whizzing up to space and dictating to our phones, our computers, our televisions, our cars and even our fridges was still something we weren't used to, and the prospect of it suddenly leaving us in the lurch was frightening.

The Bug was the biggest scam in the history of computing. So far. But hey, at least we didn't all die.

It wasn't all bad: the Four Horsemen of the Apocalypse didn't come, however thunderously their hooves seemed to beat against the back of people's heads on the morning after the night before. Cliff Richard had briefly topped the charts with the dismal 'Millennium Prayer' – dubiously hyped by the churches and later voted the worst number-one single of all time – but there was another, more authentically popular and widespread millennium prayer that was heard on the first day of the new century, spoken spontaneously as millions of muddle-headed people reached for their hangover cures: 'Oh, Jesus.'

So ended the Decade of Evangelism. What a disaster. After ten years of trying their hardest to get the message across, praying and pleading and calling for the people of Britain to come back to the Lord, there was a simple, devastating fact that church leaders could not deny: instead of adding new members, they had seen more than a million people leave. More than a million.

Nearly half of them were Catholics. The Church of England had started its great evangelistic crusade with 1.2 million people at services on a Sunday but finished it with fewer than a million. The row over the ordination of women, the row over the collapse of its finances, the row over the future of the monarchy, the growing row over the treatment of homosexuals, these had all been damaging. The English God was evolving beyond the understanding of a Church obsessed only with itself. The biggest achievement of George Carey's tenure as Archbishop had been to change the management structure. He would leave his Church broke, battered and bewildered. As a whole, organised Christianity in England had lost one in five of its followers.

I was one of them. When people talk about how they were

converted to Christianity, they often describe a moment in which the world suddenly made sense. John Wesley experienced this as he listened to a preacher on the night his life changed for ever, and said he felt his 'heart strangely warmed'. One Christmas Eve, as I sat in church, I felt my heart strangely chilled. This anti-conversion experience happened quite against my will. I had been struggling to make sense of all that was happening around me, and the way the description of the world that I heard from the pulpit seemed so out of kilter with my own personal experience. We had also been trying for some time to have a baby, enduring all the frustration and misery that is involved in attempting to get fertility treatment on the National Health Service. The brutality of making childless couples sit in a paediatric waiting room packed with toddlers' toys while they wait to be told it will not be possible to treat them this month, or next month, or any time soon because of underfunding is just one example. That particular session ended with the consultant, who could see from his notes that we were professionals, telling us we were never going to have a baby on the NHS and the only way to stand even the slightest chance was to go private. While we were recovering from that bombshell, he handed us the number for his private clinic, just in case we wanted to get in touch. And doctors wonder why we don't always trust them.

I once heard an expert suggest that six out of seven couples who have IVF treatment split up, regardless of whether they have a baby. Given the drugs, the mania and the pressure, I can well believe it. You will know from the beginning of this book that things changed for us, eventually, but at the time there was no hope, only hurt. We did all we could to avoid being anywhere near children, because it was too painful, but you can't escape the Baby Jesus at Christmas. He's everywhere: on cards, on the telly, in the papers, in shop windows, in charity shop cribs. Fair

enough. It is His birthday . . . sort of. We always went to the
midnight mass on Christmas Eve, and so we did again. 'O Little
Town of Bethlehem' was fine. 'Rejoice, rejoice . . .' No. I didn't
feel like it. I felt cold. I kept my gloves on. We were sitting right
at the back, the church was packed with people who never went
near the place most of the time, all beery and cheery and swaying from the dinners and pub sessions they had just left, to the
derision of others, to follow family traditions. People still go, in
their millions, once a year. It is tradition. It is home. Once is
more than enough, but you've got to be there at Christmas,
haven't you? Certainly, when your father-in-law is the vicar and
your relatives are waiting in their roped-off pew. 'Emmanuel has
come to thee, O Israel.' We stood for the reading, the words
coming into focus: 'For unto us a child is born.' Unto us a child
is born? The words rose from the lectern, danced around the
head of the golden bird on whose back the Bible was supported,
and flew over the heads of the congregation like a heat-seeking
missile, seeking the last vestiges of warmth in my heart and faith
in my soul and blowing them to bits.

People say conversion is like someone shifting furniture in the
attic of their mind. It's nothing to do with them, not their choice,
but a sudden coming together, an illumination, like a circuit
being completed and a light going on. Well, in that case, the furniture in my attic was smashed, the circuit in my brain overheated
and suddenly, without doing anything and utterly against my will,
for all my trying to hold it together, everything was broken. I just
didn't believe in it any more. Baby Jesus was a character in a fairy
story. God was a construct. I was so angry. I had struggled so hard
to keep my faith, despite everything that was happening to us,
and to believe that there could be a rescue, a way forward, that
God could come down into our lives and work His magic. And
now, without warning, it was over. Hopeless. I didn't get up from

the pew. I couldn't force my way out past a row of creaky, sherry-soaked knees, under the eyes of the wardens. Not on that night of all nights. So I stood when everyone stood and I sat when they sat, and I didn't fidget during the sermon, even though the small of my back burned. But I didn't sing the words of the hymns, and I thought, When this is over, I am never coming back.

The Church was also losing priests. A friend of mine, Simon Parke, had been ordained after a career as a comedy scriptwriter. When I persuaded him to talk about the state of the Church for a newspaper feature, he said this:

> To say that something is dying is not to say that it is bad. Jesus died and He was good. Poverty is thriving and it is bad. Of course, enthroning middle-management in absurd bishops' clothes, that is embarrassing. And Christian communities more aware of what and who they are against than what and who they are for – these are depressing.

Simon, then vicar of St George's, Tufnell Park, was often asked whether faith had a future:

> The important question is whether it has a future that is worth anything. That will depend on the nature of its energy. High-quality energy comes only from the human soul finding itself at the end of its tether, forced into a confrontation with the self and the search for God. A painful but joyful business. It is as a cradle – or manger – for this elusive energy that the Church has a future that is worth something.

Some time after saying those words, Simon left the priesthood.

25

Stop living the lie

One month after the attacks on America, when the everyday life of every city felt more full of danger than before, a young mother from Birmingham stood up to make a speech. She was on a platform in Trafalgar Square, next to one of the huge black lions, speaking into a microphone so that she could be heard by all the people who had gathered there. Twenty thousand had come to express their opposition to the bombing of Afghanistan. She had never spoken to a public meeting before, let alone one of this size. The usual suspects were present – anarchists, Socialist Workers, hard-left sects – but so were thousands of Muslim men and women who had arrived by coach from Southall, Bradford, Leicester and elsewhere. The speaker was one of them. Her head was covered by the hijab, and they said her name was Salma.

She was extraordinary. Her voice was calm, strong, compelling, and she had an authority and intensity that made it impossible to tune out. More than that, I had the sense of hearing for the first time a voice which was new and demanded respect. The voice of an eloquent, passionate Englishwoman who was also a Muslim and who was not prepared to let the Prime Minister go to war in her name. How many English Islamic mothers had spoken out in this way before? None, as far as I knew.

Tony Blair had talked of standing shoulder to shoulder with the Americans because of our common culture, language and heritage, but listening to Salma reminded me that he had told only part of the story. He failed to acknowledge the large numbers of people in our country who saw themselves as standing shoulder to shoulder with men, women and children in Afghanistan and other countries in the East, either because of their family or religious ties or because the notion of the world as a global village was real to them. The notes I made that day, in preparation for a newspaper report, give only the barest flavour of what it was like to hear Salma Yaqoob, but here is what I recorded her saying:

> If only the leftists had been here today, people would have said we were all lefties. If only CND had been here, they would have said it was the middle-class elite. If it was only the Muslims, they would have called us extremists. If it was only Asians and black people, they would have said it was the ethnic minorities. Tony Blair, we are here united against this war. You cannot dismiss us all.

He could and did, of course, but at that moment it was hard to believe he would. The following week I travelled up to the Midlands to find out more about Salma. Bradford born, she was a trained psychotherapist who had not been political at all before 9/11. As a specialist in psychological trauma, she had watched events unfold in America with a trained eye and had been alarmed at the politicians' overreaction. 'Scared people do irrational things. They act in ways that would not be acceptable in the cold light of day, and allow their leaders to do the same.'

Stop living the lie

A few days after the attacks, it became personal. She was walking in the city centre with her son, who was three years old, when a man spat right at her. 'I was just so shocked,' she told me. 'I was shaking with fear. It's so humiliating. Although it's not your fault, you feel as if it is. People just carried on walking. That really upset me. I thought, What if he had got violent? On the bus home, one of the passengers shouted, "Stab all Muslims!"' In the school playground, mothers who had always chatted to her turned away. Later, she found out her younger brother had been bullied, a friend who was a lawyer had been attacked and a woman she knew had been pushed in the street. 'I knew racism happened but I'd never experienced it.' Salma was English, she had been educated at university, and she considered the claims of Christianity quite seriously before deciding that Islam gave women more rights. She had started wearing the hijab at eighteen. Now neighbours who had seen her as the quiet, friendly wife of their local GP were equating her with the murderous intent of Osama bin Laden, because she had the same skin colour as a terrorist and wore Islamic clothes. 'After that day, I decided I was not going to be passive any more.'

Salma 'stumbled into' a small meeting of people opposed to military action. 'There was such a sense of relief. Until then I had felt overwhelmed, but in that room there were all sorts of people who felt strongly about it.' The others calculated, no doubt, that having a Muslim woman as the leader of their local anti-war group would get their cause noticed, and she was elected chair. 'Everyone was applauding but I was thinking, Oh my God, what have I got into? It's not as if I've got any credentials.' She did it because she was not prepared to shrink away. She could see that everything was changing, a new England was emerging, and she was not prepared to let the racists have control of it. That meant speaking out despite what people expected of a woman in her position. She later became a city councillor. Getting involved did stop her feeling so afraid, she admitted, but there was no going back. 'I feel like a character in the film *The Matrix*, who moves between a world that is comfortable, but an illusion, and reality, which is much worse. I cannot choose to return to the way I was before I woke up.'

Eighteen months later, I listened to another speech, heard on the radio in the kitchen of a friend who lived in the stockbroker belt in Surrey. Her three-year-old twins were scattering cornflakes all over the breakfast bar and their au pair was gathering up coats and hats and boots for a day in London. It was February 2003. Tony Blair was telling Scottish Labour supporters why the imminent invasion of Iraq was necessary, even as a million people were preparing to protest against it. My friend and her husband, a financial adviser, were not the sort of people who usually went on peace marches, which was why they had agreed to let me write about them. They were going to join in, and take the girls, because they felt it was right. Irresistible, even. Tony Blair spoke out via the BBC, telling us that leaving Saddam Hussein in place as the leader of Iraq would be inhumane. My friend was not impressed. 'So it's his conviction against all of ours, is it? He's in a very scary place just now, isn't he? That's where Mrs Thatcher was before the end.'

I suspected that she would know, having probably voted for her. We had both been part of the March for Jesus team in the eighties, so it felt strange to be going on another walk across the capital together in an entirely different cause now. We talked about how the City March of 1987 had grown into a worldwide movement, and how in America it had become a campaign to have one day of public holiday set aside for people to think about Christ. I'm not sure what the campaigners thought Christmas

Day was for, but in any case they were not very successful, except in one state. The Governor there could see the advantage of having Christians on his side, and he was promoting his own status as a born-again to great political advantage. His name was George W. Bush. He signed a proclamation declaring 10 June 'Jesus Day' in Texas and calling all to 'follow Christ's example'. There was outrage, as you might imagine, from people of other faiths. The American Jewish Congress called it 'an egregious and blatant violation of the First Amendment'. Bush was unmoved, but, as it turned out, events overtook the Marches for Jesus. After 9/11, mass demonstrations in the name of Christianity looked confrontational and dangerous. Anyway, by then, Bush had become President and was equipped with more direct ways of asserting the will of God.

The scale was different, but the theology was much the same: it was still about conquering the world for Christ. Instead of – or as well as – fighting demons in the heavenly realm, Bush was fighting insurgents on the ground. There was no doubt that he would have expected people like our old selves to support him, and that was profoundly disturbing. We had sung about unbelievers having to make way for the King of Kings, but now the Almighty had an advocate who seemed to take that idea literally and was commander-in-chief of the mightiest army on the planet.

'The liberty we prize is not America's gift to the world,' he once said. 'It is God's gift to humanity.' According to the BBC, Bush told Palestinian leaders he was on a mission from God. They quoted him as saying: 'God would tell me, "Go and fight those terrorists in Afghanistan." And I did. And then God would tell me, "George, go and end the tyranny in Iraq."'

My friend and I were horribly aware that the cause we once promoted had been used by this warmonger to justify actions we now opposed. We walked across Waterloo Bridge, not behind a rainbow banner proclaiming 'Jesus Loves You' but in the shadows of black flags and Socialist Workers' Party placards. There were so many others there, too. 'House Music Against War', said one placard, while Cornish Ravers had a board declaring: 'Clotted cream not ruptured spleen'. I heard a young Goth tell her friend: 'I just saw a banner that said, "Arse!" I told the guy I agreed with him. Absolutely.' The scale of the march was stupefying: there were so many people. Nobody seemed to know which way we should be walking, but it didn't seem to matter. The helicopters clattered overhead. 'The march is everywhere,' said my friend. Surely this couldn't be ignored?

Cue hollow laughter. What good did any of it do? For those who wanted to see it this way, the alliance between Bush and Blair was Christianity as a bloodthirsty, crusading and imperial-istic faith led by hypocrites and liars. In this country, church leaders had spoken out against the invasion of Iraq, but they had been ignored like the rest of us. The Church of England made a point of praying for Saddam Hussein as well as Blair; and the man who was about to become Archbishop of Canterbury, Rowan Williams, sought to stamp out all talk of a crusade. 'There is no war that is holy and good in itself. It is the last resort, not an end in itself. To bring in heavy artillery of a religious kind, to say that this is the only way to resist evil, is something that has to be watched for.'

There were protesters outside Canterbury Cathedral when Dr Williams was enthroned in February 2003, a month before the invasion. Some denounced this Welsh theologian, poet and lin-guist as a false teacher because he believed in women bishops and had once knowingly ordained a gay priest; but the bigger pres-ence was that of people angry with one of the 2400 guests, the Prime Minister. One of the placards read: 'Blair – heed the sane Archbishop not the mad March Bush'. There was no chance of that. Those days were long gone. As Stephen Bates of the *Guardian* put it: 'The Archbishop did not even have the power to irk, as Runcie had irked Thatcher.'

There were rumours that Rowan Williams didn't want the job, but he still struck his staff three times on the door of the cathedral to be let in, still sat on the marble chair of St Augustine and still took the vows that made him the youngest archbishop in nearly two centuries, at the age of fifty-two. He was the first since the Reformation to come from outside England, having been the leader of the smaller, disestablished Church in Wales. Williams wore gold silk robes hand-woven on a loom in Monmouth for the ceremony, with a gold and silver clasp that showed the white dragon of England being defeated by the red dragon of Wales. The service included his own translation of a Welsh poem about the presence of Christ that ended: 'I know what I have longed for. Him to hold me, always.' There was a song from South Africa and a tune from India; there were Jews, Muslims, Sikhs and Buddhists present; and the Pope had sent a warm personal message of support. The new Archbishop was an engineer's son from Swansea who had been a radical in his youth, even getting himself arrested for reading out psalms on the runway at the American Lakenheath air base in Suffolk in 1985 as part of a protest by CND. Those who knew him described a serious, thoughtful, sensitive man who understood that the world was changing. In the past he had spoken in favour of breaking the Church's ties with the State and the Crown, so he was not going to fret particularly that disestablishment appeared to be happening by default, as those ties snapped all by themselves.

Keeping the Church and the worldwide communion together was going to be a bigger challenge, particularly as some were already calling him a heretic. He had written about 'the sheer difficulty of talking about God' so those who had very clear views of the Bible thought he must be agnostic. That was certainly not the case, he insisted. 'You would expect some difficulties in talking about it. It's a great deal bigger than the words you can use.'

The press liked Rowan, at first. People liked his Gandalf beard, his eagle-wing eyebrows, his sonorous voice and his obvious sincerity. They would take a while to criticise the density of his prose, the caution in his delivery and the fact that sometimes, dammit, he insisted on thinking things through for an interminably long time before giving his views. But they didn't have to wait long for a scandal, which came within months. It involved one of his friends, a fifty-year-old theologian called Jeffrey John, who was appointed the next Bishop of Reading. He was gay. All the people involved in the selection process knew that and they also knew John had been in a relationship with a man for twenty-seven years. The lovers had met while John was at theological college, where he was advised that if celibacy were not possible, the next-best thing was to take a long-term, faithful partner. That was what he chose to do. Instead of asking his student to leave, the principal at the time congratulated the ordinand on a decision that would make him 'a better human being and a better priest'. That principal was David Hope, who went on to become Archbishop of York.

'It seemed there was a private morality, a Christian one, but one that could never be talked about openly,' John later said. 'There have been centuries of double thinking.' The policy outlined by the bishops in 1991 had created an 'evil' situation which led to 'personal disintegration and loneliness' but he felt he had to obey those whom God had put in leadership over him, so he had been celibate ever since. This was not a flighty man, clearly. Still, archbishops in Nigeria and Australia demanded that his appointment be stopped. Evangelicals in this country threatened yet again to take their congregations out of the Church of England, removing their contributions from the central pot. That was quite a threat, given that a church of six hundred people might pay £100,000 a year, and there were said to be a thousand priests ready to lead an exodus. Nobody really knew whether that was an exaggeration, but another thousand – including Anglo-Catholics – were also said to oppose the inevitable appointment of women bishops. The new Archbishop had a serious problem, made worse when sixteen of his own bishops signed a statement opposing the enthronement of the mild Dr John. The Bishop of Carlisle felt compelled to go on television and say: 'Obviously, the penis belongs to the vagina.'

That was a pretty weird thing to hear from a bishop, even if all he was really saying was that he didn't think gay sex was natural. Yah booh sucks, as it were. Or not. More seriously, people were arguing over the interpretation of certain Bible passages. Those who thought homosexuality incompatible with Christianity cited the reference in Paul's letter to the Romans to 'men committing shameless acts with men' and being filled with 'all manner of wickedness'. Dr John was among those who believed Paul was writing not about 'two men or women who fall in Christian love' but about the models of homosexuality that had been most visible in his own society at the time, 'prostitution and pederasty'.

Jeffrey John's dignity in the face of hatred was impressive, particularly when he was summoned to Lambeth Palace and told by his distressed friend the Archbishop that he would have to resign before he had even started, to save them all from chaos and schism. So much for love conquering all. Having abstained from sex for a decade just because a bunch of bishops said he should, Jeffrey John was hardly going to deny the spiritual head of his Church, so he withdrew. The crisis was over, until the next time. The Americans were about to appoint as a bishop a gay man who made no secret of having sex with his partner and that would create an even bigger stink, on a worldwide scale. But as far as

England was concerned, the sorry affair of Dr John only con-firmed that the Church was on a different planet to the rest of us.

'If anything good has come out of this,' said the Bishop of Oxford, 'it is that the nomination of Jeffrey John has shaken up Middle England and forced it to ask itself where it stands on the issue of homosexuality. I think, rather to its surprise, it has come to stand with Jeffrey John.' But the Bishop was wrong. The more innocent churchgoers apart, nobody in Middle England was very confused about where they stood. They didn't care. It was none of their business what men got up to in bed. The Church was beginning to resemble a demented dog, chasing its tail with ever more insane barks, while the rest of us looked on, bewildered.

A man can abuse his children, beat up his wife and destroy other people's lives with his business practices, but if he is careful, when he goes to church on a Sunday morning, nobody need know. Such things can be invisible. They are between him and his Maker. He can cut his neighbour's throat, wash off the blood, go to sit in a pew and sing 'The Lord Is My Shepherd' and he will be treated like any other respectable human being. But if he hap-pens to be gay, and if he turns up holding the hand of a man he has loved faithfully all his life, he will be shunned.

He will be made about as welcome as Gary Glitter offering to do Sunday school. I know because I have seen it. Never mind all that bull about loving the sinner and hating the sin: Jesus never says a thing about this alleged sin anywhere in the Bible, yet in word and deed it is often singled out above all others. How loving is that? The Lord was silent on the subject, but His people dare to speak for Him. What they say is full of hatred. The body language, the looks, the silence, the outright hostility and the rant in the parish newsletter make it clear to gay men that they are not wanted and never will be. Not unless they hide what they are.

Stop living the lie

I have seen people I love and respect treated in this way several times, in parish churches whose historic reason for being is to serve everyone in the community. It is a violation of that principle for a vicar to set up his congregation like a club, to which you can belong only if you believe in his own narrow interpretation of Scripture, and then to make it obvious that some people are not wanted at all. Christians who sit there in the pews week after week endorsing it with their silence should be ashamed of themselves. To treat people like dog dirt on the shoes of humanity because of a sexuality they have not chosen, which may even have been given to them by God, is outrageous. To make something Jesus never mentioned into the worst 'sin' of all, and put hate-filled words into His mouth, is surely blasphemy. Is it really any wonder that so many people stay away?

Then again, is it any wonder that the English have stopped going to church and stopped believing in their long-established God when you consider all that has happened in this story? The royal family presented itself as a model of good old-fashioned Christianity, but then smashed that model to pieces. Authority figures betrayed our trust, Margaret Thatcher told us to be more individualistic, to put ourselves and our families first, not to be afraid of making money but to exercise our right to shop where and when we wanted, including on the Sabbath. And what was the response of the State Church? Not to resist this new materialism but to open enormous and profitable shopping centres of its own. To agree with the gospel of greed. The Church was revealed as obsessed with money, yet disastrous at keeping hold of it. Its grip on our lives, as the institution to which we once turned to be named, married or buried, has been prised off by laws introducing the free market to an age-old system. Not because of religion, but because of politics.

The voice with which the Church had once spoken out so clearly against poverty and injustice was lost, at first because it became besotted with the spirit of the age but then because it grew full of self-disgust and turned away from the rest of us, to go off and squabble about sex. More strident preachers stood up and began to shout louder in the marketplace. Faith was privatised, like everything else. We stopped seeing it as part of our identity, something communal that was passed on from generation to generation, to be tended with discipline and a sense of duty. We were told that was wrong, nominal, no longer enough. Instead, we were sold faith as a leisure pursuit, a choice to make in the expectation of a thrilling, meaningful experience. Then many people were disappointed by the experience not happening as they felt it should, or not lasting. Even those who were convinced felt let down when the promised revival never came.

In politics, likewise, the promise of a new start gave way to the same old bitterness and disillusionment, only worse, because the euphoria had been so intense. The end of the millennium, about which we had all been urged to get so excited, came and went. Not with a bang but with a whimper. Nothing changed.

Except us, perhaps. We changed. Our eyes began to be opened by the arrival of new neighbours with new faiths and cultures. We began to realise there were more gods than just our old one, and that even if we didn't follow any of them, we felt in our bones that others had the right to do so. That was only fair. Some people decided they didn't believe any of the stories any more, while others let slip their sense of belonging but kept on believing in God in their personal, private ways, more confident in their own good sense than in what any priest might say.

The flowers at the palace gates marked the death of the old English God, in the sense of the traditional, Establishment values that were once expressed so powerfully in the trinity of the

Church, the State and the Crown. We'd had enough. It was over, for ever. So much for that. The English are no longer the people we were, within living memory. So what, instead, are we becoming?

REVELATIONS

Faith is the great cop-out, the great excuse to evade the need to think and evaluate evidence.

Richard Dawkins

Faith is, in the end, a kind of homesickness . . . for a home we have never visited, but have never once stopped longing for.

Philip Yancey

26

Is God still an Englishman?

Is God still an Englishman? Well, yes, but He (or She) is also an Afghan, a Bosnian, a Croat, a Djibouti, an Ethiopian, a Finn, a Greek, a Hungarian, an Indian, a Jamaican, a Kurd, a Lebanese, a Moroccan, a Nigerian, an Omani, a Pole, a Qatari, a Russian, a Saudi, a Turk, an Uzbek, a Vietnamese, a Walloon . . . Well, you get the point. (Yes, I know it's cheating to stop there, but can you think of a nationality beginning with X?) The point is that the monoculture is over. The Anglo-Saxons have just got to get used to it – but then they do have Celts and Danes and Germans and Gauls and Normans and Vikings and so many others in their blood anyway. England has always been a rainbow nation, it just didn't want to acknowledge the fact. Now there is no denying it.

There was strength in pretending to be pure, but now we have to find strength in acknowledging our variety. If all immigration stopped tomorrow, our country would still be a human soup. As it is, two million more new people will arrive over the next decade, and that's just those who will be legal. The last census showed that while the North-East and South-West of England were still nearly 95 per cent white, overall it was 87.5 per cent. That was mainly because of the increased number of black and Asian people in the cities. Since the survey was taken, we have also been joined by hundreds of thousands of people from Eastern Europe.

'England is a memory now,' the singer Morrissey was quoted as saying in the *NME* a while back. The son of Irish immigrants took legal action against the magazine and stressed he was no kind of racist at all, but beyond the misquote he had a point. England *is* a memory, if you mean the old England with one culture and one faith. We have a new England, in which young white boys on the streets of Melksham try to talk and walk like gangsta rappers and Sikh football fans turn up to watch the national team in turbans with their faces painted in the colours of the flag of St George.

When Charles and Diana got married there was one black player in the England squad, as a reserve. Now you could fill the whole first eleven with non-white England stars: James, Johnson, Cole, Lescott, Ferdinand, Lennon, Jenas, Walcott, Young, Heskey and Defoe as an example. Among them are several young men who represent something so new that it has yet really to register on a census: the rise of the mixed-race English.

One in five children are now from an ethnic minority and they are six times more likely to be mixed race than the adults around them, according to the Equality and Human Rights Commission. In Britain, half of all children with a Caribbean parent also have a white one. Half of black Caribbean men are seeing someone from a different background, as are one in five black African men, and two out of five Chinese women. These are mostly people under thirty, who are much more likely to cross the old race and cultural barriers than those who are older. 'The old polarising debate about black and white is changing and the next generation will not see race in the same way we see it,' says the Commission, enthusiastically. 'This is hugely positive and we can afford a moment to celebrate: Britain's diverse culture is becoming all the more fascinating and inter-connected.'

Is God still an Englishman?

Hooray for us and our broad minds, then. But what about the ghettoes? They are still there, and growing, as any teacher will tell you. The divisions are most obvious in schools, because people from Pakistan and Bangladesh are having more children than those people who identify themselves as white British. The number of faith schools has grown, and they are no longer just Christian. The Church of England does still run a quarter of all primary schools as well as a couple of hundred secondaries, but it is facing a big challenge. In Blackburn, Birmingham, Bradford, Oldham and parts of London, there are church schools with student populations that are now 99 per cent Muslim. In two schools, it is 100 per cent. The legal requirement to hold a daily act of recognisably Christian worship is often quietly sidestepped and instead the heads talk about their calling to serve the communities around them. 'My Muslim families want their children to be here because they want them to be encouraged to be honest, true, respectful, loving, generous,' one head teacher told *The Times*. 'You don't have to be a Christian to want that, but they are Christian values nonetheless.' She wanted pupils to leave feeling that faith of any kind was of value. 'It's important that the children understand that no one has to be right or wrong in this.'

There are people who don't like it: the British National Party secured a million votes in the European elections in 2009, the biggest support ever seen for the far right in this country. That was despite some spectacularly inept campaigning by its leader Nick Griffin, who chose to launch his efforts standing in front of a picture of a Spitfire, the ultimate English icon. However, the code number on the side of the plane revealed that it had been flown during the Battle of Britain by a Pole, the heroic leader of a Polish squadron that fought for this country to the point of death. The squadron may well have contained the grandfathers of some of the young immigrants Griffin so wants to keep out.

If the defence of the realm had been organised by the BNP, Hitler would have kipped down in Buckingham Palace on the first night of the war.

The BNP picked up votes because people felt threatened by incomers or abandoned by all the other parties. These real concerns are only made worse by writing off BNP voters as racist, chain-smoking, benefit-scrounging chavs with devil dogs. The BNP leaders are knuckleheads, but they show respect and understanding for the white, working-class people whose support they want. Most politicians don't. That is dangerous.

Lately, another group has emerged which is less predictable than the BNP and harder to pin down. Within a few months of starting up, the English Defence League had already created riots and provoked a foolish cabinet minister into comparing it with Oswald Mosley's Blackshirts. League members do wear black polo shirts with a little flag on the chest. Their target is Islamic extremism and their placards say 'No More Mosques' and 'Sharia Out'. The intriguing thing about the League is that it includes black and mixed-race lads as well as white ones. It insists that it is not a fascist organisation, even filming members in balaclavas setting fire to a Nazi swastika flag.

The League was started through the social network Facebook, where its page warns: 'We are not here to turn people against Islam, just Islamic Extremists. Anyone who cannot control their feelings and feels the need to write insulting comments to people with different beliefs or skin colour [to] their own [is] not welcome, and will be deleted without warning.' The League is trying very hard not to be dismissed as part of the far right, even though some of its named members have belonged to the BNP. The story that its leaders tell is that they got together in reaction to a protest by Islamists in Luton, during a homecoming march by the Second Battalion of the Royal Anglican Regiment. The soldiers

were booed and hissed by a few young Asian men carrying placards that read 'Butchers of Basra' and 'Go to Hell'. They had
been ostracised by other Muslims in Luton, but they made the
front pages.

'We're a community,' a League spokesman told a BBC reporter
while hiding his face behind a hoodie. 'The Islamic community
has so many voices to come and speak for them. We have none.'
Protests in Birmingham city centre were supposedly meant to be
peaceful, but there were running battles with Asians in which
punches and bottles were thrown. Dozens of people on both
sides were arrested. John Denham, the Communities Secretary,
compared such skirmishes to the fascist street battles of the thirties. 'The tactic of trying to provoke a response in the hope of
causing wider violence and mayhem is long established on the far
right.' That really wasn't helping. It was just stoking the fires.

In Birmingham, some councillors had tried to warn young
Muslim men not to be provoked. They included Salma Yaqoob,
the anti-war speech-maker from 2001, who was not surprised the
warnings didn't work. 'Racism is becoming more open, more
direct and more vicious,' she wrote in the *New Statesman*.

Salma is now the leader of Respect, the political party over-
shadowed by its involvement with the controversial MP George
Galloway. She intends to stand as an MP, and has a strong chance
of winning. For a young English psychotherapist, working
mother and Muslim to achieve that kind of political profile can
be seen as part of what the veteran politician Shirley Williams
describes in her recent autobiography: 'The tide rolls steadily in.
There are few areas of life in which women do not play an
increasing part, reaching the highest positions in once wholly
masculine areas like banking, policing, judging, even in the military.' But, of course, that is far from the whole story.

Salma is an example of how some people refused to be

marginalised or give in to prejudice after 9/11 but instead sought to engage with the power structures and gain an influence on the way we think, behave and make policy. I don't agree with her politics at all, but I do think that England is being remade, and women like Salma Yaqoob are helping to make it happen. Her article lamented the way a couple of hundred determined young men could make it look as if we were heading for a racist civil war:

> On the day the first small group of English Defence League protesters came to Birmingham, I spent a pleasant afternoon at a community festival in my ward. It was one of those days when people who can trace their origins to every corner of the globe joined together. This is the society we must defend. No country is truly an island any longer. We are all connected. This is a good thing, a source of strength and unity. But people must speak up for it.

The trouble with that happy thought is that so many people are telling us their way is the only way. The young men who protested against the homecoming of the soldiers in Luton believe, as others do, that England should become an Islamic nation, under the rule of Sharia law. They do not reflect the views of many English Muslims, but they do generate fear, and therefore get attention. More than anything, attention is what true believers crave right now. There used to be no argument about faith in this country – you either accepted Christianity or you rejected it – but now that is over and faith is a marketplace, the followers of every kind of creed quite rightly feel that they are entitled to set out their stall.

Since they are competing for the attention of the 39 million adults who live in England, with 12 million children, they ought to realise how much we have changed. There are nearly five million more of us than there were in 1981. Space is becoming an issue, particularly since we became divided between home-owners and people who can't afford to get on the property ladder. Signing a mortgage contract together is seen by many as a bigger step to take than having a wedding. Marriage is in decline. That is not going to change. The number of new mothers has outstripped the number of brides, and half of all babies are born to unmarried women. That is not surprising, because more than four million of us are doing what the preachers used to call living in sin. Two million families are led by lone parents. Very few of us live up to the marital ideal that is proposed from the pulpit. Still, the perception remains that we will be made to feel bad about our lifestyles if we go near a church, mosque or temple, and many people use that as an excuse not to. They're not afraid; they just don't need the grief.

We have stopped belonging to clubs, trade unions, political parties and many other institutions. Instead, we go online or watch television, which continually tells us we are only an audition or a lucky break away from fame and fortune. We all potentially have the X-factor. Unfortunately, that is a lie, and few of us have the talent to do anything other than embarrass ourselves in the cause of helping a showbusiness entrepreneur make a lot more money. But our children don't see that, so they go into school and tell their teacher they want to be famous, be it as a performer, a footballer, a presenter, a reality show star or a model, like the Princess of Permatan, Katie Price.

When boys and girls grow up a bit and realise their dreams are not quite within reach, some of them get very angry and feel there is no justice, at which point they start stealing, dealing in drugs or running with gangs to get the clothes, the jewellery, the cars and the gadgets they feel they deserve. It works, as long as they don't get caught or killed. The sense of injustice is fuelled by a warped version of the traditional view held by the working men and women of England – nobody should be allowed to get above themselves, those who do should be brought down a peg or two, and I'm as good (and as worthy of a bit of bling) as the next person. Ain't I?

The National Lottery reinforces the feeling of imminent wealth, while at the same time taxing the poor. There are more millionaires than three decades ago but the poor feel poorer (although they've got more stuff), and between the two there are anger, alienation and rudeness, which escalate into violence. This is fuelled, of course, by drink. We are much more likely to find ourselves lying in a pool of our own vomit in a city centre gutter with our knickers round our ankles than we were in 1981 – particularly if we are young, female and have just drunk a dozen vodka mules.

There are also more drugs around at more affordable prices, but the nation's favourite path to oblivion is through the high-speed consumption of very powerful drink, which is much easier to buy than it was. As was hoped, we have become more like continentals since the introduction of twenty-four-hour licensing. Unfortunately, though, the continentals we most resemble are the ones Cezanne painted in *The Orgy*.

'The English are noted among foreigners for their persistent drinking,' according to one commentator. But hang on just a Technicolor-yawning minute ... that was said by John of Salisbury in the twelfth century. That's what some of the new Puritans forget: the English were binge drinkers long before we even had pubs. Back when we lived off the land, when the grain supply was vulnerable to flood and drought, the harvest was unpredictable and its produce would not keep for ever, people learned to make merry while they could. It was a way of relieving stress indoors, by the fire, while the weather raged outside.

Depression and drinking increase when it is cold and dark, and it was cold and dark a lot of the time before electricity.

One in four houses in parts of London had their own gin still when Hogarth was scratching out his famous engravings in the eighteenth century. Half the population was drunk, either on a lethal version of the fancy juniper-flavoured spirit we have today or on Hogarth's favoured alternative, jolly old beer. The drinking water was foul, so it made sense – until Victorian Christianity came along with new sewers and imposed its morality. The temperance movement told us that ruin lay at the bottom of the glass, and at the same time there were laws to control the production of alcohol. God was a disciplinarian and the law was the instrument by which He kept us from disgracing ourselves. The Establishment decided which drugs we could have – tobacco freely, alcohol in moderation, cannabis not at all – on the basis of who controlled the markets and how much money could be made by the right fellows.

The system couldn't hold once people stopped believing in the Establishment God. The People's England had always been on the ale, knocking back gallons of the stuff on VE Day or going on a booze cruise to Calais, but as the downward pressure of Victorian morality decreased and the laws changed, so the knees up really began.

We fell quickly for cheap booze and alcopops. As true believers in the free market, the government didn't interfere. In the old days we could drink ourselves silly only at harvest time, but now it was harvest time any time. The only reason it was not a perpetual happy hour in the nineties was that young people wanted to be fit and thin, so they took to abstaining from alcohol during the working week and going for spectacular lash-ups at the weekend. Which we all know starts on a Thursday night and lasts until the hangover from hell on Tuesday morning. (Time for the hair of the dog.) For the first time, boys *and* girls were doing this. But they were just being true to the bawdy, lusty, life-loving spirit of England that had been submerged for so long under an austere and fearful Christianity.

Our drink problem is usually blamed on a profound social disease – the English inability to cope with talking to strangers, or even friends, unless we are off our heads. This, as it happens, is also an explanation for the fact that nobody in the world sends more text messages per person than we do. The two things may seem unrelated, but consider the frantic thumb action in any bar on a Saturday night. We have only been able to do it for a decade, but 56 billion texts are now sent from UK phones every year. All because we don't want to talk. We would rather wear out our digits struggling against predictive text than dial a number and get our thoughts across in an instant. We would also rather email our ideas, comments or saucy flirtations to the colleague sitting two feet away from us than say anything to their face. Talking would be embarrassing. Somehow, if it's on screen, it's not. It is considered private – even though the boys down in IT are probably reading the message right now and having a chuckle. On our phones, by email, on Facebook or Bebo or MySpace, we would rather communicate in a way that does not require face-to-face contact, any day.

This addiction to privacy also helps to explain, perversely, why so many people visit cathedrals or attend church at Christmas. The impulse is nostalgic, a desire to reconnect with something lost. Or it is a rare chance to step outside a busy life and contemplate something bigger and older and more meaningful. Every year, about twelve million people visit cathedrals, which are among the top tourist attractions in the country. They offer fine art, magnificent architecture, mesmerising colour and inspirational music, with a stillness that is rarely available elsewhere.

They have come full circle: built to impress a population that could barely read, they can still get through to us today. Grace Davie, the sociologist of religion, says: 'The point is that we feel something, We experience the sacred, the set apart.' They are ideal, she says, for people 'for whom membership or commitment presents difficulties. They are places where there is no obligation to opt in or to participate in communal activities beyond the service itself.' Many of the visitors are tourists, but for local people cathedrals can be the antidote to those churches that want you to sign up straight away and give your life. Instead, you come and you go. You walk into a cathedral, you have the experience, you walk out again. You don't have to talk to anybody, if you don't want to.

It may sound counter-intuitive, but this is also true of going to church at Christmas. More than three million people attend a service on Christmas Eve or Christmas Day. This is often seen as a remnant of our emotional attachment – but it is also a sign of our estrangement from what church usually is. Christmas religion can be impersonal if you want it to be. You turn up with your friends and family (there is safety in numbers). You may well have a drink inside you (releasing inhibitions). You nod to familiar faces (but don't have to say much). You sing familiar songs and hear a familiar message. Then, when it's over, crucially, you can bolt for the door. No need to talk to anybody but the people who came with you. That's it, over for another year. Ho ho ho.

Not everybody feels this way. Some people want strength and certainty in their lives, not the stress of ambiguity. They want the security of knowing exactly what they are supposed to believe. The desire for that kind of fixed meaning is the reason why the faiths that are now receiving the most attention are those that are absolutely sure of themselves. They shout loudest. London, in particular, is now a cacophony of faith. Besides the countless churches, it has the largest Hindu temple outside India and plans for the largest mosque in Europe, next to the Olympic site. That is not far from the largest church in the country, the Kingsway International Christian Centre, which attracts twelve thousand people every Sunday. Led by the Nigerian pastor Matthew Ashimolowo it has a predominantly black congregation representing forty-six nationalities. This is bold, unapologetic Pentecostal Christianity of the kind that was given such a boost by Morris Cerullo, and it believes that God wants His followers to be rich . . . in loose change as well as spirit. Miracles and healings are promised and pursued. Other black-majority Pentecostal congregations are also growing in the cities, and the Church as a whole in this country is slowly changing colour: the latest figures show that the number of white churchgoers has dropped by a fifth over the last decade, while the number of black, Asian and other non-white people in services has risen, by a quarter in each case. Most new arrivals are choosing to worship with people from their own backgrounds, giving confidence to leaders like Ashimolowo.

He doesn't really need any more of that, but even he is not nearly as confident as the loudest voice in the marketplace, a megaphone of a man whose fundamentalism seeks to demolish all opposition. No, he is not among the 1.5 million Muslims in England, or the 500,000 Hindus, but is instead the acclaimed leader of the nation's seven million committed unbelievers: the Ayatollah of Atheists, Professor Richard Dawkins. If you think it is unfair to call him such a thing, take a look at the YouTube clip in which he speaks from the lectern at a college in Lynchburg, Virginia, on 23 October 2006. A young woman in the audience asks him what she acknowledges is probably the 'most simplest' question he will be asked all night: what if he is wrong? 'Well, what if I'm wrong?' The professor shakes his grey mane a little and collects his thoughts, before going on the attack:

Well, anybody could be wrong. We could all be wrong about the flying spaghetti monster and the pink unicorn and the flying teapot. You happen to have been brought up, I would presume, in the Christian faith. You know what it's like not to believe in a particular faith, because you're not a Muslim. You're not a Hindu. Why aren't you a Hindu? Because you happen to have been brought up in America, not in India. If you had been bought up in India, you would be a Hindu. If you were brought up in Denmark in the time of the Vikings, you'd be believing in Wotan and Thor [some members of the audience giggle]. If you were brought up in classical Greece, you'd be believing in Zeus. If you were brought up in central Africa, you'd be believing in the Great JuJu up the mountain. [There is open laughter now, although not, presumably, from any Africans present.] There's no particular reason to pick on the Judaeo-Christian God, in which by the sheerest accident you happen to have been brought up, and ask me the question: what if I'm wrong? What if you're wrong about the Great JuJu at the bottom of the sea?

Wild applause follows, for the intellectual equivalent of a seal cull. The logic is indisputable but the delivery is devastating. He knows nothing about the girl who asked the question, beyond being able to deduce that she is nervous and not his intellectual equal. So few of us are. Still, Dawkins falls on her like a ravenous dinosaur devouring some helpless little creature unfortunate enough to have evolved at a slower pace. The point is not just that he is rude and ungracious, but that Dawkins entertains people, in prize-fighting terms, by knocking down bums. He does it with the girl, and he does it in his writing by seeking out the most extreme religious dogma to attack. He's absolutely right that it seems 'a preposterous, mind-shrinking falsehood' to believe the creation story in Genesis is literally true and the earth is younger than the scientific evidence suggests, but that is why so many thoughtful Christians also reject those ideas. His demolition of intelligent design is convincing, but anyone who has seen someone they love die of cancer is going to struggle with it anyway. There is a great deal of truth in his attacks on indoctrination, fanaticism and bigotry, although his own scientific fundamentalism is as merciless as that of most hardcore religionists.

Professor Dawkins acts as if all scientists agree with him that science is incompatible with faith, when they most certainly do not. Some are wary of presenting science as rigid truth – as he often seems to – when they know and love it as a fluid thing that changes as each new proof or theory comes along. The middle ground is not fertile for Professor Dawkins. Like all extremists, he needs extreme opponents to put him at his best. He's not so good at convincing those who accept evolution but still won't give up the possibility of the divine.

Still, he's very popular, isn't he? Who would dare take him on? Not Rowan Williams, who is too clever to be drawn into that kind of battle. In any case, the Archbishop of Canterbury is not as important as he was. He has been knocked off his perch by someone who has more people in his pews than there are at Anglican services on a Sunday and who is now without doubt the most authoritative spiritual leader in the country. His rise is evidence of a profound and historic shift in the nature of English faith. This man speaks powerfully and clearly and has a confidence to match that of Richard Dawkins any day, blow for blow.

Who is he? Let's meet him, right now.

27

Meet the new boss

To get to the Archbishop of Westminster you go round the back of his magnificent, imposing cathedral and up a side-street, press a brass buzzer, and persuade the Irish nun who is the doorkeeper that you are expected. The doors are massive, heavy, dark wood. The staircase beyond them would suit the Addams family, and all the way up it are the shadowy portraits of previous cardinals and archbishops, each with the same smile, halfway between welcome and indulgence. It is easy to be wary, if you are not a Catholic. If you are, please forgive me the sin of cynicism, which I am fighting as I climb the stairs.

The Pope may be visiting this country soon after this book comes out, but my mind is full of an image of a recent papal visit to another land. His Holiness is standing at the top of the steps to his private jet, his hands in the air as if he is the champion, the greatest, the big news, the answer. Pope Benedict XVI is a German academic, and a former member of the Hitler Youth, who allows his bishops to say that condoms are wrong even while Aids is engulfing Africa. In the picture in my mind's eye he is all in white, of course, shining in his papal finery, while behind him stand two cardinals in black and purple, caped, wearing mirror shades, their hands clasped together in front of them like bodyguards, like

303

Mafiosi. How can an unbeliever help but think of dodgy money, of sinister mutterings, of power games, of Dan Brown plots? They don't exactly help themselves, do they?

Then again, high-level Catholic leaders don't often show much sign of caring what other people think of them. Why should they? More than any other, their Church knows what it is, what it believes, what it stands for and what it thinks you should do with your life. Confess. Obey. If you are looking for certainty in a confusing world, you will find it here. That is one reason why the Archbishop of Westminster, Vincent Nichols, has become so much more than the most important Catholic in England and Wales. His confidence, his clarity and the collapse into chaos of his rivals have left him as the most authoritative spiritual leader in the land – the first time anyone in his position has enjoyed that status since the Reformation. It's not just the force of his personality, nor even his willingness to attack. (MPs, he says, have fiddled the expenses system and given in to 'the easy temptation of greed'.) In 2006 the *Sunday Telegraph* declared: 'Britain has become a Catholic country.' This was on the basis of research showing there were more Catholics at Sunday services than Anglicans. It was a tight call, at 861,000 compared to 852,000. The Church of England said the comparison was unfair, because its people did not have the same obligation as Catholics to go every week.

Both sides were splitting hairs, though. Seven million people go shopping on a Sunday, and if you counted every person at every kind of church in the country there would still be nowhere near as many as that. The *Telegraph* was making Christmas mischief, but also reflecting a widely held perception that something had shifted, partly as a result of people coming to this country from abroad. The report was published the day after Tony Blair became a Catholic. With typical flair, he had chosen to make the move just before Christmas, when religious stories always get publicity. Catherine Pepinster, editor of the influential Catholic magazine the *Tablet*, said his conversion 'must be a sign that Roman Catholicism really has come in from the cold in this country'.

Vincent Nichols doesn't want to appear smug. 'What we strive for is one Christian voice,' he says, but then he can afford to. The decline in attendance has been slowed by the arrival of immigrant believers. 'There is one parish here with a thousand people going to mass on a Sunday and one hundred different nationalities represented,' he tells me, as we sit together in his enormous but sparsely furnished study. 'That is duplicated across all the big cities. From a Catholic point of view, it is really very good.'

The books on the Archbishop's shelves are all about politics and power: *The Pope and England*; *The Catholic Church and the Second World War*. The decor and furniture in his office – walls in neutral colours, a big desk, four capacious armchairs arranged around a cold hearth – have an air of faded grandeur, as if the room is inhabited by an aristocratic but threadbare aunt. Nichols himself is an earnest, attractive sort of man. Youngish looking for his sixty-three years, calm and confident, with a handshake to match, he's almost Peter Perfect in a dog collar. Almost. Other priests manage to make the all-in-black, semi-off-duty ensemble look like it is saving them from dressing as a tramp, but Nichols makes it look elegant. There are some in his Church who think he's a little too well presented, a little too ambitious. Some of his senior bishops apparently wrote to the Papal Nuncio, the Pope's man in London, to say, for goodness' sake, don't pick this man to be our leader. One source told a paper, anonymously, 'He could do with learning a little humility.' If that is so, it is hard to imagine him learning anything of the sort while he is the king of Westminster Cathedral, arguably the stateliest of the capital's many stately buildings.

Nichols has also been accused of shifting views and picking battles with the government on abortion, contraception, BBC bias and adoption by same-sex couples just to impress the Vatican. 'That would be a stupid thing to try to do,' he says, which is not quite denying it. 'Fortunately, in the Catholic Church, decisions about who is asked to do different jobs on the whole are made a long way from here. I was a bit confused by the continual accusation, it didn't correspond to how I understand myself. The only thing that I am ambitious about is to live a good life. Full stop.'

The son of two teachers from Crosby (also, curiously, the birthplace of Robert Runcie), he reluctantly gave in to his calling at the age of sixteen while standing at the Anfield Road End watching Liverpool play. 'I was protesting to God and saying, "Will You please leave me alone? Why can't You just let me be like everyone else in this crowd?" I don't want this notion of being a priest.' How exactly was God making His will known? 'It was . . . a nag. At times, just a nag.' A voice in his head? 'It's a feeling in the pit of your stomach, it's a conviction when you wake up in the morning, it's an anxiety.' His brother Peter was with him on the night before he was made a priest in Rome. 'With typically impeccable timing, he said to me, "What are you doing this for?" I said, "Well it's a bit late to ask now. But I think it makes sense of who I am. I think this is my road to being happy."' His Merseyside lilt comes across very well on the radio and television. Once, during the funeral of Pope John Paul II, he was asked by Huw Edwards to explain what was happening. 'No, Huw,' he said, quietly but firmly. 'This is an important part of the mass. We will be quiet.'

For all his confidence, attendance at mass is down 40 per cent since the sixties. Three-quarters of his flock of 4.2 million people are lapsed or lost, but Nichols sees a form of salvation in the new England:

We have Poles outside our churches on a Sunday, kneeling on the pavement because there isn't enough room inside. That's good for the cause of religious faith. It's good for the Catholic community which has to open its doors and its minds. And I hope it is good for the people who have chosen to come here to get settlement, to know that there is a welcome for them here and that they can play their part in this society.

The worldwide Catholic Church totals more than a billion people. It feels no need to apologise or adjust. It has a strong product to sell. 'The Catholic Church has some strong cards in its hands, when it comes to holding together and being clear in its principles,' Nichols says, and it's hard not to hear that as a critique of the poor, squabbling Anglicans. He insists it's not a competition, but later damns them indirectly as he tells me with happy enthusiasm that dealing with the State is a bit like lighting a gas fire: 'If you are too far away from it, the spark goes out. If you are too close to it, the spark goes out. The trick is in keeping just the right distance, and nearness.'

As we speak, advertising authorities are considering whether to relax the rules on when commercials for condoms and abortion can be shown on TV. This very modern Archbishop is mobilising his forces to write letters and emails and sign online petitions. 'If you don't make your voice heard, then, quite understandably, it's not attended to.' Don't condoms illustrate a huge problem for the Catholic hierarchy? Frankly, when the priest comes into the bedroom, even the most devout ignore him. 'What's being ignored is that the proper place for sex is within a stable, permanent, lifelong, faithful relationship sealed by marriage,' he says, and there is no question of compromise here. Nichols fought hard to try to stop the government allowing same-sex couples the right to adopt. 'Sexual living is a reflection of God's love for us. It has two key qualities, which are faithful-ness and creation of new life. That is the heart of what I want to be saying.'

That is hard to take seriously when it comes from a celibate, but then I'm not a Catholic. Vincent Nichols is unafraid of talk-ing frankly to unbelievers, which is just as well, because as the most high-profile, most convinced Christian in the country, he has to take on the likes of Dawkins. Catholic bishops wear their anachronisms like badges of honour, but what answer would he give to the question asked by that poor, unfortunate student in Virginia? Isn't it possible that everything Nichols does is based on self-deception? That there was no God nagging him, on the ter-races at Anfield, and his calling was just the fretting of a teenage boy overwhelmed by hormones and the powerful example of the priests he saw every day? The Archbishop doesn't raise his voice. Why should he? He knows he's right. 'Then it is a very remark-able pattern in life, repeated millions of times over, that people give themselves to following a call in God, and live fulfilled and happy lives. Are you saying it's all a myth?'

'I might be,' I say.

Vincent Nichols, the leading spiritual figure in this country, the man with the largest and best-upholstered stall in the mar-ketplace of faith, smiles that indulging smile. 'I don't think so.'

Hold on to your ermine, there is talk of Nichols' predecessor, Cormac Murphy O'Connor, being given a seat in the House of Lords. Constitutional experts are trembling over their post-lunch port at the prospect of this daring appointment, which would overturn five hundred years of history and make him the first Catholic bishop in the Upper House since Henry VIII snatched control of the English Church. Can't you feel the earth shake beneath your feet? No? Perhaps that's because it doesn't really matter as much as some of the more antiquated historians claim. Thirty years ago it would have done, but not now. There appears to be agreement that the Act of Settlement of 1701 should be abolished so that a future monarch can marry a Roman Catholic (as well as making it possible for women to be first in line to the throne). The Pope has already begun to steal priests from the Church of England, telling those who are upset about the idea of women bishops that they can come over to Rome instead and keep their own traditions. That includes the right to be married. Oh and they can bring their own people too. Hundreds of congregations are believed to be taking this unprecedented offer seriously.

Whatever happens, the argument for England continuing to have an established Church, with unique privileges in the making and approval of laws, the appointing of monarchs and the great ceremonies of our national life, is over. It's just that many of those involved do not realise it. When members of the Church of England fret about whether it should be disestablished – prised away from the State and the Crown and left to fend for itself like any other beleaguered Church – they fail to see that this is already happening, by default. The claim to care for every soul in every community is now absurd, thanks to the shortage of money, priests and congregations. The idea that the next monarch will copy his mother and vow to preserve and protect the one true Protestant faith as upheld in the Thirty-Nine Articles is laughable, given the need to reflect the spirituality of the whole nation and the desire of the heir to the throne to be named Defender of Faith. All faith, in all its variations. The coronation service will surely have to be multi-faith, removing the Church of England's historic claim to be the sole conductor of all the great national religious ceremonies. If Charles is still going to be Supreme Governor, it will require a great deal of knuckle-gnawing by

constitutionalists and liturgists and almost certainly mean a separate service from the coronation. In any case, nobody will be
able to pretend that he embodies Anglican faith as his mother did.
We know too much about him to say that.

The Prime Minister has always appointed bishops on behalf of
the monarch, but that particular intimate link between Church,
State and Crown has already been broken by Gordon Brown. On
coming to power he asked for just one name to be presented to
Downing Street in future, so that it could be rubber-stamped and
sent on to the Queen. Since she was unlikely ever to reject the
name, he had effectively placed the decision back into the hands
of the Church itself. 'We should not have rolled over so feebly on
this,' said the agitated Peter Bruinvels, a Church Commissioner.
'We will wind up as an irrelevance in the constitution if we're not
careful.' Too late, Mr Bruinvels. Too late.

In the Commons, very few MPs now see the point of the law
that requires them to accept or reject what the Church decides,
so that's just a rubber stamp, too. Eventually, Parliament will stop
finding the time. The House of Lords includes twenty-six
Church of England bishops who enjoy status and influence not
given to the leaders of any other faith community, but those bishops are going to get their mitres clipped. As I write this, the long
debate about how to reform the House of Lords seems to be
coming to a head at last. The Lords Spiritual are likely to be abolished completely, unless their selection is altered to include
leaders of other faiths. In any case, there will be a massive loss of
status and influence for the Anglicans.

In all these ways, the ties that bind the Church to the State and
the Crown are unravelling. However long it takes, the process
cannot now be stopped. The principle is settled. The argument
is over. The Church of England as we knew it is finished. It's like
Wile E. Coyote just after he has run over the edge of a very deep

canyon: hanging in mid-air with his legs whirling furiously, trying desperately not to look down.

So much, then, for the people who know exactly what they believe. What about the rest? If the polls are right then there are about 26 million people in England who believe in some kind of God but don't belong to a religious institution. They get ignored in the debate about what kind of country this is now, because they have no collective voice – but they are still present and in the majority. You could say that they make up the biggest group of believers around, a new national faith which has no money, no premises and holds no meetings, except by accident. If it ever does so the opening hymn should be Scott English and Larry Weiss's 'Hi Ho Silver Lining' because 'we're everywhere and nowhere baby, that's where we're at'. That's where they come from, too. People of all faith backgrounds and from all over the world make up what we might call The Church of Everywhere (or to give it a full and proper title, The Church, Temple, Mosque or Other Affiliated Building of Everywhere and Nowhere, Baby). The question is, do they have anything in common? Is there anything identifiably English about this loose gathering of believers? Is there a common spirituality at work that embraces all our competing visions of the divine and yet is still ours? In other words, is there still an English God?

28

Goodbye England's Jade

Jade Goody was accused of being the worst of us. She was branded thick, vulgar and gobby, and with good reason. That's what happens when you go on prime-time television and say you think 'East Angular' is abroad and Rio de Janeiro is a person. Ha ha, look at the daft cow. The dental nurse from Bermondsey made a laughing stock of herself on the 'reality' television show *Big Brother* in 2002, but she also became a star. Not everybody sneered. Some laughed, because they recognised themselves and they liked her. She trained for the London Marathon by eating Chinese takeaways and curries, then collapsed on the course, saying she hadn't known how far it was: 'I don't really understand miles.' That was quite funny, actually.

The stories the tabloids told about her childhood were not. The one-armed, drug-using mother, the useless-junkie dad, the aggro and the abuse made people sympathise and like her even more. They bought ghost-written Jade Goody books, and the weight loss videos that made no mention of her liposuction, and the perfume that had even less to do with the real person but still sold nearly as many as the scents by Posh and Kylie. She opened a beauty salon and had her own television series. This girl whose agent had once hired a tutor to help her read and

write began to look tough and street smart. Here was the
underdog, the survivor, a woman worthy of respect for what she
had made from her one little slice of good fortune. She wasn't
thick at all, just under-educated, and the chaos of her family life
explained that. Gobby, undeniably, but vulgar is just what posh
people say when they don't like you, isn't it? She was taken up
as the ultimate proof that we're all just a lucky break from untold
wealth and stardom. What a lie that is, but Jade Goody made it
seem true. If she could do it, blimey, anyone could. Why not
you? Why not me?

Then the silly woman went and lost the lot. She let another
set of *Big Brother* cameras catch her being a snarling racist and
bully. She was expelled from the house, and from our good
books. Her defenders said she wasn't really being racist when she
abused the Indian actress Shilpa Shetty; she was just being herself. That was all Jade could do, that was why she was loved, she
meant no harm. It was true. She was a girl from Bermondsey
who had bettered herself and moved to Essex, and in both
places the culture was still in transition from the deep prejudice
of the recent past to the mixed-race future. I know the area of
Essex she called home, I grew up with those people and I know
they happily have close friends who are black or Asian, but
when they get rattled they might still call them 'black bastards'.
It's fear. It's secret. Jade let everyone see the fear, and you can't
do that. Particularly not on telly.

She apologised frantically, through the magazines and television shows that had made her famous, but it wasn't enough. Not
until she agreed, out of bravery and desperation, to go to India
and appear under the extreme scrutiny of that country's *Big
Brother*. Scrutiny was never more extreme than on that day in
August 2008 when she was called to the diary room and picked
up a mobile phone and heard the voice of her consultant back

in London, who had demanded to break in to the show, telling her that she had a cancer that could kill her. The images of her emerging from that room, dark eyed, dishevelled and in pieces, are devastating to watch. We did watch. She was ours. This was where it had always been leading, towards someone dying for our entertainment, voyeurs that we are. Not so happy to take part in life outside our own families any more, but happy to watch. Jade didn't withdraw. She understood and she let us have it all: the pictures of her chemo-induced baldness, on the front of all the tabloids; the tearful fretting about her boys; the tele-vised wedding to her Jack, her jack-the-lad, only six weeks before she died.

So what? Well, the funeral was an unusually public display of new English spirituality. Not the clever middle-class kind, but the folk faith of the majority. It's an improvised faith, an inven-tive one, sentimental and tacky but real none the less. For the first time, it was televised. Sky News cameras saw the hearse – a Rolls-Royce, of course, because brands are a guarantee of quality if you don't know any better – stop by the market where Jade's family once ran a stall, and a single white dove was released. Up it flew, over the heads, over the buildings, escap-ing, like anyone with any sense. The coffin was taken thirteen miles to the north, along the migratory route taken by so many families, including my own. Out to the suburbs. There were hundreds of people waiting to see her funeral on the huge screens that had been erected outside the church, mostly women and children, and I understood why.

That part of Essex, the East End transplanted to the edge of the forest, is a place where even the smart kids have to pretend to be stupid and the only thing that really matters is money. The Essex boys and girls who live there know that the world thinks they are brash and materialistic, and they play up to it, partly

314

because they are those things but also because they are hustler smart. Nobody was a better hustler than Jade. Every time the sneering classes laughed at her, the people she left behind and those who lived close to her nice big house pulled her closer to their hearts.

I was there, in the crowd, as the men in black shouldered her white and silver coffin and carried it into the church, the lilies on it trembling. 'Jade from Bermondsey', said a pink wreath on the hearse; 'East Angular', said the one on the car behind it. This was an Anglican church, but for once the institution seemed to understand that it was only playing host to a faith it could not define. If it gets that message, it may yet remake itself. There is nothing in the Thirty-Nine Articles about a dying twenty-seven-year-old giving bracelets to her very young boys, so they can rub them when they want to feel her near; nor in her telling them that she is going to be the brightest star in the sky. That's the sort of stuff we've been doing for ever, mostly with the Church's disapproval.

'Be strong, Jackiey,' someone shouted to her mother, 'she's looking down on you.' Flowers had been thrown into the path of the hearse, of course. The great Stephen Fry, who is not above sentimentality, called her 'a Princess Diana from the wrong side of the tracks'. It says a lot about us now that this great man of letters, a modern Dr Johnson, gave his verdict via Twitter.

There was a choir, but not a chilly Anglican one. The mostly black London Community Gospel Choir added soul to the ceremony. Gospel has woven its way into English life through the American culture we seem so desperate to copy, so that every wannabe who auditions for *X-Factor* imitates the vocal stylings that only Whitney Houston knew how to do not so long ago. No white church choir singing traditional music could have produced as much emotion as gracefully as the LCGC did, singing 'Amazing Grace' while the coffin was carried in. Jack-the-husband read a poem which was full of bad rhymes and seemed to have borrowed its faith from *The Lion King* – 'When we look into the sky for the brightest star above/Bobby, me and Freddie will send you all our love' – but it was applauded warmly. Then came the pictures, the videos and the music that have become such important parts of modern funerals since Diana, as well as a tribute from her publicist, the king of spin, Max Clifford. Jade was now famous all over the world for the manner of her death, he said. She would have loved all the attention. One of her former teachers told funny stories about what a terrible student she was, but how she was 'open and true to herself' and 'had more front than Selfridges'. He read the poem 'Do Not Stand at My Grave and Weep' by Mary Frye, suggesting Jade was now at one with the divine, in the natural world: 'I am the starshine of the night./I am in the flowers that bloom.'

As all this happened in the church, the large crowd that had gathered outside was silent. You could hear the news helicopter clattering overhead, but the spectators were absolutely caught up in what was happening, hardly saying a word. Until the churchy bits. Then they didn't close their eyes in prayer; they stood watching, as if this were a show being put on for their behalf. This was 'vicarious religion', as Grace Davie calls it, when we are happy to let other people pray on our behalf. They didn't sing 'The Old Rugged Cross', but then they didn't know the words. People just don't know that stuff any more. Whenever the service became even a little religious, in the language of the readings or the liturgy, the people switched off. Or rather, they switched on their mobile phones and rang their friends. The low murmur of conversation became louder. Some people even walked away, because this religious stuff was not part of their lives. They didn't get it and they didn't want it.

When the sermon started, they shut up. Why? First, because the priest was a woman, and looked vaguely like the Vicar of Dibley. Second, she had not assumed that she had the right to be heard, but rather focused everything she was saying on the Jade she had come to know personally, as her death had approached. 'We don't expect, do we, to be celebrating a wedding and then to be saying farewell to the bride just six weeks later? We don't expect to have to bury our children, whatever age they are. We don't expect those who are so young and so full of life and love to be taken from us. And yet that is life – that is the reality we face today.' She even produced the copy of the Bible that Jade had read on her hospital bed. 'To me, the fact these verses are underlined means . . . that when the last column inches have been written about Jade's unforgettable life, then that in no way is the end of her story.'

The sermon was brilliant, because it was very short and poignant and personal. This was the Church as servant, willing to offer a place for ritual and reflection to those in need, whatever they believed. And what they believed, judging from the content and the cards and flowers and balloons outside, and the things people in the crowd said afterwards, was what Max Clifford said: 'Jade has moved to a better place.' She had been given an upgrade, to a VIP suite without pain. It was folksy, it was humorous, it was irreverent at times and highly emotional at others. It was pagan in the way people enlisted the beauty of the natural world in defence of Jade and talked of her being up with the stars, burning bright, and throughout most of it anyone of any kind of faith could have agreed with its sentiments and prayers. Family first. Friendship as strength. Love beyond death. It was personal, yet inclusive. It was deeply sentimental but also inspiring, whatever might be said about the way in which Jade became famous. Her fame revealed the worst of us and her death was appalling; but her funeral, beyond the sentiment and the showbiz, showed glimpses of our best.

29

And did those feet?

Think of the perfect English village. Go on, be as obvious as you like. There's an ancient parish church, isn't there? The bells are ringing, echoing around a churchyard. There are lovely old houses, made out of local stone, in a street where bicycles lean against a flinty wall, and there are hardly any cars. Let's have lads playing football in the road, undisturbed. What about a red telephone box, we need one of those, and a little post office that sells groceries, and, of course, a welcoming pub where they serve hearty food in front of a roaring fire. Now, let's look at it from above, perhaps from high on the ridge of a nearby hill, which could be on the South Downs Way. A wide sky, a patchwork of shades of green stretching out below us, and there in the valley is the village, its church tower cuddled by trees, looking just like the idyll you see in the opening titles for *The Vicar of Dibley*, that gently funny celebration of the way we think we used to live.

The place you have just imagined is called Firle. It's real, it's in Sussex, and it looks as much like the perfect English village as anywhere could. If the soul of England is anywhere, it's here, wouldn't you think? A few years ago the people of England were asked to name the icons they felt defined them as a nation and a list was made. Obviously, the Angel of the North is far away, but as I walk towards the pub (that's one ticked off), past the phone box (2) and the church (3), I realise I am surrounded. There will be stamps bearing the Queen's head (4) in the post office. The name of the village comes from the Old English word *fierol*, which means overgrown with oak (5), and there will be a robin (6) somewhere in the hedges (7), even if this is not the season for roses (8). The lovingly replicated rustic kitchen that I can see through one of the cottage windows surely contains a copy of Mrs Beeton's *Book of Household Management* (9) and someone here will have *Pride and Prejudice* by Jane Austen (10) on their bookshelves. Morris dancers (11) come and perform in the summer, and no doubt they are occasionally watched by a woman in a miniskirt (12). She would be pretty cold if she turned up now, on the first day of November, so I would invite her into the Ram Inn to sit by that fire and have a nice warming cup of tea (13) and a cheese sandwich (14). Meanwhile, I'd have a roast beef dinner (15). Later, we could drive to the coast, which is only a few minutes away, and watch a Punch and Judy show (16) while sharing fish and chips (17). We could listen to an FA Cup (18) commentary on the car radio on the way back, unless she preferred *The Archers* (19).

Okay, I'm starting to get carried away, but Firle does feel like the spiritual home of a certain kind of Englishness, the kind that is nostalgic and idiosyncratic and gets flogged to death by the Tourist Board. Soon there will be coachloads of visitors coming to the village every day, when the landscape around it is designated part of a new national park, the closest to London – but for now, out of the summer season, not many outsiders turn left off the main road and find their way past the dead-end sign and the left-hand bend that makes you think you are entering a secret place, probably owned by a lord.

You are. You just passed the entrance gates to the big house,

And did those feet?

Firle Place, a proper stately home which has been run by the same family for five hundred years. Up in the church there is the alabaster effigy of Sir John Gage, who was close to Henry VIII and took charge of the disbanding of the local monasteries as part of the King's Protestant revolution, even though he himself was a Catholic. And a pragmatist, I think we can safely say. Later, during the reign of the Catholic Mary, his son oversaw the burning of Protestant heretics. Even later, they converted; so the family clearly had the ability to roll with the times. The present Lord Gage has members of the royal family for sleepovers. The house is allegedly open to the public, but only for something like two hours a day on certain days in the summer, and you can't just wander about, you have to go on a guided tour. It's marvellous. You buy a ticket from a woman behind a counter, who then calls you into a different room and takes it off you again, thank you very much. Then she locks the door so that it is impossible to get out.

If she thinks you might run away with the silver, or with an Old Master under your arm, her fears are not misguided. On the day I had a look around there was a policeman with a dog on the lawn, sniffing clues as to who had stolen some porcelain worth a million pounds. They thought the thieves had come on the guided tour first. A police sign on the community noticeboard asked if anybody had noticed any 'suspicious people' in the village. Would that be them strange folk with the eyes that glow red in the dark?

I'm not going up to the big house today. I'm going to the pub, where they are serving pints (20) of Harveys, the finest beer in England, at ten o'clock in the morning. This is not because Firle has more alcoholics per pretty cottage than anywhere else (it doesn't); nor is it because the weather (21) on this first Saturday in November is agonisingly cold, with a really annoying mist of rain that gets under your clothes and fogs your glasses. The pub is open because the hunt (22) is coming. It will assemble here today, before thundering off in search of a fox. Or rather not, because it is not allowed to do that any more. Instead, a fox's brush dipped in fox urine will be dragged across country by a willing gal on a horse, ten minutes ahead of the pack. 'It's not the real thing,' says a hunt grandee, a man of Hogarthian girth who would make any right-thinking horse rear on its hind legs, 'but it's the best we can do.' He is talking as the horses begin to arrive, clopping out of trailers parked haphazardly in the surrounding lanes. There is a queue (23) of Land-Rovers (24) now backing up to the main road. Soon the space outside the pub is filled with what feel like hundreds of mighty mares and geldings, all big and strong enough to jump hedges and rip through ploughed fields. 'Are you frightened?' asks a horsey woman with a little whinny. The answer is: yes, I flaming well am. Will that hoof kick back and smash my kneecap? Why has this enormous honey-coloured horse just lurched sideways, knocking me over with its flank? Where the hell did that big black head come from and why is it staring like that?

'And who are you?' says a red-faced man who must be ex-military. 'Not an anti,' I say quickly. They hate the campaigners who come with cameras, hoping to film a real fox being torn apart when the law says the hounds should be called off. It hasn't happened so far, because the hunts follow the law, at least when people are watching. Who knows what happens on a wet Wednesday afternoon in the woods? And, frankly, who cares? An extraordinary amount of parliamentary time and energy was spent introducing a law that the average bobby (25) considers unenforceable and which hasn't saved the foxes, because farmers just shoot them instead. The farce happened because the English are so sentimental about animals that the ban was an easy vote winner, and because it bought off a few simple-minded back-benchers who might (and should) otherwise have made more of a stink about going to war. The words 'Ban the Ban' were burned into the side of the Downs in letters one hundred feet high at the height of the fight, but now the hunt is just waiting for the Tories to come in and overturn it.

'The antis really are pests, with their abuse,' says Julia, one of the three Masters of the Hunt, a redoubtable sixty-seven-year-old woman who makes me think it is the riders who are more likely to flick V-signs (26) at the antis. I'm talking to her boot, because she is high above me on the back of Priscilla, a bay mare of similar vintage, in equine terms. 'What do people do if they fall off while jumping a hedge?' 'Get back on.' The stiff upper lip (27) is mandatory here, even if it has disappeared elsewhere. 'Apart from anything else, the antis look awful in those balaclavas.' Right. I regret my mud-spattered oilskin, which looks as if it has been bundled up damp in the back of the car for months. This is because it has.

The huntsman on the next horse is immaculate in his scarlet coat, despite almost certainly being paid less than a dustman for keeping the hounds in good order for this gathering of aristos, landowners, company directors and farmers. He is preparing to parp his little horn. Usually at this point the Reverend Peter Owen-Jones would climb a little wooden platform outside the Ram Inn to make a short prayer, blessing the hounds. 'Amen.' He can't be here today, so off they all go anyway in a thunder of hooves and howls, barks and bugle soundings, leaving me alone to reflect on something I have seen so often before among the landed and horsey classes who still have such influence over rural life, and which has been confirmed again in conversations here today. They are as confused and fearful of the future as the rest of us.

Up in Yorkshire, handing me a pheasant sandwich and a hip flask of whisky one misty morning, as she prepared for a hare-coursing event that wasn't supposed to be happening in the eyes of the law, a weathered woman in a Barbour and headscarf asked if I thought it was 'all going to be over soon'. She meant her way of life. I didn't know. She was local, she said, and I asked for how long. 'Eight hundred years.' The look on my face made her laugh. 'Not me personally, you understand.' That was how long the local manor house had been in the family. 'We're selling. Going to be a ruddy hotel. Breaks my heart.' She looked like she had a stout heart, but it was hurting. People like that feel the loss of the old certainties that shaped their family histories as much as any of us might feel the sudden withdrawal of electric light. They're afraid, because they are not immune to change and they have stopped believing in the old-fashioned God, just like everyone else.

In Yorkshire, and in Firle, I saw that something else had taken the place of God. They still had faith, but now it was in tradition. To them, field crafts, rural sports, hedgerows and stately homes represent, in real terms, what it means to be English; and they have collaborated with the likes of the National Trust to sell this vision to day-trippers, too. It's like farmers becoming stewards of the land: reassuring for the rest of us who live in dirty, frantic cities and a source of income for them, but ultimately hollow. That is what has happened to faith in rural England, as far as I can see, now that the churches have only a few faithful but ageing supporters left. Once, the countryside was taken as a sign of the glory of God. Now that the old God is all but out of the equation, people worship tradition and the countryside itself.

That's what it seems like to me, anyway, but what do I know? The man I need to see is the vicar, but we don't get to meet until the following summer. Peter Owen-Jones arrives at the Ram Inn just after noon wearing a big floppy hat that is part Indiana Jones and part Tom Baker's Dr Who, as well as a long, tan leather coat, a bluish tartan waistcoat and a French-blue clergy shirt with one of those dog collars that go all the way round, like a proper dog's collar. The vicar is quite the character, and, of course, the people in the pub know him well. No Harveys this time, but rock shandy. He is fitting me in between preparation for a charity game of cricket (28) – Firle Cricket Club being one of the oldest in the world – and a funeral. I don't know if he's going to read from the King James Bible (29) or lead the singing of 'Jerusalem' (30), but speculating on it does give me a chance to shoehorn them in here. What is it about that hymn, by the way? It is our real national anthem, sung at cricket and rugby matches and by public schoolboys, although nobody really knows how it came to be so important to us. As other people have pointed out, it has the structure of a peculiar joke. 'And did those feet in ancient time/Walk upon England's mountains green?' Er, no. 'And was the holy Lamb of God on England's pleasant pastures seen?' No, 'fraid not. 'And did the Countenance Divine shine forth upon our clouded hills?' Have a guess. 'And was Jerusalem builded here, among these dark satanic mills?' No, Billy. Sorry. Enough. Incidentally, if and when we do ever get to that 'builded' place, I sincerely hope it's not like Jerusalem at all. Watching suicide angels trying to blow up celestial tanks as they mow down the cherubim is not my idea of heaven.

Shall we leave the icon thing alone now? You get the idea. For a village with a population of 170 to be able to claim half the items on the list, it must be pretty darned English, mustn't it? 'This is not England,' says the vicar, calmly. 'If you come from a thousand miles away and you want to see the real England, then you might come here and think that you have found it. You have not.' That's enigmatic. 'Real England is a thousand different things. This is a tiny part of it. Walking up the High Street in

Bromley by Bow at one o'clock in the morning is just as much real England.' That's easy to say when you are living in a beautiful house in a beautiful village in a beautiful part of the country, where the only living thing in danger from knife crime is the pheasant about to have its throat cut, but Owen-Jones is saying something else, too. Firle is not what it seems. The hunt was chasing a fox that wasn't there. 'I know this looks like a picture of beauty, but we're dealing with the reality and the mess of life. What makes it beautiful are not the bricks and mortar but the people who live here. This is the strongest community I have ever lived in, and I think a great deal of that is down to the fact that people don't own their own houses.' That's a surprise. It turns out that the half-flint houses look similar because they are all owned by Lord Gage. You have to apply to the estate office to get one, and you can't change the look of it without permission. At first glance, this is a place where the envious English obsession with property prices should be rampant, but in fact it's non-existent. 'It's a level playing field.'

Well, it is if you're not his lordship, I'd say. It sounds feudal to me. Then again, the vicar is not even really the vicar, not in the old-fashioned sense. He's a television presenter who attends to the spiritual welfare of the village when he is not away making programmes for the BBC. Owen-Jones is one of the growing number of non-stipendiary ministers who are not paid by the Church but are trained for the priesthood and do other work for money. Their goodwill is extending the death throes of the established Church in places like Firle, for now. He gets a house, but that's all, and in return he is the vicar not only of Firle but of the nearby villages of Glynde and Beddingham. He is supposed to be God's man in each of them, all the time, without pay. That's exhausting, but he likes it. 'I am in no way perfect parish priest material, but the Church of England can't afford to have that any more. Within the next ten years, in the countryside, most vicars will be like me and won't be paid.' He quotes a scene from *Lark Rise to Candleford* where the schoolmistress calls in the local vicar to deal with unruly pupils, and he beats them. 'I think that notion of being a parish priest – as Jean-Paul Sartre noted, a policeman in a dress – has thankfully gone. But there is still a very deep affection, especially within the countryside, for the one man or woman whose head is in the clouds. Really, a spiritual shaman who cares for people and keeps their secrets.'

'Shaman' is not the sort of word that his boss would use. Wallace Benn is the determinedly Evangelical Bishop of Lewes. I wonder how they get on, and I tell him a story about Christmas. We were down at our local bandstand, which is situated right on the beach, by the crashing waves. Every Christmas Morning a silver band plays a selection of carols and a couple of thousand people turn up to sing along, wearing Santa hats and taking surreptitious nips from flasks of mulled wine. It's a cheerful occasion, unique to an English seaside town, and it attracts all ages. This time, somebody had asked along Bishop Benn.

Anyone other than a bishop with an overdeveloped sense of his own status would have realised that the thing to do was greet everyone, remind us why we were there, maybe say a quick prayer and get off. Two minutes, maximum. As the sermon that the Bishop chose to bring us that morning passed the tenth minute, people who had been happily singing Christian carols found the warmth of their goodwill disappearing and the December cold creeping up their legs. By the time he passed twenty minutes, they were walking away. Actually turning their backs on the Bishop, giving up on the event they had been enjoying so much before he arrived, and going off to do something else. Perhaps half the crowd did that. The mood was ruined. It was a parable of the way the Church behaves in the dog days of its establishment, pretending it has not lost its status and still assuming it is entitled to berate and define us, even as people turn their backs and walk away in droves. We don't want that, isn't it clear enough by now? Why could the Bishop not realise that he was there by invitation, not by right? Who in the name of his own God did he think he was?

The vicar of Firle seems to quite like his bishop, but he does say this: 'The Church of England, because it is wrapped up in the Establishment, has wrongly assumed that it has the right to bludgeon people with the Word of God. The whole parish system is underpinned by the assumption that we have a right to be there. That approach has been a huge failure.' And this is a man who still loves it. 'I came back from being away with renewed respect for the shambles and the dust that is the Church of England, because it's still something fluid. It still has within it the germ of believing in universal love and tolerance. That is a fine thing.'

We can agree on that. Despite all the decline and disaster stories, for the last little while in our national history, the actual parishioners have provided a model of decency, respect, community, tradition and commitment to those around them, in particular the less well off. They will continue to do so, even as the churches empty and the institution gives in to rigor mortis. They have been pathetically served by their leaders, who have broken something valuable and betrayed the very real good they do, which means their mild goodness is no longer seen as the main incarnation of Christianity in this country. That leaves a vacuum which people with more extreme beliefs are rushing to fill. If we are not careful, extremism will dominate the character of England.

We also have to face another question: who is going to look after the buildings? The Church has 16,200 places of worship, including some of our greatest architectural treasures, but it cannot afford to keep them open on its own. The parishioners who do the day-to-day work and pay for most of the repairs are ageing, and dwindling in number. Peter Owen-Jones is relatively lucky in running his in a gorgeous village that will attract a lot of visitors when Firle is enclosed within the new South Downs National Park; but just a few miles away there is another church with a negligible congregation that is losing £400 a month and will probably have to close soon. Across the country, away from the tourist spots, there are hundreds like that. Boarding them up or selling them off as flats is not a disaster in the city, but losing the church hits a village hard when it has already lost, as so many have, the post office, the general store and the pub.

One in five will go within a generation, according to a recent forecast. Hundreds of others have already turned into dysfunctional museums, in use for no more than a couple of hours a week but kept open at great expense because people love them and feel that they should be preserved. Doing so costs £200 million a year, of which about £40 million comes from English Heritage and the National Lottery. The Church is left to find the rest but has started pointing out that it owns nearly half the Grade I listed buildings in the country and doesn't see why it should drive itself to the edge of bankruptcy in order to preserve treasures that belong to everybody, not just believers. The government doesn't think it can help. And why on earth should it, given that they're not all lovely and many of them have outlived their use by congregations that have vanished?

So there is trouble ahead. The pace of closure is increasing. What will happen, once the Church is unable to keep these buildings that help define the English landscape? Do we want them? We will have to decide.

When a vicar compares himself to a shaman, you can usually guess he doesn't know what he's talking about. Not this time.

Peter Owen-Jones has met more than a few during the extraordinary journeys that he undertook for the BBC to film a television series called *Around the World in Eighty Faiths*. With only his floppy hat for protection, the wandering priest met whirling dervishes in Syria, brawling Shinto fire carriers in Japan, trans-gender Islamic mediums in Indonesia who stabbed themselves to prove they were possessed, and neo-Catholics in Brazil who made him take part in their sacrament, the drinking of a tea made from a root that causes hallucinations. 'It's quite intense,' he said on camera as the tea, known as daime, worked on his brain. 'Everything seems closer. Your sense is being heightened, your sight, your sound.' After filming an episode in Japan, he said: 'Wherever I have been in the world there has been a sense that there is a divine. An other. I know that those who are atheists would say that's a human disease that we all suffer from, but it seems to be universal, this craving for God.' His global adventure has given those words some authority. So when I ask which country has the most fascinating spirituality, and the most compelling changes in culture, he surprises me by saying, 'England.'

'Really?'

Yes. You walk down the main street in Cairo or most of the world's cities and it is predominantly uniform, in terms of its culture. You go to London, Birmingham, Manchester, and it is truly cosmopolitan in a way it wasn't when I was ten years old. You look at the football team and it is clear that what it is to be English is not white and tea-drinking and bowler-hat-wearing any more. There isn't a blueprint for how to become a society like the one we are becoming, as our whole value system is contradicted by this wonderful influx of different ideas, different cultures, different cuisines, different musics. Everything. We have a chance to become something

we haven't consciously been before. This is an influx from
the world.

'Not to Firle,' I say. It's only a few years since the bonfire society here made an effigy of a caravan with a family inside and
gave it the number plate P1KEY. Then they set it on fire. The
police investigated but made no arrests. The society apologised
for any offence, and said it was only meant as a comment on the
council not finding anywhere for travellers to live, but it's not
exactly open-minded and welcoming, is it? Owen-Jones does
not answer directly, but he does say the village is nowhere near
as all white and insular as that story may suggest. 'The influences
of London and Brighton are alive and kicking.' The 'dogs of the
National Party' are not winning here, he says. 'Even from the
depths of this beautiful little Sussex village, I don't think that's
what we want to become.' Instead, he detects 'a growing awareness and tolerance of each other's tribe, and a growing
understanding that other religions – which previously were perceived as a threat – actually have a great deal to teach us.' He
would say that. It's his day job. He believes it, though, and he
thinks the English do, too. 'If to be English means we're going
to be tolerant, peace-loving, open-hearted and generous, then,
yes, I want to be part of it.'

Here endeth the sermon, but I want something more profound. What does this man who has gone in search of God all
over the world think is happening here, right now? 'There is a
huge spiritual change taking place,' he says. Oh no. I've heard that
before, from the lips of everyone from Billy Graham to Morris
Cerullo, but I don't interrupt. He's not talking about Christianity,
at least not in the way we have known it. The loss of the old
imperial model of Englishness that was 'about ruthlessness and
the lust for power' has created space for something else:

A new manner of approaching nature and the divine is coming up through the earth, through many of the emerging communities. It began with the arrival of the environmental movement. Friends of the Earth and the other NGOs have set out their stalls for a big change in our consciousness. It is happening under the radar, and it is going to be the defining feature of the next fifty years.

Now he really does sound like a shaman, but I'm not going to stop him. 'We are realising that we cannot keep taking from the land without consequence.'

What does that mean here, in this village? They have been debating whether they should go on using gravestones, given that they have to be imported at great environmental cost from South Africa and India. He talks about methods of farming, and how to treat the Downs: 'Do we want marble white butterflies in ten years' time?' He talks about the harvest feast the village is having, using only food that has been grown or produced locally.

There is a deep, resonant spirituality in this village, as there is emerging elsewhere in England. It is a contemporary spirituality, earthed in creation, influenced by Buddhism and a resurgent druidic paganism. The future, with all the difficulties we face, is not going to be sorted out by the scientists. It's going to take a complete change in our value systems and how we deal with each other – and, more profoundly, our relationship with the environment, moving from a position of dominance to one of harmony. That is the only way we will save ourselves.

People like Peter Owen-Jones are often accused of not really believing in anything, but from the look in his eyes I know that's not true. 'We are on the cusp of a huge awakening. A spiritual renaissance.' I have heard that before, but he means it. And I have also heard a rumour of something intriguing happening in the dark of night, in the countryside not far from here, which might just fit in with what he says. It will be easy to find, I am told.

Just follow the light of a hundred flaming torches.

30

A pagan place

Walk with me through the tunnel of fire, between the flames that light the way in the darkness, held up on either side by huge men and wild-eyed women. They are dressed in black boots, black trousers and black hats, with black coats made from rags, and their faces have been blackened by paint. They look as if they would give you a black eye in an instant. But these are not Hell's Angels charred on a satanic spit-roast, they are Morris dancers. The members of Hunter's Moon are unlike any Morris side you have ever seen: they smash huge sticks together instead of waving wimpish hankies and they have come to this place on a winter's night to take part in a pagan ritual.

'Oh, apple tree, we honour thee,' says an imposing woman in a velvet robe, who has separated herself from the crowd in order to stand alone by a massive, cold bonfire. It will be lit in a moment and the flames will leap and the night will crack as shot-guns are fired into the air. 'Each golden apple you bring forth, a gift to Aphrodite, has at its heart a pentacle, the symbol of her mystery,' the priestess declares, leading a ceremony she believes is older than history. There has been no publicity, but more than five hundred people have gathered in the shadows at this farm anyway, including several children who have climbed up into the branches of the trees. They are under strict orders to leave alone the apple cakes laid around the roots of the oldest tree, as both a sacrifice and a pagan equivalent of the bread in a communion. The silver chalice in the hands of the priestess contains mulled cider, an equivalent of communion wine. She holds the great cup above her head, like a football trophy, and declares: 'We call upon the old ones.'

This is a moment of high drama. It could not be more serious. 'Bless this cup, and bless the trees, and all that stand here among them.'

'And the tree monsters!'

What? The shout came from the leader of the Morris dancers. That can't be in the script, can it? The children in the trees are poking out their tongues. They're blowing raspberries. What in the name of Gaia is this all about? The laughter is loud. The priestess doesn't mind. Shouting rude things at her is not just okay, but celebrated. Can you imagine doing that at mass, or making some crude joke about booze or blood? Here, they think it's brilliant, and the priestess is smiling as the bonfire is lit and goes up with a whoomph to great cries of 'Wassail!'

That word is a very old one – even the Normans called it typically English – and here it refers to the tradition of blessing the orchard every year, usually with a good old drink-up. Modern pagans go beyond historic scholarship in connecting this rural custom with what they call the old religion, the one said to have existed in these isles before Christianity. 'I was making a libation,' the priestess tells me afterwards. 'Every tree in the orchard gets something. We are making offerings to the ancestors, the spirits and the old gods to ensure a good crop.'

The ancestors, the spirits and the old gods? That suggests a faith with a big cast list, an impression reinforced on the website of the Pagan Federation. 'Paganism is the ancestral religion of the whole of humanity,' it says boldly, linking it with the beliefs of ancient civilisations in Egypt, Greece, India, Japan, Persia and Rome. This reads very much like an attempt to portray the pagan creed as the one true way, as almost every other group of believers does – but the good news on that score is that getting modern pagans to agree on their beliefs is impossible. There are almost as many 'paths' as there are people: including druids, who see themselves as heirs to the priests of pre-Christian England; Wiccans, who practise modern witchcraft; shamans, who seek to engage with the spirits of the land; and heathens, who worship the gods of such North European tribes as the Vikings. Then there are those who make up their own paths. Paganism is an individualistic faith, which encourages each person to respond in his or her own way. At the heart of every variation, though, is the idea of a divine force inherent in nature. They are all 'followers of a polytheistic or pantheistic nature-worshipping religion'.

The census in 2001 recorded forty thousand pagans, but that is considered a huge underestimate. Activists say there were lots of them among the 300,000 who declared themselves Jedi, as in *Star Wars*, because pagans don't like telling the government what they are really up to. They would say that, though, wouldn't they? A more authoritative estimate comes from Ronald Hutton, a professor of history at Bristol University, who calculated a decade ago that there were 120,000 people going to pagan rituals or meetings. That was before *Harry Potter*, *Buffy the Vampire Slayer*, the *Lord of the Rings* films, *Charmed* and *Sabrina the Teenage Witch* made pagan spirituality and mythology part of pop culture. The Pagan Federation thinks the figure has trebled as a result: 360,000 would put them ahead of the Sikhs and in fourth place behind Hindus, Muslims and Christians. Professor Hutton tells me he can accept the figure may have doubled to 240,000, but that represents only those who participate in organised events.

Much more interesting is the extent to which pagan beliefs have become accepted among the wider public. 'It is best to think in terms of concentric circles, from those who are initiated members of a group such as a coven, out to those who go to Stonehenge for a drink and a party,' says Hutton. At the last summer solstice there were 36,500 people at Stonehenge, the most since the stones were reopened to the public nearly a decade ago. They were not ravers seeking a free party, as in the old days, but mostly people who saw some real spiritual significance in watching the sun come up between the stones. Unfortunately, it didn't show. The dawn was too cloudy. There was no doubt that people would be back next time.

Away from Stonehenge, much smaller groups of people marked the solstice by gathering before sunrise in gardens or woods, on beaches or hilltops across the country, some for organised rituals; and some, like my friend Cath, just responding to their own understanding of a spirituality that seems to work best in the open air. 'We went out in the garden to sit on the grass, in the dew, and tune in to things,' says Cath, who works at Canary Wharf and lives in a crowded street in Peckham, so she was not revelling in some rural idyll. 'The pursuit of the natural feels more urgent in the city,' she explains. 'You have to get it where you can.' She calls herself a pagan and has done a lot of research into the faith but never so much as attended a meeting, let alone signed up for anything. She is far from alone.

'What we believe is suddenly everywhere,' says Bantu, a dread-locked twenty-nine-year-old who was on a hill in Wales when the solstice came. He started to worship Gaia, the earth goddess, after learning about Her in a workshop at a climate camp. Bantu is a full-time environmental campaigner, moving from protest to protest, finding community and a common spirituality with the many people in the camps who wouldn't think of belonging to any kind of federation but who pursue a rainbow of revived, recreated or invented beliefs with nature at their heart.

Another protester, Caroline, became a pagan after taking part in the anti-road demos of the nineties. 'I was at Twyford Down, standing on the trees to stop the bulldozers,' she says. 'That big wave of eco-protest got squashed but it is coming back now with a vengeance, with G20 and the climate camps at Heathrow and Kingsnorth. Something new is happening.' That again? I keep hearing it. Now in her fifties, Caroline runs a publishing company in Brixton that specialises in urban music, so this is not just about people who live in pretty villages. Nor is it all white. At a pagan festival recently in Holborn, in the centre of London, I met Mani, a Sri Lankan who used to work on asylum cases for the Home Office and now helps Tamil immigrants. 'I was taken to the temple at the age of six and religion was something I respected. Sometimes I still go, but paganism is more empowering, because there is no boundary between you and the divine. I came to England and got pulled into a spirituality which is local to this land.'

The link between spirituality and the environment was made explicit for modern times by James Lovelock in the seventies, in his influential description of the earth as a living, self-regulating organism which he named after the Greek goddess Gaia. Some take his theory more theologically than others, but it remains the most famous example of the desire for new forms of spirituality that work together with a reappraisal of how we treat the planet. You certainly don't have to be pagan to be green, or vice versa, but the two movements have given each other energy, as each has grown. For many pagans, becoming a green campaigner is a way of demonstrating faith through practical action. For many activists, the pagan idea of an ancient and universal spirit that animates the earth gives their actions a personal, spiritual framework.

A pagan place

Not that you have to read eco-theory to get the message these days. 'I watch a lot of CBeebies with my youngest child,' says Catherine, a druid from Kent.

You see the indoctrination starting at an early age: recycle your rubbish, don't waste water, all of that. It's about how to live your life in a more friendly way towards the earth. It has been fantastic, watching the rest of the world catch up. If you start off trying to be environmentally aware, it is not much of a step to seeing all of nature as sacred, and from there to becoming a pagan.

Perhaps. It depends what you mean by 'a pagan', and that's where we really get to the point.

Some paths are 'mystery religions', like Wicca, which are hard to join. Once initiated, you become as vulnerable to exploitation as any other member of a closed religious group whose self-elected priests offer secret truths. Keep away from those, and the Pagan Federation says all you have to believe to be a pagan is this: that each of us has the right to follow our own path (as long as it harms no one); that there is a higher power (or powers); and that nature is to be venerated. The first of those is accepted wisdom in modern, anti-authority, individualist England. The second is a massively popular belief, with two-thirds of us saying we have faith in God, or gods. The third has become, within a generation, a sacred truth. The earth is dying, we are to blame, we need to repent and change our ways to have any hope of salvation: this is the gospel according to environmentalism, and to oppose it is considered blasphemous. It is what we believe, and it dominates the way we are told to live, from the price of petrol to what we are allowed to put in our wheelie bins. So, look beyond the witches and wizards and other hardcore practitioners for a moment to the countless people like Cath who are privately finding their own paths, and to the way pagan beliefs have become part of all our lives. It is not quantifiable, in a census or a survey, because our new way of believing does not want to sign up or be pinned down, it is elusive and private, but it is also obvious and all around us. We want a spirituality that relates to the earth. We need room for multiple gods, because we have multiple cultures. We go in for believing, not belonging. We want a faith with no formal structure, no domineering priests, no difficult creed, one that does not require us actually to do anything or go anywhere, if we don't want to. For all of that, paganism is perfect.

If you could stand on the white cliffs of Dover with a huge megaphone and ask everyone in England to put up their hands if they believed in live-and-let-live, looking after the planet and the existence of some kind of God, millions of hands would be raised. Most of the 26 million people who believe in a higher power but don't belong to an organised religion would probably raise their hands. We're still haunted by Christianity, but in its loosest sense our new national faith is also pagan.

The soul of England is in the fire and the cider, the laughter and the dancing. The flames first: we are a Northern European people who rebelled against the winter with festivals of fire, and we are still afraid of the dark. One in three people still believes in the Devil in some form and he still lurks in our imaginations as the one who gave the apple to Eve, was created out of smokeless fire, made a pact with Faust, or rode a tank and held a general's rank while the Blitzkrieg raged and the bodies stank, if you believe the Stones. The police have detailed dozens of cases of extreme abuse in which adults thought they were beating the Devil or evil spirits out of children, the most infamous being that of Victoria Climbié. Christians differ as to whether he really

exists, as a personality active in the world, or is merely a repre-
sentation of all that is bad, but both the Catholics and the Church
of England still have exorcists. Those who want to see the Devil
in their lives can point to the rape, torture and bloody horror that
have become parts of our culture in films and computer games,
or the lies we are constantly told about fame, celebrity and our
inadequacy as sexual beings. Or maybe that's just us, doing it for
ourselves. The Devil is a terrorist: he doesn't have to do much or
even exist for the fear of attack to cause havoc and oppression.
Sometimes, just the dark is enough.

Our other form of resistance throughout history was to eat and
drink heartily when we had things to eat and drink, knowing we
would go hungry and thirsty once they had gone. Better that
than to let them go off. If we drink a flagon of scrumpy (or a
bottle of Malibu) and spew all over the farm track (or the high
street), it's not because of some modern plague of misbehaviour;
it's what the English have always done.

The laughter, too, has always been there. Poking your tongue
out at the master and undercutting everything with humour are
pagan and English. They are what Hallowe'en is really about:
laughing in the face of death, the ultimate master. We didn't go
in for it much while the Church was in charge, but that has
changed spectacularly in recent years. We spent £12 million on
Hallowe'en tat like Frankenstein masks and blood-dripping vampire teeth in 2000, but within five years that had soared to £120
million. This happened because a research team from a supermarket chain went off to America to see how it was done over
there, came back and flooded the shelves in October, and found
themselves being copied by every rival. The team was from
Woolworths, which has since gone bust, so they got what they
deserved. Hallowe'en – like the pagan festival of Samhain, from
which it originates – takes the things we are afraid of, like bats

and zombies and the Grim Reaper, and makes fun of them. There is also a bit of sex thrown in, for the parents, who can vamp it up as Morticia Addams or the dashing Count. This is another example of how we are returning to an Englishness that existed a long time ago, before the Church became dominant. Bawdy, loud, lusty, full of jokes and beer, instinctively against authority and rules and people who think they're better than us, feeling a link to the land and the animals, liking a good laugh and a mighty fart but also fond of wordplay, intricate dances and dressing up in costume. Being silly. Doing all the things the Victorians didn't want us to do. The lid has come off. We no longer have to do what we're told, keep our elbows off the table and chew with our mouths shut. The People's England is having its way, even if those who think they know better don't like it.

The dancing shows this most of all. The Morris we all think we know, performed by hankie-waving men with beards and beer guts, all dressed in white with bells on their ankles, was popularised by the folklorist Cecil Sharp in the early twentieth century and taken up by the churches and village societies as a clean, healthy way of letting young men burn off energy. It reached its peak during the folk revival of the sixties, but then became a bit of a joke. That was that, until the emergence over the last decade of a new generation of Morris sides who take a completely different approach, with spectacular costumes and overtly sexual dances. 'You'd have to be an innocent not to know what was going on,' one of Hunter's Moon tells me as half the side leans back with their legs spread and holds up their sticks like massive dicks, and the other half thrashes them with their own bits of wood. Their style was invented by people with an interest in pre-Christian beliefs, who accused Cecil Sharp of removing all the sex and ritual from the dances he recorded. They thought the dances could be remnants of sacred rites – and even if they weren't, they could be made to look like it and used that way. It's all made up, of course – there is no documentary evidence nor any reason to believe that the faith and practice of the ancients have been passed down unbroken by word of mouth – so they are both celebrating tradition and inventing it at the same time. It works for some people, though, in a way organised religion just doesn't. 'The moment you stand easy, ready to dance, you are grounding yourself, partaking of the ground on which you stand,' another member of Hunter's Moon tells me. He is an office manager by day. 'You get so detached from the natural cycle of life that it is nice to be part of events that remind you. Forming the circle can be quite profound.'

Initially, Hunter's Moon got together to dance the John Barleycorn ritual at Lammas, the pagan harvest festival, when it was first held on the promenade at Eastbourne, one of the most conservative Christian towns in the country. The council hated the idea and threatened to call the police. 'We quoted the law that says we have the right to perform our religion unmolested and in public,' says Lynda, the priestess who led the Wassail. That clash was nearly ten years ago. Since then, Lammas has become one of the great local draws of the summer, promoted by the council as a tourist attraction, which is a demonstration in itself of the way England has changed.

Other new Morris sides include the extraordinary Wolf's Head and Vixen of Rochester, whose members dress as Goths in black crushed velvet, black lipstick and mirror shades. 'We are self-consciously working with shamanism and ideas of sacred space,' their founder says. 'The set dances are set up to be like a magical operation.' Cecil Sharp would have had a fit, but the Morris revolution has run in almost perfect parallel with what has happened to religion, with a long-accepted tradition dying off and new ideas flooding in, some of them seeking to reconnect with the ancient past and with nature. All this laughing, drinking, dancing and waving phallic sticks in the air is about liberation, in the end. 'I am astonished at the way things have grown,' the leader of Hunter's Moon tells me. 'What we're doing is small, but the reaction from people everywhere suggests we are in tune with something really big.'

According to Professor Ronald Hutton, the English pastoralist Harold Massingham 'foresaw a time when his compatriots would recover their appetite for natural beauty and natural living' and 'the divine spirit of the land would awake'. Massingham wrote in 1932: 'The Lord of Misrule will be proclaimed and all the blessed sons and daughters of men will gather to the Feast of Fools.' This was a response to the strident Christianity of his day 'and then to the more sustained phenomena of urbanisation, industrialisation and rapid social change . . . it was also very much an English one'. That is all very familiar, and prescient. Massingham was possessed by nostalgia for a lost rural landscape: he could not have imagined a webbed world in which the old boundaries of taste, decency, morality and nationality evaporate in a permanent, chaotic and glorious feast of fools that is online but also internal; it's happening inside the mind of the bloke browsing his iPhone on the bus, the neighbour up all night staring at pixels, the teenager in her bedroom. But Massingham would have loved to see the English God throw off His cricket gear and run naked into the forest to frolic for a while.

For five centuries, give or take a few wobbles, the faith of England was a given: sometimes enforced, sometimes the cause of persecution, sometimes a matter of social conformity, sometimes just something we had without thinking much about it. Always, it defined our lives. Now we have lost the downward pressure of the old stifling, conservative, complacent faith, and thank goodness for that. We are returning to what we were, but also becoming something new. Richard Dawkins is right to say that we follow the stories into which we are born, but our children are being born into a place where there are many stories.

The English God appeared to be dead, but it wasn't true. He was just regenerating. The obstinate way in which people refuse to stop believing has given Him new energy, but He has also changed so much. He looks both male and female now. He quotes from the Quran as well as the Bible, and many other books besides. He doesn't care whether you are straight or gay, married or cohabiting, because there are much bigger things to worry about, like the sins or mistakes that are causing the seas to warm, the ice caps to melt and the crops to burn. The new English God wants us to work with nature, not seek to dominate it. He still believes in fair play and good versus evil, but also in free choice, mutual respect, equality, open emotion, sexual fulfilment, loving your neighbour who lives on the other side of the world and having a darn good party while you can. If you listen carefully, you can hear him humming 'All You Need Is Love'. He's a bit of a sentimentalist, but he can also laugh at himself.

I'm not advocating this picture of God, only describing the deity that seems to inhabit the minds and imaginations of the English now and informs our cultures, whether we're conscious of Him or not, and whatever we call Him. Or Her. Or Them.

We don't all believe the same things anymore. The English and the British are no longer all following the same fierce creed, and conquering the planet in the name of Christ. An optimist might say we are gentler, friendlier, more compassionate, more emotional, more feminine, more diverse, more interesting, more open, a more questioning bunch than when we were so sure of ourselves. We think we have lost our way, but we may actually just be finding it.

England is so full of troubles just now, so full of sound and fury, yet it is also surely full of possibility. We can choose to lament the loss of our old certainties, or look instead for ways to celebrate what we are becoming, as Englishness opens up.

We may have lost our faith in the old-fashioned God, but we have also found new soul.

31

The second summer of love

Death unravels us all. When they carried my friend Ali to the church in her wicker basket, I found myself returning to the story I knew best. The Jesus story. The promises of life after death and, underneath us all, the everlasting arms. It felt like home, to hear that story again and to sing those old songs, but it was like the family home you return to after a journey around the world: the smallness is stifling even while the familiarity is comforting. I was coming home with a new awareness that there were so many other homes in the world, so many other ways of seeing the same thing, which may or may not be there, and may or may not offer hope to those who are dying, for whom the question is no longer hypothetical. What happens now? We will know, all too soon. Christians, Muslims, Buddhists, Hindus, pagans, atheists, agnostics, we all ask the question that Ali asked and we're all heading somewhere. I don't know where, but I do know where I hope it might be. Ali grew increasingly convinced of her destination as the day of her departure approached. She knew where she was going.

There is a theological term that describes what happens to people who have been committed believers, who have been hurt by the widening gap between the story they tell themselves and the lives they lead, who have fallen from faith and seen that the world is a dark and broken place, who have torn down their old gods and questioned everything and can no longer bring themselves to trust the story in the way they used to, however much they want to, because life is not like that, and who speak with irony and fear certainty but cannot resist the pull of the divine. If they are fortunate, they reach a state of wonder that has been called the 'second naivety' or the 'second innocence'. People caught up in this state don't turn their back on the questions. They continue to put great value on critical thinking, they recognise that the claims of science are strong and that the accusations made against their old faith and the people who follow it may well be true, but they cannot leave it there. The rabbi and philosopher Neil Gillman writes: 'I cling by my very fingernails to the realisation that my rational self is not the whole of me . . . that the world remains for me a realm of enchantment. I do science but I also appreciate poetry; I work but I also play.' This sense of wonder is not just for Jews or Christians. It is for all those who have believed – whether it be in Islam or revolutionary socialism or the old England – who have struggled and who have grown tired of their tears. People who find this elusive second innocence recognise that each of us is born into a story, as Richard Dawkins says, as an accident of class, culture, geography and time. They see that there are many other stories, and seek to learn from them, becoming open to people and ideas that they used to think were threatening; and yet they also begin to acknowledge, after surfacing from the anger and disappointment they felt towards their original story, that there is still power for them in many of its symbols and myths.

In his description of the stages of faith, James Fowler says that people can see 'powerful meanings' in the old ways, 'while simultaneously recognising that they are relative, partial and inevitably distorting apprehensions of transcendent reality'. I do believe that when the trauma of losing our old faith lessens, and as we grow up into what we are becoming, the English may enter a second innocence, charged with confidence and optimism and a new sense of wonder.

As for myself, how could I not feel that way, as a thousand of us gathered together to celebrate Ali's life? The address was made by another cherished friend, Doug Gay, the former minister of her church and now a lecturer in theology at Glasgow University. He admitted that it hurt so much to be there, said we were all dumbfounded by the question of why it had happened. But he also had something else to say:

> In faith we speak of things we cannot see. We gather up the brightest fragment of material we can find in the Scriptures and we piece together a patchwork vision of heaven, of paradise, of Ipharidisi . . . And we say to Ali, 'You have gone home, you are in glory, now you live in a country called No More Death, No More Crying, No More Pain.' And we are comforted. We say, with the eyes of Narnia, you with your love for life, you have said, 'Goodbye Shadowlands, the term is over and all the holidays have begun.' Now you are where every beauty is brighter and every pleasure more intense. You are where there is the best wine, the finest food, the funkiest music, the brightest clothes, the wildest dancing, the kindest laughter, the deepest joy. Life is more, where you are. And we are excited.

There were tears in every eye by now.

> We say with the jeweller's eye of Revelation that you, Ali, the magpie girl who loved stuff that flittered and sparkled and

shone, you now live in the city whose four walls are set with jasper, sapphire, agate, emerald, onyx, carnelian, chrysolite, beryl, topaz, chrysoprase, jacinth, amethyst, and where the gates are pearls and the streets are pure gold, transparent as glass. And we are dazzled. We say, with a mind to the sceptical Marxists among us, and within us, that to talk this way of heaven is no opiate. It is not spiritual heroin or crack which will drug us into oblivion. Wherever the Church has fought hardest for justice and liberation down through the centuries, it has done so because it dreamed of heaven and it prayed for heaven's kingdom to come now on earth. We say, with the voice of Dr King still ringing in our ears, this is where you are. Ali, who adopted Hackney and who loved living here, you are where there is every tribe and tongue and nation, where every language is spoken and every colour and culture fully respected. You are where every oppression is ended and every potential filled. This is where you are, and this is where we want to be. One day, we will follow you.

Everything has a season, or so the saying goes. There is a season for darkness and tears and there is a season for sunlight and laughter. So it was that two and a half years after her death, I found myself standing in a park with Ali's husband Chris, looking up at a bold blue sky. It was late September, it should have been windy and cold and autumnal, but instead the day was warm and bright, with the scent of late flowers carried on the breeze. 'This is like my life,' Chris said, and I knew what he meant, immediately. 'You think the summer has gone, that's all there is, then it surprises you by coming again.'

Unusually, Chris was wearing a suit. A silver grey one, with a flower in the lapel. It was his wedding suit. He was going to get married within the hour, here in this park, to a lovely woman called Naomi who had been strong enough to take on this widower and his children and open the door for them all, as he was going to say in his speech, to a new life. His little boy was the best man, in the same kind of silver suit, and his daughter was a bridesmaid in an Oriental dress. We were surrounded by friends, on the slope of a hill in this open space in East London, where the concrete floor of an old bandstand had been strewn with petals. The black wooden railings and posts, tagged with graffiti, had been wrapped in purple and gold chiffon and clothed in vivid garlands, sprays and blooms. This battered old shelter had been transformed into a temporary, verdant temple of life.

When the bride arrived, she was serenaded to the platform by an acoustic guitar and a violin playing 'Here, There and Everywhere'. A trio took up the mandolin, the accordion and the djembe drum for the first song of the service, which had a verse in the Shona language. The next was a gospel setting of 'The Lord is My Shepherd'; and the last was 'Come Go with Me to That Land'. None of these was sung with the reticence you get when a congregation tries, barely, to follow a booming organ; this singing was loud, ragged but energetic, because we were out in the open air, there was an easy, hip-swaying rhythm to them and these songs were common ground.

The congregation looked as if someone had gathered up a random sample of people from the streets of Hackney: there were young black men and women, Caribbean matriarchs, a couple of families in splendid traditional dress from Nigeria, women in saris, white middle-class media types and social workers, some very cool Scandinavians and a large contingent of wandering Aussie citizens of the world. Because it was a wedding, there were also quite a few bemused relatives dressed in those back-of-the-wardrobe suits, summer dresses and hats in which the English, in particular, like to look awkward on such occasions. The younger women were slightly more glamorous versions of their mothers, but the younger men wore chinos and untucked shirts, a sign of the abandonment of formality in all but a few situations. People don't even wear suits to court appearances any more.

The service was led by the minister of a church about a mile from the park, which had employed Chris as a community worker. That had been when Ali was alive. Even now, she was not far away: some of her ashes had been scattered under a tree planted in her name, in another part of this park. Her mother and her sister were among the guests. Thinking of Ali, and looking at so many of her friends who had been brought back together for this unsettling but nevertheless happy occasion, I was reminded of the way that she, Chris and the church had chosen to mark the Queen's golden jubilee in 2002. They held a street party right outside the church, on a road so violent the local paper called it Murder Mile. They strung out bunting in red, white and blue but also in black, green, gold and all the colours of all the flags of the countries of origin of people living in the area. The Victorian town houses and flats around the Lower Clapton Road contained men, women and children from all over the world – from Afghan and Rwandan asylum-seekers to elderly survivors of the *Windrush* generation or the wartime East End, as well as young migrants from the Home Counties who had come in search of a more exotic life. All were welcomed, including a large number of people from the local mosque. 'We want to insist on the possibility of diversity and togetherness, despite the circumstances,' Chris said at the time. 'We're celebrating a different kind of commonwealth from the one Her Majesty is most familiar with.' This was, he said, about the commonwealth of humanity.

Yes, I know it all sounds painfully right on, doesn't it? Perhaps it was. Naive, maybe. Hopelessly idealistic, a ridiculously high-minded way of looking at a bit of a knees-up with a few unwitting locals. Chris would admit all that – I know, because I put it all to him – but he would also say it was worth doing, if only for the sake of doing *something*. There was an Englishness about the way it was done, with as little fuss as possible and in a quietly, stubbornly inclusive way. Of course, everyone was invited, whatever their affiliation or background: that was only fair and right. And this was absolutely not a stunt pulled by the church in order to convert people to its creed. It went deeper than dogma.

The wedding in the park was like that, too. I stepped back from the crowd for a moment, to make a little video of the scene on my phone, panning slowly in a circle. There was the bandstand in the shadow of huge trees, then the lawn on which we would eat cake and drink champagne, and the hole where the bride and groom were going to plant a hornbeam as a marker of this day. Beyond that were benches where women in Islamic dress were having a picnic, looking over at canal boats on the River Lea and distant abstract shapes on the skyline where the Olympic site was under construction. In the middle ground, spread out like a cliché, was a cricket pitch on which men in white were playing out the afternoon. I stopped filming and saw that a pair of Haredi Jewish men in black clothes and wide-brimmed black hats, members of a community that occupied many of the surrounding streets, had slowed down their Sabbath walk to take in the wedding. A woman with a little dog stopped and asked what it was all about. When somebody told her, she beamed. 'How lovely. Does that happen often here?' It didn't. Hardly ever. They hadn't particularly asked permission to do it either, beyond checking with the park staff that they wouldn't mind and asking the council if they could plant the tree. 'Aren't they brave,' the woman said, and she had a point. Someone might come along and stop them, she said, 'and the weather and all that'. But nobody did, and the weather was glorious. She stayed for a piece of cake and a paper cup of chilled champagne.

This was a difficult day in some ways, but it was also beautifully life-affirming. We were out in the open air, under the swaying trees and the clear sky with the sun on our faces and the colours of the flowers in our eyes, recognising the splendour of creation and – in the planting of the tree – the need to respond to the planet with care. The love that Chris and Naomi had found spoke of redemption, a season of light and life after sadness. There was a boldness, a directness, about declaring that in a public place like this, where anyone of any faith or none could step into the congregation, then afterwards share the sweet food and drink. One of the readings was a passage that could surely find agreement among all those with different approaches to the divine: 'Summing it all up, friends, I say you'll do best by filling your minds and meditating on things true, noble, reputable, authentic, compelling, gracious – the best, not the worst. The beautiful, not the ugly. Things to praise, not things to curse.'

Maybe I'm just a sentimental old fool who got caught up in the moment, still cherishing the memory of Ali while full of happiness and optimism for my friend, his children and his new wife, but I did look around me that day – at the bandstand, the variety and generosity of the people taking part or watching and the gorgeous late summer setting – and think, Yes, this scene contains something old, something new, something borrowed and something beyond the red, white and blue. A glimpse of a new England. An England to believe in.

That was yesterday. Early this morning, I went down to the beach. I took four of the largest pebbles and made a circle. I took flat stones and piled them on top, then fatter ones, then white chalk lumps, then dark grey stones the size of your fist, then flinty golf balls; and I placed them all carefully on each other, stone upon stone upon stone, until the pile looked like a rough-shaped pyramid, there on the beach, a dozen feet or so from the approaching tide. I did it because someone once told me that much the same was done by Columba, a saint on the run from his past who found peace with his back to his native land, on a Scottish island called Iona. It is said that Columba built a pile of stones on a beach to mark an ending.

I am not sure whom my marker was for, but I built it, and I stood there and looked at the waves that would come in and remove the stones one or two at a time, wave by wave, under-mining, pushing, prodding, pulling, until the marker would be gone – underwater or flattened or both. And I prayed to . . . well, I don't know. God. Allah. Jehovah. The life force. The universe. Whatever. Actually, I didn't pray, not with words, because I didn't have them. I was silent.

After all this thinking and writing, fretting and fiddling, that's what it comes down to: silence on a beach. Not wordless wonder, that's too romantic, but something more ordinary and, because of that, more profound. Standing there, in the early morning, looking at the horizon, scenting the sea, feeling the salt spray on my face, breathing deeply. Saying nothing.

Fancy some more? Want to respond? Please come
and join the conversation online. The blog of the book
features exclusive extra content including interviews, images
and videos – and a chance to have your say.

www.isgodstillanenglishman.com

A note on chapter headings

Some of the references may be more obscure than others, depending on your age and tastes, so here they are. Most of the songs quoted were popular in the year under discussion. 1. The title of this book, as well as the quote from George Bernard Shaw. 2. The standard fairytale beginning. 3. 'The Land of Make Believe' by Bucks Fizz. 4. 'Ghost Town' by the Specials. 5. A headline in the *Sun* after the sinking of the *General Belgrano*. 6. 'The Final Countdown' by Europe. 7. 'Two Tribes' by Frankie Goes to Hollywood. 8. 'Doctor! Doctor!' by the Thompson Twins. 9. 'This Is England' by the Clash. 10. Speaking in tongues. 11. 'Walls Come Tumbling Town' by the Style Council. 12. 'Make Way' by Graham Kendrick. 13. 'You'll Never Walk Alone' by Richard Rodgers and Oscar Hammerstein. 14. 'Hallelujah' by Leonard Cohen, as covered by John Cale. 15. 'I Will Always Love You' by Whitney Houston. 16. 'Ain't No Doubt' by Jimmy Nail. 17. The root of all evil, according to the Bible. 18. 'Everyday is Like Sunday' by Morrissey. 19. A line in the ZooTV shows by U2. 20. 'Everything Changes' by Take That. 21. 'Seven Ways to Love' by Cola Boy. 22. 'Candle in the Wind 1997' by Elton John. 23. 'Perfect Day' by Lou Reed, as covered by various artists for Children in Need. 24. 'Millennium Prayer' by Cliff Richard. 25. 'Stop Living the Lie' by David Sneddon. 26. Another reference to the title of the book.

27. 'Won't Get Fooled Again' by the Who, which came out when the future Archbishop was at university. 28. A play on the lyrics of the Elton John song again. 29. 'Jerusalem' by William Blake, as set to music by Sir Hubert Parry. 30. 'A Pagan Place' by the Waterboys. 31. 'The Second Summer of Love' by Danny Wilson.

Acknowledgements

Ali Adeney Lawrence, 1967–2007

Many thanks to Camilla Hornby and Tim Whiting, who made the book happen. To Rachel and the kids, for putting up with me while I wrote it. To Andy Turner for his wisdom and advice. To Chris and Naomi Lawrence for not minding. To the following people who helped in specific ways they may only be dimly aware of: Michael and Stephanie Cole, Chris Crowley, Grace Davie, Andrew Davies, Lewis Doney, Malcolm and Meryl Doney, Doug Gay, Jennie Gilhespy, David Gillard, Katy Guest, Paul Handley, James Hanning, Gareth Higgins, Iain Hunt, Hunter's Moon, Simon Jones, John Mullin, Mike and Liz Newing, Peter Owen-Jones, Martin Palmer, Philip Parr, Alastair Pearson, Catherine Pepinster, George Pitcher, Dave Roberts, James Thornton, Nick Thorpe, Martin Wroe and Salma Yaqoob. And to all those people I have not mentioned, but who shared the many moments and conversations that led up to this. Thank you.

Further reading

Some of the book grew out of articles I wrote for the *Independent on Sunday* over a number of years. The passages on Morris Cerullo, John Wimber and NOS are based on my own reports in the mid-nineties for the *Church Times*. A different version of the interview with the Archbishop of Westminster appeared in the *Guardian* in May 2009. For the sake of their privacy, I have changed the names of most of the people mentioned in the passages relating to my own personal experiences. 'All Souls' is an amalgam of several churches, but otherwise the events did take place as described. The last time I looked, the encounter between Richard Dawkins and the student in Virginia was available on YouTube. All the books listed below are useful and interesting (some more than others), but I was particularly grateful for the insights of Andrew Chandler, Grace Davie and Kate Fox.

Alexander, H.G., *Religion in England 1558–1662* (Hodder and Stoughton, 1968)

Arden, Paul, *God Explained in a Taxi Ride* (Penguin, 2007)

Armstrong, Karen, *A History of God* (Vintage, 1999)

Bates, Stephen, *A Church at War* (Hodder and Stoughton, 2004)

Beckett, Francis and Hencke, David, *Marching to the Fault Line* (Constable, 2009)

Bierley, Peter, *Pulling out of the Nose Dive* (Christian Research, 2006)

Brown, Andrew, Robert Runcie obituary, *Independent*, 12 July 2000

Brown, Callum G., *The Death of Christian Britain* (Routledge, 2001)

Brown, Mick, 'Unzipper Heaven, Lord', *Daily Telegraph*, December 1994

Bruce, Steve, *God Is Dead: Secularisation in the West* (WileyBlackwell, 2002)

Bruce, Steve and David Voas, 'Vicarious Religion: An Examination and Critique', *Journal of Contemporary Religion* (2010)

Butcher, Catherine, with Coates, Forster, Green and Kendrick, *March for Jesus* (Kingsway, 1992)

Campbell, Beatrix, *Diana, Princess of Wales: How Sexual Politics Shook the Monarchy* (Women's Press, 1998)

Cannadine, David, 'The Royal Dilemma That Won't Go Away', *Financial Times,* 12 December 1992

Carey, George, *Know the Truth* (Harper Perennial, 2004)

Carpenter, Humphrey, *Robert Runcie: The Reluctant Archbishop* (Hodder, 1996)

Chadwick, Owen, *The Reformation* (Penguin, 1964)

Chandler, Andrew, *The Church of England in the Twentieth Century: The Church Commissioners and the Politics of Reform, 1948–1998* (Boydell, 2006)

Cole, Michael, *Make Way for the Spirit* (Highland, 1988)

Cole, Peter, *Religious Experience* (Hodder Murray, 2005)

Davie, Grace, *Religion in Britain since 1945* (Blackwell, 1994)

Dawkins, Richard, *The God Delusion* (Bantam, 2006)

Fowler, James W., *Stages of Faith: The Psychology of Human Development* (HarperCollins, 1981)

Further Reading

Fox, Kate, *Watching the English* (Hodder, 2004)

Hampson, Michael, *Last Rites: The End of the Church of England* (Granta, 2006)

Heathcote-James, Emma, *Seeing Angels* (John Blake, 2002)

Howard, Anthony, 'Why Her Will Wasn't Done', *The Times*, 4 May 1996

Howard, Roland, *The Rise and Fall of the Nine O'Clock Service: A Cult Within the Church?* (Continuum, 1996)

Husain, Ed, *The Islamist* (Penguin, 2007)

Hutton, Ronald, *The Triumph of the Moon* (Oxford, 1999)

Jenkins, David, *The Calling of a Cuckoo* (Continuum, 2002)

John, Jeffrey, *Permanent, Faithful, Stable* (DLT, 1993)

Kaye, Bruce, *An Introduction to World Anglicanism* (Cambridge, 2008)

Lacey, Robert, *Royal: Her Majesty Queen Elizabeth II* (Little, Brown, 2002)

Lofland, John and Rodney Stark, 'Becoming a World-Saver: A Theory of Conversion to a Deviant Perspective', *American Sociological Review* 30 (1965)

Lynch, Gordon, *Losing My Religion* (DLT, 2003)

McGrath, Alister E., *A Brief History of Heaven* (Blackwell, 2003)

McGrath, Alister E., *The Dawkins Delusion* (SPCK, 2007)

Moorman, J.R.H., *A History of the Church in England* (Black, 1952)

Moreton, Cole, *My Father was a Hero: The True Story of a Man, a Boy and the Silence Between Them* (Viking, 2004)

Morrison, Blake, 'Take Two Days', *Guardian Weekend* magazine, 1 April 2006

Morton, Andrew, *Diana: Her True Story* (Michael O'Mara, 1992)

Owen-Jones, Peter, *Small Boat, Big Sea* (Lion, 2000)

Orwell, George, *England, Your England and Other Essays* (Secker and Warburg, 1953)

Palmer, Martin, *Living Christianity* (Element, 1993)

Paxman, Jeremy, *Friends in High Places: Who Runs Britain?* (Penguin, 1990)

Pimlott, Ben, *The Queen* (HarperCollins, 1996)

Roberts, Dave, *The Toronto Blessing* (Kingsway, 1994)

Ruthven, Malise, *Fundamentalism: The Search for Meaning* (Oxford, 2004)

Tomkins, Stephen, *A Short History of Christianity* (Lion, 2005)

Voas, David and Alasdair Crockett, 'Religion in Britain: Neither believing nor belonging', *Sociology 39* (2005)

Williams, Shirley, *Climbing the Bookshelves* (Virago 2009)

Wimber, John, *Everyone Gets to Play* (Ampelon, 2008)

Wimber, John, *Power Healing* (HarperOne, 1991)

For more by me, go to: www.isgodstillanenglishman.com.

Index

Index

Index

Index

THE EVOLUTION OF GOD
Robert Wright

'Persuasive' *Sunday Times*

'Enthralling' *New Yorker*

In *The Evolution of God*, Robert Wright, award-winning author of the bestselling books *Nonzero* and *The Moral Animal*, takes us on a sweeping journey through religious history, from the Stone Age to the Information Age, unveiling along the way an astonishing discovery: that there is a hidden pattern in the way that Judaism, Christianity and Islam have all evolved.

Through the prisms of archaeology, theology, evolutionary psychology and a careful re-reading of the scriptures, Wright's findings repeatedly overturn conventional wisdom and basic assumptions about the great monotheistic faiths.

ABACUS
978-0-349-12246-5

Now you can order superb titles directly from Abacus

☐ The Evolution of God   Robert Wright   £8.99

The price shown above is correct at time of going to press. However, the publishers reserve the right to increase prices on covers from those previously advertised, without further notice.

───────────────── ⟨ABACUS⟩ ─────────────────

Please allow for postage and packing: **Free UK delivery.**
Europe: add 25% of retail price; Rest of World: 45% of retail price.

To order any of the above or any other Abacus titles, please call our credit card orderline or fill in this coupon and send/fax it to:

Abacus, PO Box 121, Kettering, Northants NN14 4ZQ
Fax: 01832 733076   Tel: 01832 737526
Email: aspenhouse@FSBDial.co.uk

☐ I enclose a UK bank cheque made payable to Abacus for £ . . . .
☐ Please charge £ . . . . to my Visa/Delta/Maestro

Expiry Date ☐☐☐☐   Maestro Issue No. ☐☐

NAME (BLOCK LETTERS please) . . . .

ADDRESS . . . .

. . . .

. . . .

Postcode . . . . Telephone . . . .

Signature . . . .

Please allow 28 days for delivery within the UK. Offer subject to price and availability.